I08001161

IMAGES
of America

SULLIVAN'S ISLAND

Gadsden Cultural Center

ARCADIA
PUBLISHING

ISBN 978-0-7385-1678-3

Published by Arcadia Publishing
Charleston, South Carolina

Printed in the United States of America

Library of Congress Catalog Card Number: 2004106312

For all general information contact Arcadia Publishing at:
Telephone 843-853-2070
Fax 843-853-0044
E-mail sales@arcadiapublishing.com
For customer service and orders:
Toll-Free 1-888-313-2665

Visit us on the Internet at www.arcadiapublishing.com

Dedicated to Harold Byrum

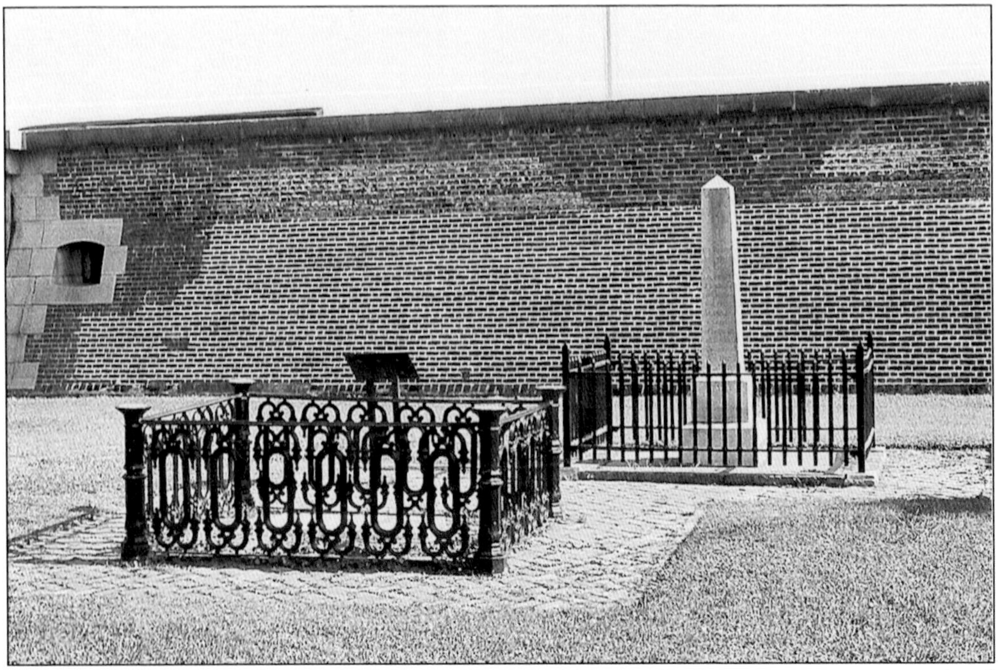

OLD FORT MOULTRIE. The grave of Osceola, Seminole Indian leader, who was imprisoned and died at Fort Moultrie, and the memorial marker to a Union ship lost during the Civil War are located near the main entrance to Old Fort Moultrie. (Courtesy S.C. Department of Archives and History.)

IMAGES
of America

SULLIVAN'S ISLAND

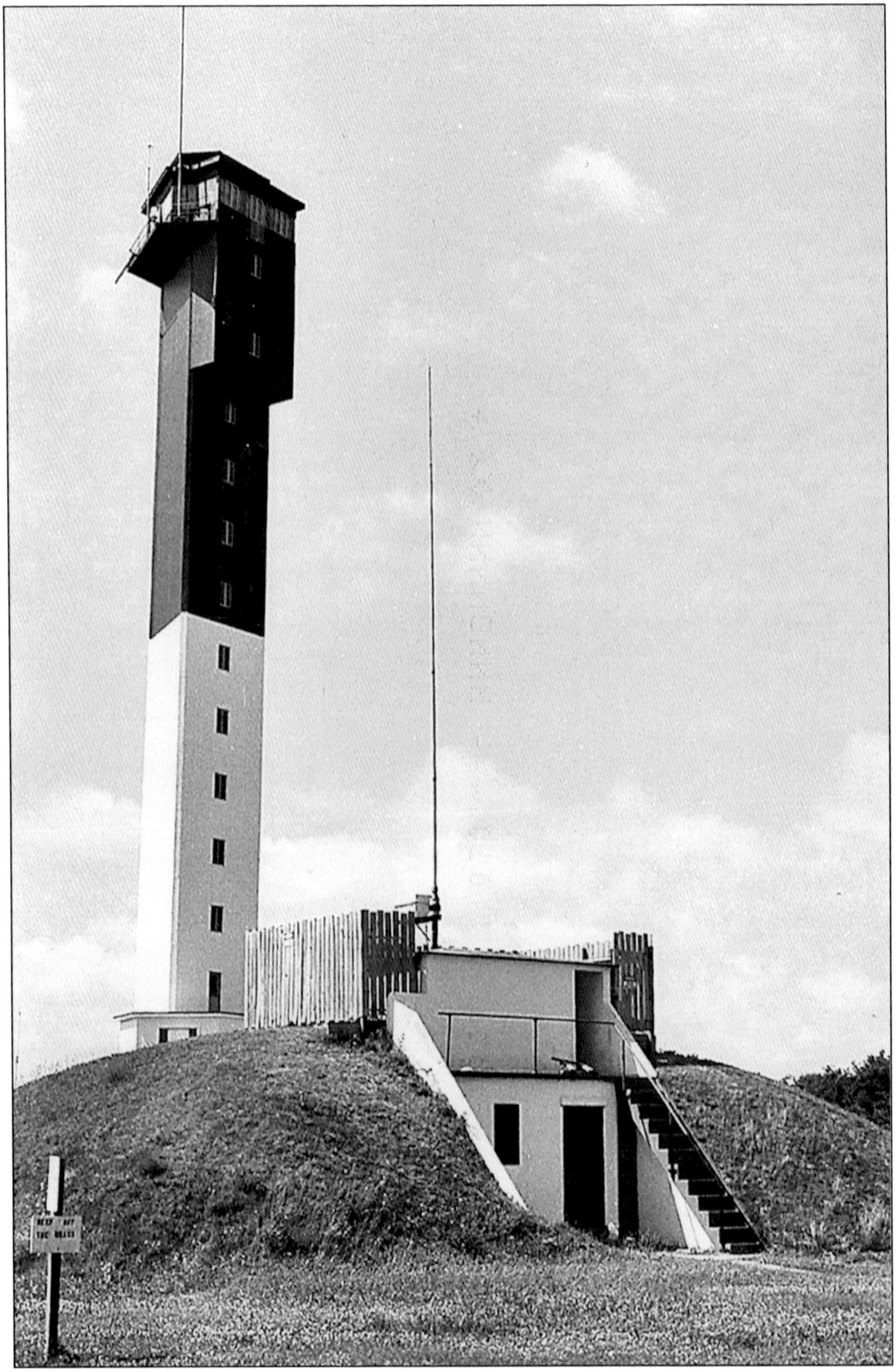

SULLIVAN'S ISLAND LIGHTHOUSE, 1962. The lighthouse is one of the most widely photographed buildings on Sullivan's Island and is frequently found on local license plates. This lighthouse, built by Cape Romain contractors, is the latest in a series of lighthouses that have stood on Sullivan's Island. (Courtesy S.C. Department of Archives and History.)

Contents

ACKNOWLEDGMENTS

This book is based on a historical and architectural inventory of Sullivan's Island done in 1987 by Preservation Consultants, Inc., of Charleston. Members of the firm included John Laurens, David B. Schneider, and Sarah Fick. The survey was done after Sullivan's Island qualified for a grant from the S.C. Department of Archives and History. The survey included all buildings, sites, structures, and objects erected or that achieved significance in 1935 or earlier. Preservation Consultants surveyed 360 properties in its inventory of historic places. The architectural rating system that they used is included in this book. Because of financial and space considerations not all properties surveyed were able to be included. There was an attempt made to include not only the large island residences but also the small endangered cottages that contribute to the uniqueness of Sullivan's Island.

The Sullivan's Island Town Council was required to match the S.C. Department of Archives and History grant. The council was reluctant to allocate its entire share from town revenues and felt it was appropriate that the private sector also contribute. I feel it is appropriate to acknowledge and thank those individuals and organizations who contributed. They are Carroll Realty; Mrs. Mayme W. Macmurphy; Leonard A. Greene; Patrick C. Ilderton Contractor, Inc.; Charles E. Sweatt; Robert P. Thompson; James C. Byrd; Raymond R. Finch; Col. John R. Johnson; R.F. Curd; Adele Deas; Agatha M. Thomas; Audrey R. Smith; Mrs. Joan C. Pittman; Sullivan's Elementary School; W.F. Lear Jr.; Charles M. Condon; Charles E. Aimar, M.D.; Dr. Ronald B. Cooper; Mrs. N.J. Ward; Dr. Ross L. Neagley; Barbara T. Kimbrell; Mrs. Jane D. Selby; Mrs. Grace S. Blanchard; Dr. Douglas Parham Jr.; Dr. George G. Durst; Samuel E. Hanvey; Margaret P. Schachte; Sumter F. deBrux; Steward W. Johnson; Mrs. Anna P. Anderegg; Judith W. Chase; Mrs. Eltress M. Dick; Mabel P. Wichmann; Andrea L. Rubin; John M. Mirsky; Carl J. Smith; Atlantic Investments (Leonard L. Long Jr.); Henry B. Smythe Jr.; W. Allison Siegling; Bailey & Associates; Mrs. Esther H. Tecklenburg; Mrs. Amalie Stone Walker; Barry Krell; Dr. Bachman S. Smith Jr.; Cameron W. Stuhr; Joseph T Newton III; Michael C. Mithoefer, M.D.; Mrs. June W. Murphy; Mrs. Charles V. Peery; Park B. Smith; and Peter Manigault, all of Sullivan's Island and Charleston; also, Arthur Sarnoff, New York, New York; and Colin W. Edwards, Bremeton, Washington.

I would also like to acknowledge my wife, Bonnie A. Williams, whose valuable assistance helped make this book possible; Sara Fick, who steered me to the right places for information; David Kelly of the S.C. Department of Archives and History for his prompt assistance and cooperation; Linda Dayhoff Smith for background material; and Carl J. Smith for additional information.

I would like to thank Mayme W. Macmurphy for spearheading the project that resulted in this book.

—Roy Williams III

INTRODUCTION

Sullivan's Island, located at the mouth of Charleston Harbor, has played an important role in the region's history since the earliest days of English settlement in South Carolina. It is a long, narrow island oriented from east to west with its western tip pointing toward Charleston Harbor, its front on the ocean to the south, and a division from the Isle of Palms to the east by the waters of Breach Inlet. The development of the community has traditionally been associated with both the harbor defense and the summer recreation habits of Charleston area residents.

The island was named for Capt. Florence O'Sullivan, who came to the colonies in 1669 and, after being elected to South Carolina's First Provincial Parliament in 1672, was appointed on May 30, 1674, to take charge of a signal cannon to be placed "near the river's mouth." This cannon was to be fired as a warning to Charles Towne, then located upriver at Albemarle Point, upon the approach of ships into the harbor. O'Sullivan's post established the island as an important component of the harbor's defenses, a role that it would retain until World War II.

Various legislative acts refer to the maintenance of the "watch house on Sullivan's Island" throughout the remainder of the 17th century. In 1700 the legislature passed an act "to encourage strangers to come to this port [Charleston] by making Sullivan's Island more remarkable, by building a new lookout and buoying channel." In 1714 it passed a further act to appoint commissioners to lay out streets and regulate police.

In addition to its role as a coastal defense and marking station, the island also served as the location for the harbor's early pest houses or "lazarettos." These structures were built as quarantine stations to hold persons, free and slave, thought to present a potential risk for the spread of disease in Charleston. A 1707 legislative act called for the construction of what was probably the first pest house on the island, and an act of 1753 called for the replacement of a pest house that had been destroyed by a hurricane.

Evidence suggests that the island remained sparsely populated in the years prior to the Revolutionary War. In early 1776 construction started, under the command of Col. William Moultrie, on the first substantial fortification on Sullivan's Island, to be built of 16-foot-thick palmetto log cribbing filled with sand. Work was completed on the beachfront and part of the northern front by June of that year, when Sir Peter Parker's British forces attacked the fort and its 31 guns. Also on the island, toward Breach Inlet, Col. William Thomson with 780 troops fought off an attack by 2,200 British soldiers under the command of Gen. Henry Clinton, who attacked from the Isle of Palms (then called Long Island). Moultrie's command held against great odds and was victorious.

An act of the state legislature in 1787 appropriated the island for public purpose and made all grants of land drawn after March 21, 1784, invalid. The result of this act was that no land acquired after that date could be owned in fee simple. Possession of lots was through the granting of "licenses"; these became "licenses to build" and led to the custom of erecting a small, two-room "keeping house." Some lots were pre-empted, a type of squatter's rights where building a house resulted in being issued a license after the fact. These lease forms of tenancy remained in effect until 1968, when the township began to grant fee-simple titles.

In 1791 the legislature passed an act that allowed those who might find it "beneficial to their health to reside on Sullivan's Island [to] have liberty to build on said island a dwelling . . . and the said person . . . shall have exclusive right to the same delivering up the same when demanded by Governor or Commander in Chief for the time being."

In 1796 the U.S. government acquired four acres of land from the state on which to erect a replacement for "Moultrie's Fort" (or Fort Sullivan), which had been washed away by advancing tides. This replacement, earthen-work fortification was itself destroyed in a heavy storm that occurred October 1–2, 1803. Plans for a third Fort Moultrie were developed by Maj. Alexander McComb, U.S. Army Corps of Engineers, in 1809. The new fort was approved by the secretary of war and completed by 1811.

By the time the town of Moultrieville was incorporated in 1817, as many as 200 houses may have been in existence. Most of the town's early population was made up of summer residents from Charleston, as the fort was not heavily garrisoned at the time. In 1819 the town's charter was amended so that in order to claim a lot, a dwelling house had to be erected. Between the Revolutionary and Civil Wars, Moultrieville's population appears to have continued to grow, although it was affected by activity or inactivity at the fort and occasional storms or other disasters.

The island has always been exposed to natural disaster. The most notable were the hurricanes of 1893, 1911, and 1916, which destroyed buildings in large sections of the island. As early as September 1752, a storm hit the area, killing about 100 people in and around Charleston, 9 of them on Sullivan's Island. In 1816 lightning struck the steamboat *Enterprise*, resulting in 2 deaths and 10 injuries. Major hurricanes damaged the island again in 1822 and 1845, and half of the fort's garrison was wiped out by a yellow fever epidemic in 1845. An article in the Charleston *News and Courier* on September 11, 1854, mentioned that the Point House, a hotel, had been destroyed in a hurricane. A cyclone did extensive damage in 1885; the Charleston earthquake of August 1886 affected several buildings on the island, and a tornado touched down in 1938 destroying at least 15 houses.

Access to the island was provided by ferries and steamboats throughout the 19th century. Hibben's Ferry operated between Mount Pleasant and Sullivan's Island from 1798 to 1821. The ferry boat *Hildegard* was operated by the Pressley and Mintz families, making trips between the tip of Sullivan's Island and Adgers Wharf in Charleston.

By the 1840s Frederick Adolphus Porcher, a St. John's Parish planter, described the island in his journal:

> The difficulty of living on the Island was great. An irregular market was held, but too uncertain to be depended upon. The steamer which came every day from the City left too early to permit any one to get his market supplies in that way, so we were obliged to depend on poultry.

The areas to the east of Moultrieville, referred to as "The Myrtles" because of the abundance of woodland and myrtle bushes found there, developed slowly during the 19th century. Porcher's journal described it:

> This portion of the island had been well peopled, but after the storm of 1822 people were afraid, and its proximity to the marshes also made them afraid of fever. It was now almost abandoned, the only houses in the neighborhood being those of Judge Huger and Col. I'On on one side, and the elegant mansion of Gen. Pinckney on the other.

On the eve of the Civil War, it appears that most of the island's population, predominantly summer residents, was still concentrated on the western end of the island. The war itself had a devastating effect, with constant bombardments resulting in the destruction of most of the island's buildings.

Fort Moultrie was all but abandoned after the Civil War and soon fell into disrepair. The last troops were mustered out on December 10, 1866, and no regular garrison was reinstalled until 1897. During Reconstruction, Congress passed a Fortifications Bill in March 1871 that resulted in sporadic work at Fort Moultrie, lasting until 1876. This work included the construction of foundations for magazines and gun platforms, guardroom, and bomb proofs, as well as the installation of several pieces of artillery. The fort was nearly abandoned again after 1876.

After the war the island's summer residents returned, and much of the western half of the island was again covered by houses by the 1870s. The first post office on Sullivan's Island, Moultrieville Post Office, was established in 1875. A bridge from Mount Pleasant was reported to have been built during the Civil War, and with the coming of the trolley line, several smaller neighborhoods began to develop on the island's eastern end during the late 19th and early 20th centuries. Maxwell Anderson, a lumber mill operator and real estate developer, floated lumber from Charleston and laid out several lots on which were constructed houses for his mother and brothers. The neighborhood was referred to as Andersonville by island residents.

The 1890s saw a major development in transportation to the island. In 1898 Dr. Joseph Lawrence became interested in developing the Isle of Palms as a resort area and therefore promoted the Charleston and Seashore Railroad Company. Lawrence became the company's first president and presided over the construction of a trolley line from Mount Pleasant, through Sullivan's Island, to Long Island (now Isle of Palms). In addition to the line's eight miles of track, a power house was built on the island, and bridges were built between Mount Pleasant and Sullivan's Island, across Cove Inlet, and across Breach Inlet between Sullivan's Island and the Isle of Palms. Early in the trolley line's history, it was also possible to bypass Mount Pleasant by taking a ferry from Charleston directly to Sullivan's Island, where it was met by a horse or mule trolley. The last trip of a mule trolley was in July 1898.

The trolley line had an important impact on the island growth as it made the eastern end of the island far more accessible and therefore more attractive for residential development. The trolleys had box cars large enough for furniture, commercial ice delivery, etc., and could be used to transport entire households to and from Charleston. On July 23, 1903, a post office was opened for Atlanticville, representing much of the land east of Station 22. (The Atlanticville Post Office was discontinued in October 1942.) The trolley's generating station provided electricity for the island for the first time, and telephone service followed in 1913. Houses continued to be built at a rapid pace, filling in between those that had predated the trolley line, so that by 1917 a plat of the island indicates houses on virtually every dry lot.

Sullivan's Island is a very different place from its rustic beginnings as a resort in the early 19th century, when Francis Hall, an Englishman, wrote about summer in the Charleston area:

> All the inhabitants who can afford it, then fly to a barren sand-bank in the harbour, called Sullivan's Island, containing one well, and a few palmettos: Here they dwell in miserable wooden tenements, trembling at every storm, lest (as frequently happens) their hiding places should be blown from over their heads, or deluged by an inundation of the sea.

The settlement did not reflect Hall's description very long. Robert Mills, Charleston architect and designer of the Washington Monument, writing about the island two decades later described Moultrieville in a far different fashion. By that time Gen. Thomas Pinckney—former South Carolina governor, American Minister to England, author of the Pinckney Treaty in American History, and Vice Presidential candidate in 1796—had built his elegant mansion as a retreat on Sullivan's Island. General Pinckney's four-and-one-half story townhouse in Charleston at 14 George Street, which still stands today, was his winter residence in the city. He was a rice planter at El Dorado Plantation in St. James Santee Parish. Mills pictured Moultrieville as follows:

> Moultrieville has a handsome appearance, particularly when entering the harbor; the greater part of the houses (for more than a mile) front the beach, which extends the whole length of the Island, a distance of three miles. This beach at low water is very firm and

wide; affords a delightful walk or ride, where the delighted visitant may inhale the pure and bracing sea-breeze, which wafts health and vigor to the system.

William Crafts of Charleston had a different opinion of the sea breezes. He wrote that the island air rusted metals, destroyed shoe leather, and inspired verse-making. He called the breeze not ocean air, nor land air, but a mixture of both, and not so good as either. He reported that the air was of doubtful benefit to the lungs but had a good effect on the appetite and was an excellent specific against the yellow fever. Crafts described the little city of Moultrieville as the sybarus of the South, which rapidly renewed its luxurious population and was the general resort of the indolent and the refuge of the invalid.

It is remarkable that any buildings on Sullivan's Island have survived the vicissitudes of time. Fire, bombardment, tornadoes, erosion, and hurricanes have all taken their toll, but Sullivan's Island shows us, in house after house and street after street, pictures of its own life through close to 200 years. These are things that we should not lightly lose, but, unless we look out for them, they can vanish little by little through thoughtlessness, ignorance, or want of a little care until the island becomes just another hum-drum, highly commercialized beach resort.

It was to help guard Sullivan's Island from such a fate that this book has been published. For in our island's case, the new era that has burst upon her need not abhor or destroy a good deal that she can now boast of. But the town is full of new blood, of people who do not know Sullivan's Island. However they may appreciate her charms, they can hardly recognize or respect what she has kept from her past unless they are given some knowledge of that past. As a graphic way of supplying a means to that end, these photographs are now published.

It should be fully understood that these photographs are only memoranda to you who see them, not works of art or even works of expert photography. Many of the original photographs were destroyed in Hurricane Hugo. What is hoped of these pictures is that anyone, with this book in hand, may see the island through the eyes of a group of disinterested people (the architectural surveyors) who would like to point out to every resident, old or new, the buildings of all sorts that they have found valuable to their community.

It is hoped that this book will be used by you as a running reference, or rather, a walking one. Take it someday and go along I'on Avenue or the street you live on and see what houses and structures it would have you look at. There are hardly any of our present-day neighborhoods such as Andersonville and none of our historical subdivisions, such as Moultrieville, Fort Moultrie, Atlanticville, or Marshall Reservation, that haven't either buildings or sites of considerable interest, historically, architecturally, or both.

Sullivan's Island built usually with such individuality that history, sentiment, and architecture came down to us hand-in-hand. Therefore, by simply indicating a building that is worthy in itself of preservation, the survey often does a double duty by helping also to mark a historical or romantic subject. If you use these photographs properly, you will find that, however they fail otherwise, they tell the story of Sullivan's Island as no words could.

One

MOULTRIEVILLE

Stations 9–12

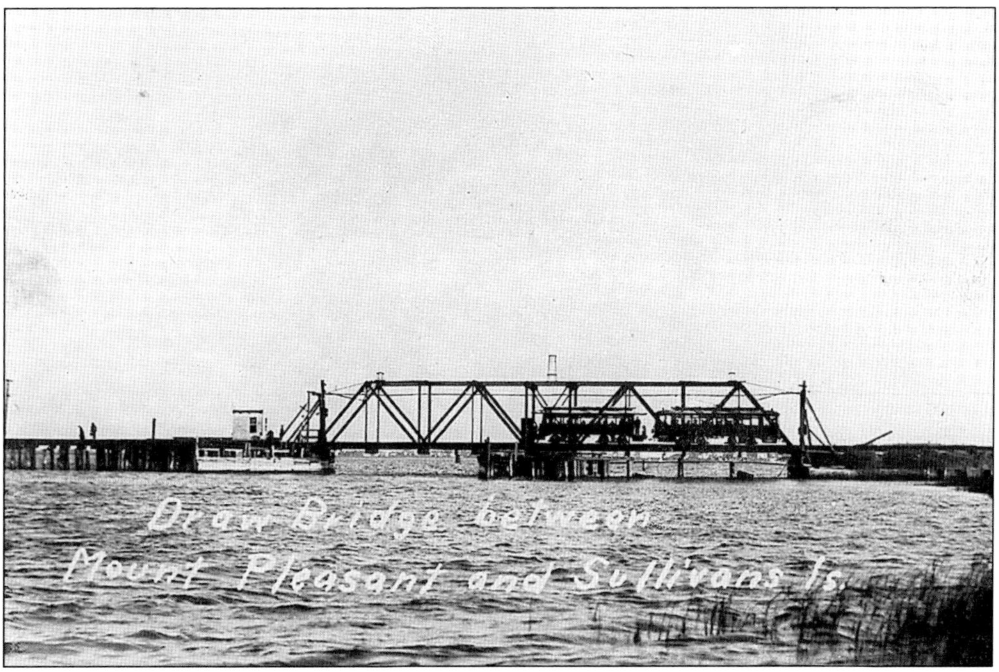

COVE INLET BRIDGE. The Charleston and Seashore Railroad Company was founded in 1898 to provide rail access to Long Island (Isle of Palms) from Charleston, South Carolina. This bridge, which replaced an earlier bridge, was constructed *c.* 1900 for the trolley line, and automobiles began using it in 1926. [Gone.] (Courtesy Marshall Stith.)

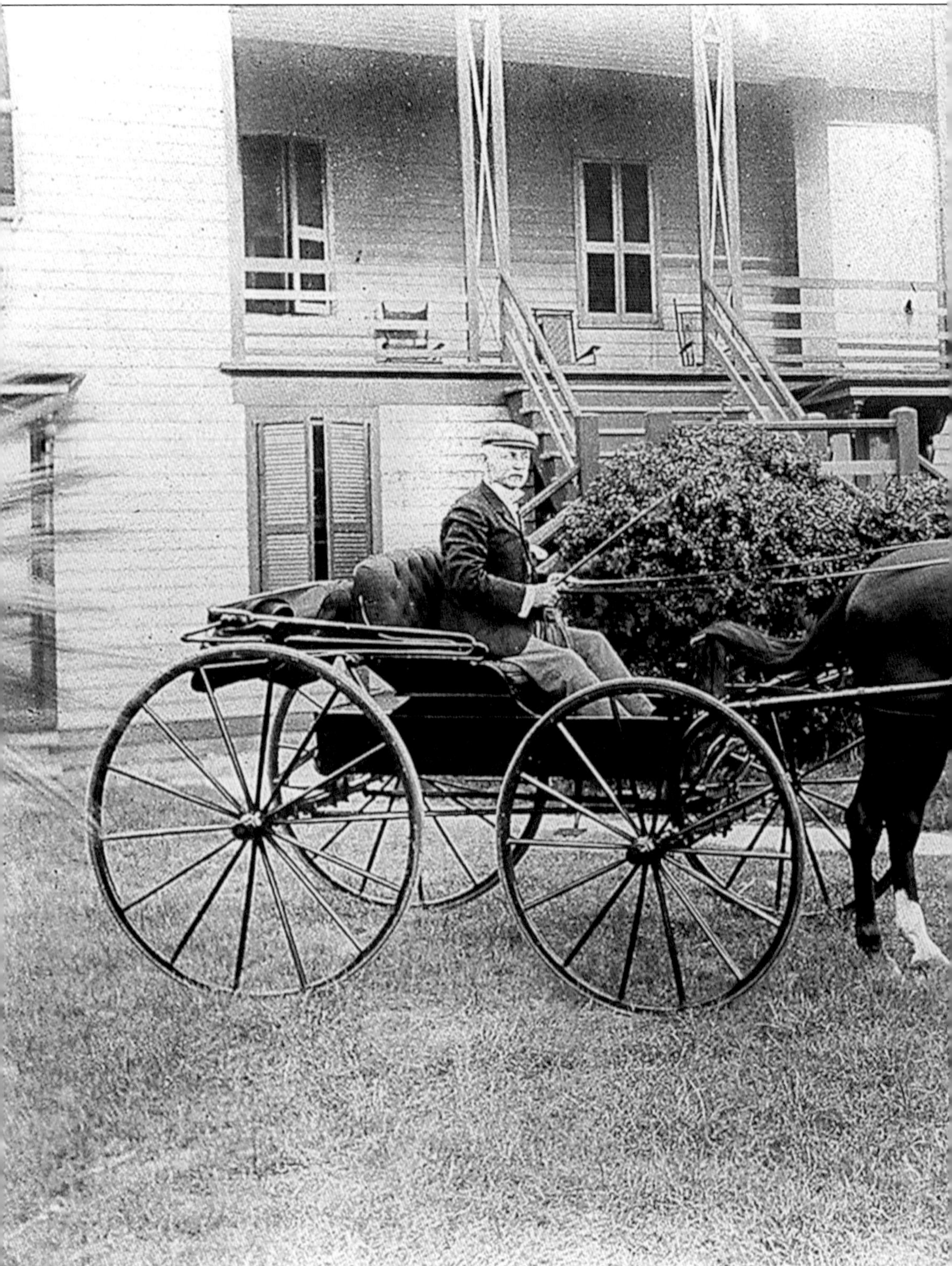

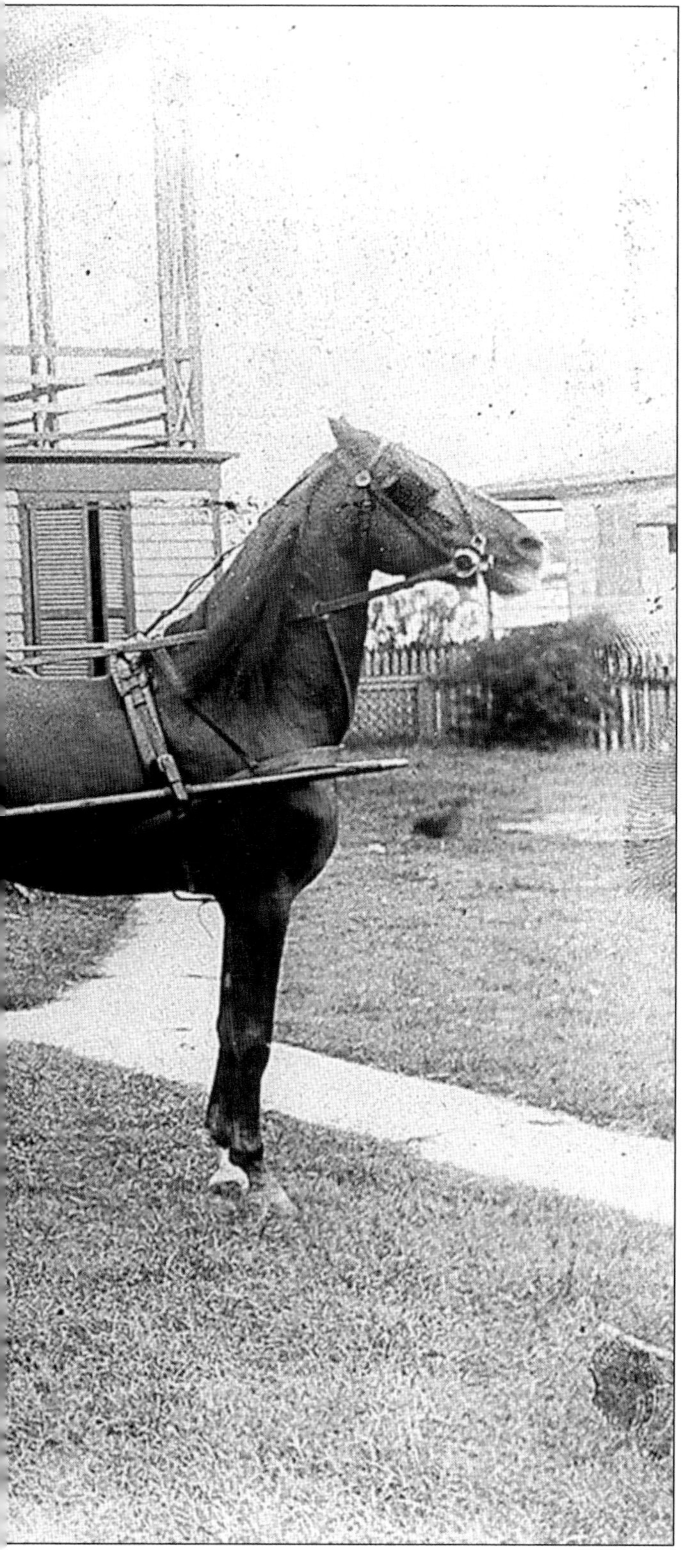

STATION 12, WILLIAM M. BIRD. Mr. Bird is shown in front of his house, known as the Bird Mansion, at Station 12. He was a Charleston merchant whose company, Wm. M. Bird & Co., was located at 205 East Bay at the corner of Cumberland Street. During the great Charleston earthquake of 1886 most of the three-story building collapsed onto Cumberland Street, including all the brick work above the cast iron storefront on the first level. Although the store was completely wrecked, by 5:15 a.m. on the morning after the earthquake, the company had rented a building at 175 East Bay Street and resumed selling wholesale paints and oils. Mr. Bird was a devoted member of the Episcopal church on Sullivan's Island and in a number of letters expressed his displeasure with the federal government when the church's property was condemned for the expansion of Fort Moultrie. [Gone.] (Courtesy Ben Hagood.)

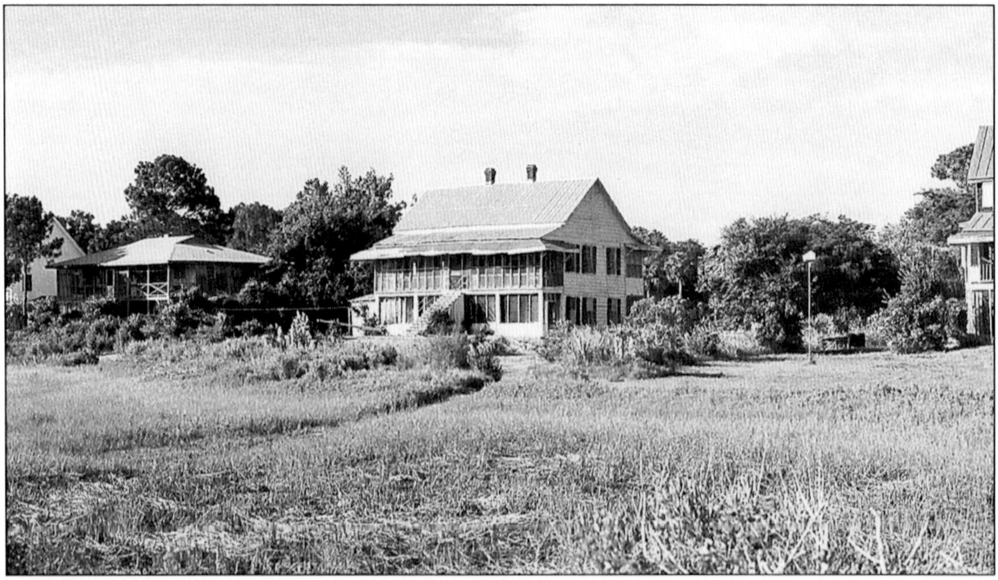

847 Middle Street c. 1870. The Lockwood House was the summer house of Henry Whilden Lockwood, mayor of Charleston (1938–1944), and his family. The house overlooked the Charleston Harbor, where Lockwood had captained a tugboat in the 1920s. [Exceptional example of 19th-century island residential architecture; Gone.] (Courtesy SC Department of Archives and History.)

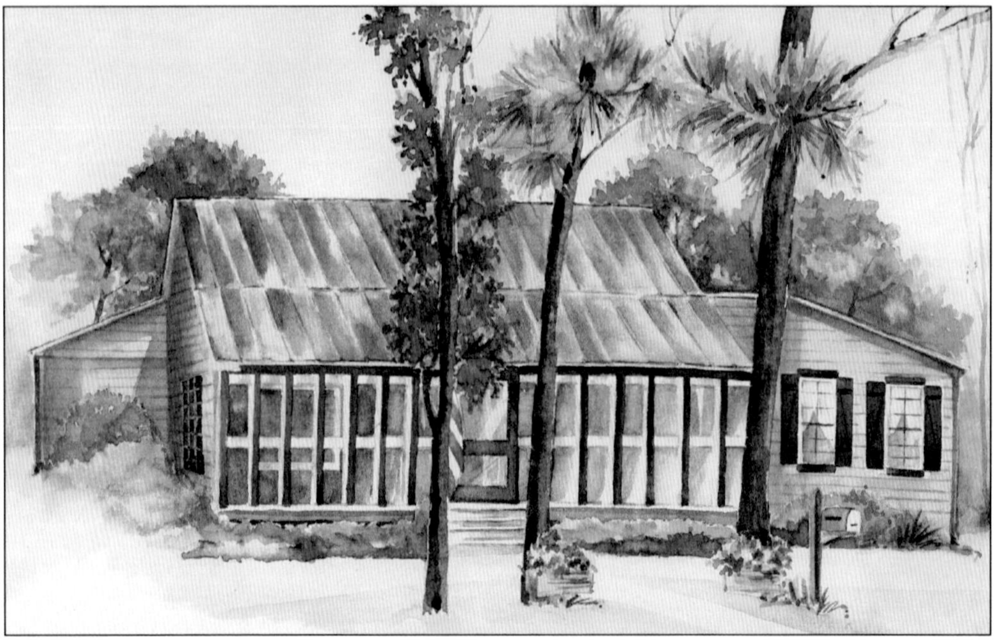

852 Middle Street c. 1890. The Moore House was bought by James T. Molony, a ship chandler in Charleston, and his wife, Margaret Hartnett Molony, from Annie Laffan in 1911. The property is said to have been the former location of Brady's Tavern. The principal entrance has a transom with sidelights. The Moore family, now in its sixth generation, still summers here every year. [Modest 19th-century example.] (Photo of painting courtesy Ann Moore, granddaughter of James and Margaret Molony.)

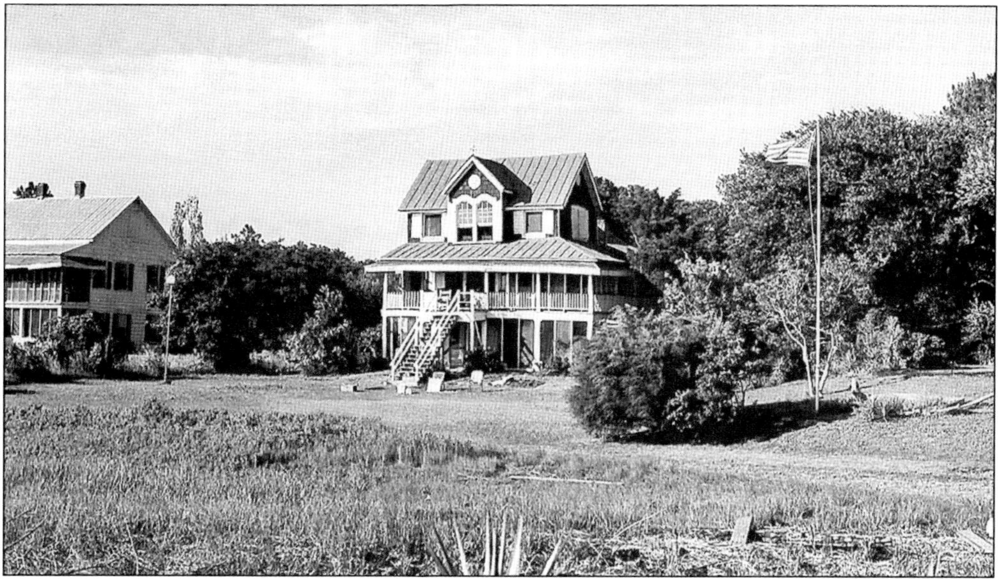

853 Middle Street c. 1880. This summer cottage (Porpoise Point) belonged to C. Irvine Walker, a partner in the Charleston firm of Walker, Evans & Cogswell Printing Co. In 1925 the Cooper River Realty Commission—made up of John P. DeVeaux, Edward Tiencken, H.T. Foster, A.O. Halsey, R.G. Rhett, and William Whaley—bought the property. The commission operated the ferry boat *Sappho* between Charleston and Mount Pleasant. The house was sold in 1930 to Ella Carter McGuire, to Franklin Robson in 1952, and to Caroline and Amy Wilbur in 1959. [Exceptional example of 19th-century island residential architecture.] (Courtesy S.C. Department of Archives and History.)

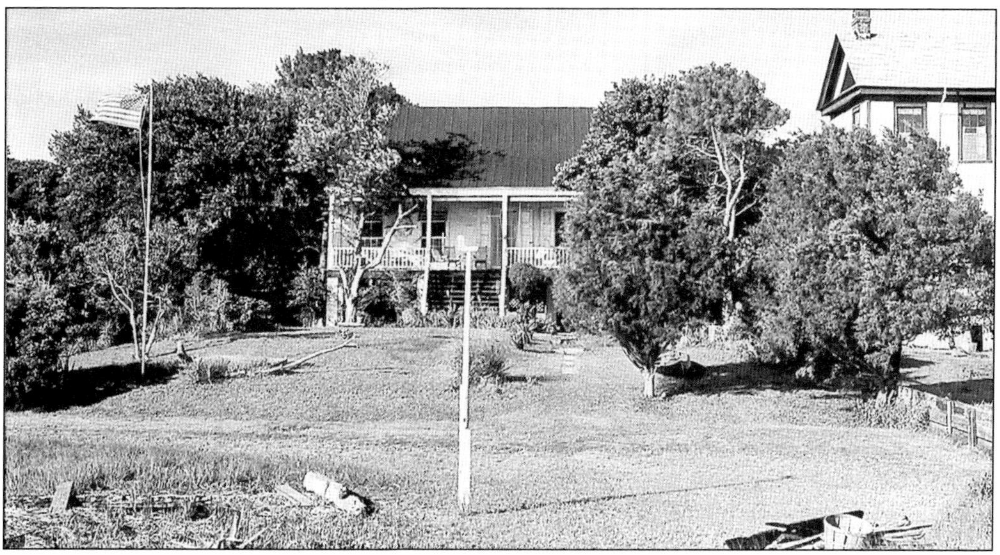

901 Middle Street c. 1874. The O'Hagen House was built by the Aichel family of Charleston. Oskar Aichel, a prosperous grocer, was affiliated with John Hurkamp Co., dealers in groceries, liquors, and wines. The house was acquired by Eugene J. DeVeaux and his family in the 1940s. To protect the interior of the house and its inhabitants from violent storms, each opening on the piazza had an inner and outer set of windows. [Good example of 19th-century island residential architecture.] (Courtesy S.C. Department of Archives and History.)

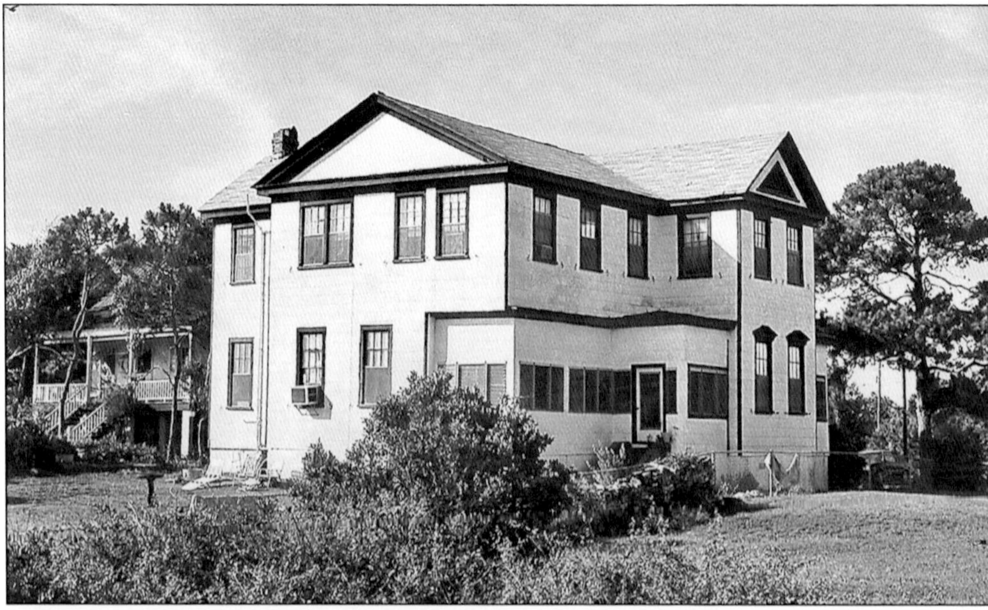

905 Middle Street, 1876. Claussen/Mahony House was constructed in 1876 by John Claussen, owner of a large commercial baking company in Charleston, who constructed the house in 1876. John R. Mahony, owner of a shoe store in Charleston, purchased the house in 1915 as a summer residence. In 1931 Mahony's eldest daughter, a widow, moved there permanently with her seven children. Her son Otis M. Pickett became a doctor. An unusual feature of the house was that the principal northern façade faced the land rather than the ocean, with a central pavilion containing a bay window at the first level. [Exceptional 19th-century example; Gone.] (Courtesy S.C. Department of Archives and History.)

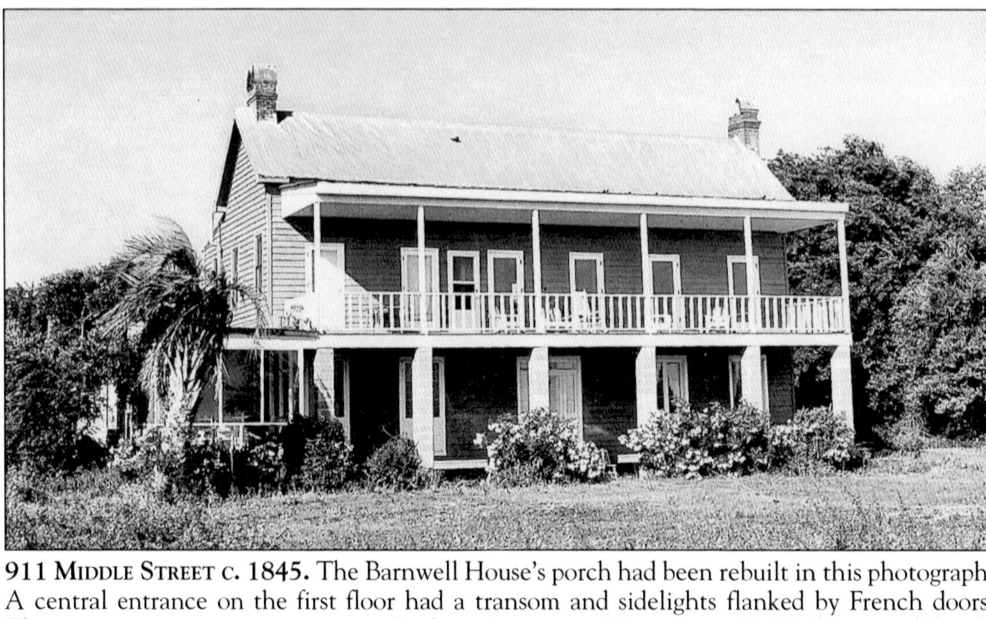

911 Middle Street c. 1845. The Barnwell House's porch had been rebuilt in this photograph. A central entrance on the first floor had a transom and sidelights flanked by French doors. The property appears on numerous Sanborn Insurance Maps. Louis E. Williams and family were the last residents to live there. [Exceptional 19th-century example; Gone.] (Courtesy S.C. Department of Archives and History.)

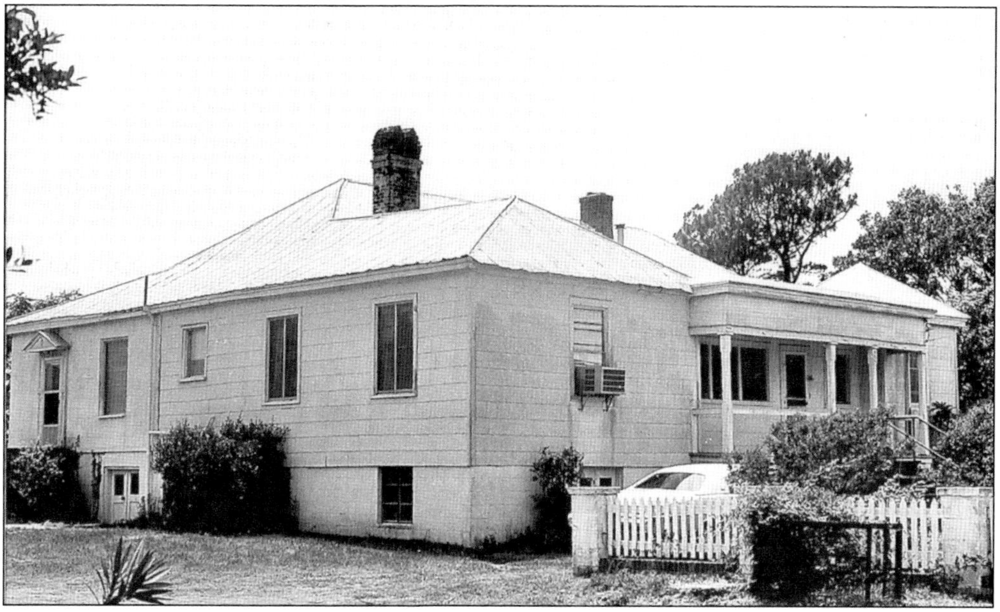

957 MIDDLE STREET c. 1870. This residence was the former location of the "Holiday House" donated by Mrs. Manning Bethea Simons as a summer camp for underprivileged Charleston children. Among the ladies who served a president of the Holiday House Association were Mrs. Thomas S. Silcox, Mrs. Dewar Gordon, Mrs. Walter Metts, Mrs. Richard Allen, and Mrs. Burnet R. Maybank. The summer of 1941 was the last year the Holiday House operated. The property was sold in 1943 and the assets of the organization placed in government bonds. The property was then acquired by the George F. Brown family, who lived there year-round. [Good 19th-century example; Gone.] (Courtesy S.C. Department of Archives and History.)

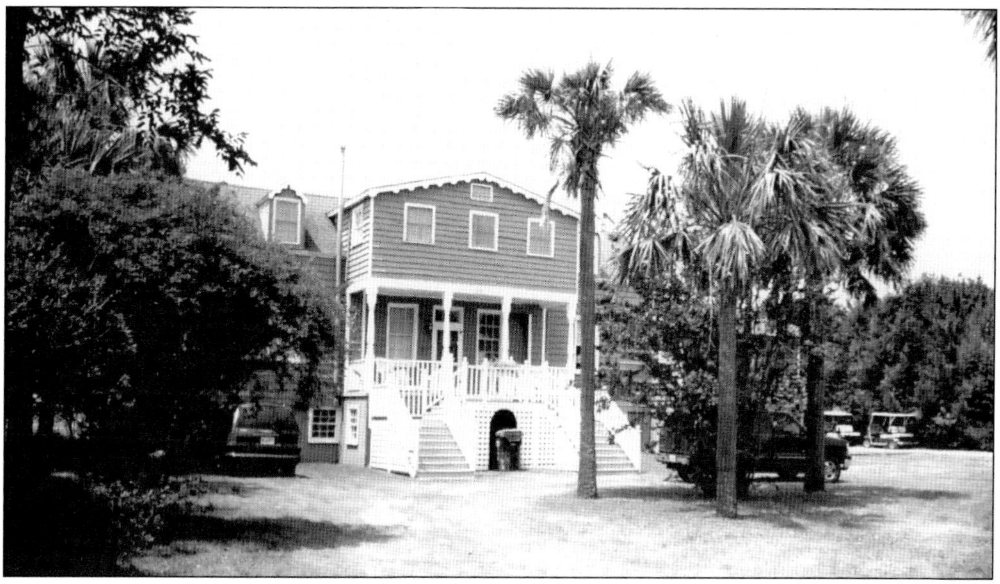

1001 MIDDLE STREET c. 1845. This house has a T-shaped block to the west and an addition to the north elevation. There are decorative sawn bargeboards at the gable ends. Jib doors were created from original French doors c. 1930. [Exceptional 19th-century example.] (Courtesy Bonnie A. Williams.)

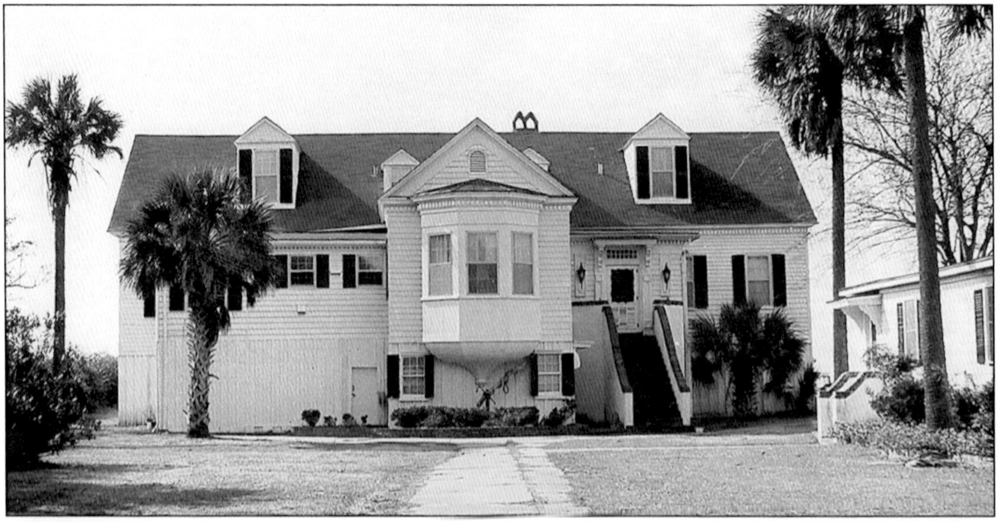

1009 Middle Street c. 1850. The Simonds House has a plaza on its south elevation that originally extended across the entire front of the dwelling. Three pedimented gable dormers with vertical band siding are also on the harbor front. The north elevation is accentuated by a bay window. Old glazing indicates early construction. The chimney has an arched rain hood. The property now belongs to the Engle family. [Very good example of 19th-century island architecture.] (Courtesy Marshall Stith.)

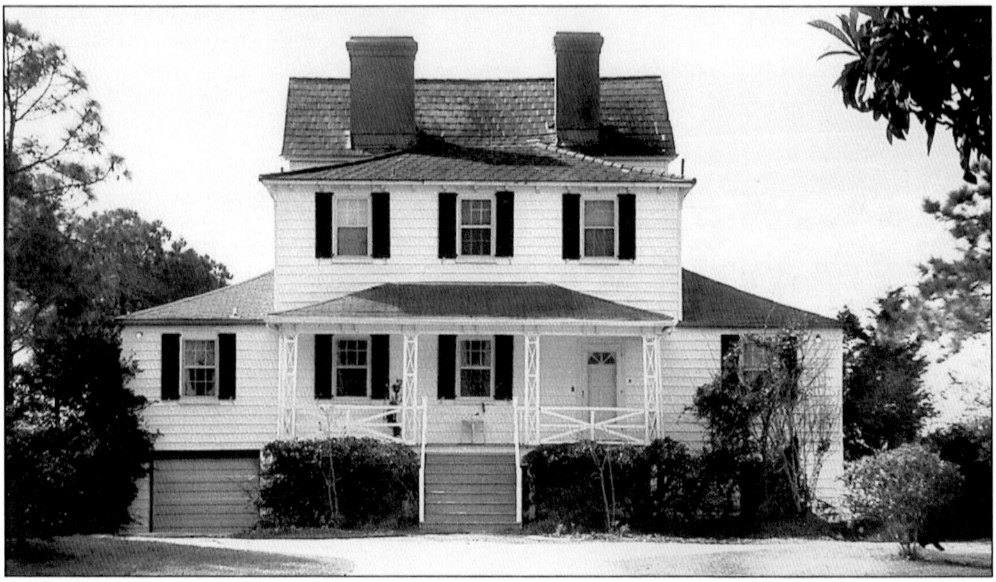

1013 Middle Street, 1834. The Pringle House (also known as Harbor View and Windy Hill) was originally constructed in 1834. The house was acquired after the Civil War by the DuPont family, who may have been related to Admiral Samuel Francis DuPont, commander of a fleet of Union ironclads that attacked Charleston during the war but were repelled. The house was later owned by the Pringle family, the Atkinson family, and Robert C. Oertel, a well-known, early 20th-century explorer. The Edward E. Crawford family now live there. Tradition holds that the rear dependency was constructed as a slave house and that a Civil War battery may have been located along the property's beach front. [Exceptional example of 19th-century island architecture.] (Courtesy S.C. Department of Archives and History.)

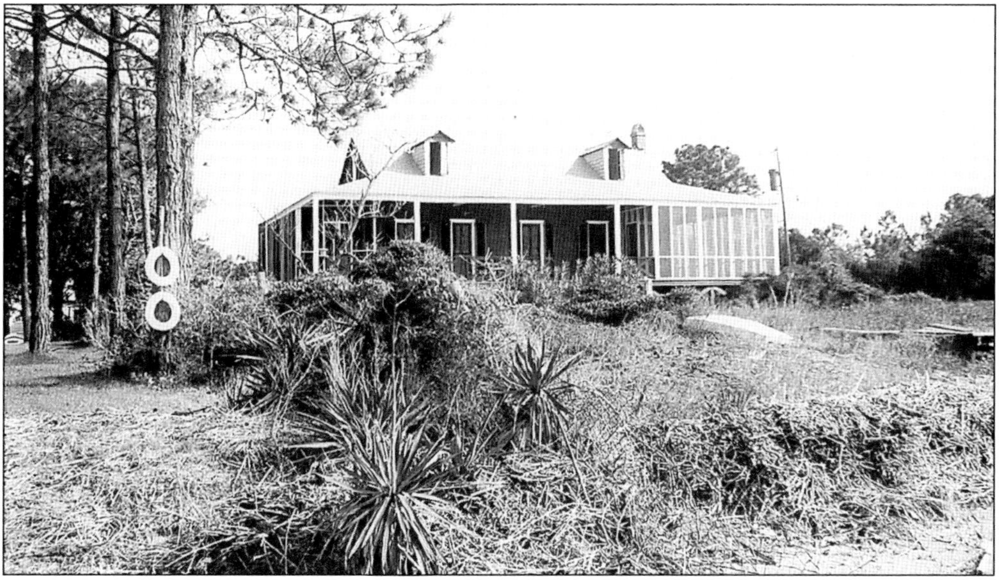

1023 Middle Street c. 1929. The Nat Barnwell House is a one-and-a-half story, rectangular-shaped dwelling with porches on all four sides. It was built with many doors and windows placed to maximize cross ventilation. A one-by-one bay kitchen house has been connected to the main house. There is a one-by-two bay servant's house to the northwest and two dormers on the south elevation roof line. [Good example of early 20th-century island architecture.]

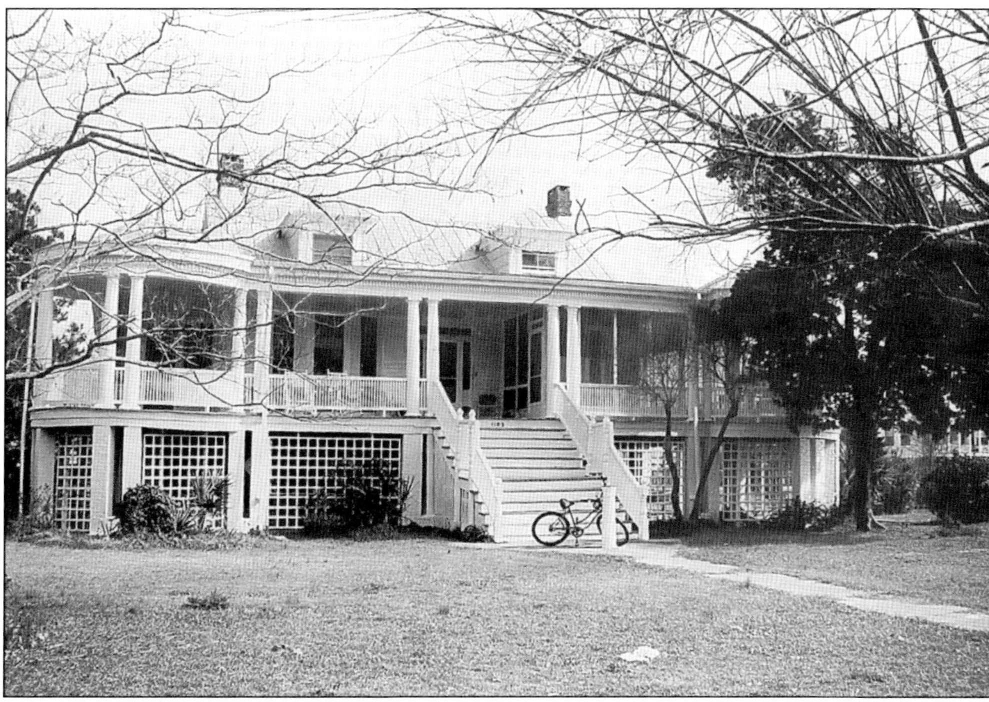

1102 Middle Street c. 1890. The Cosgrove House's original owner is said to have been James Cosgrove. The dwelling is rectangular in shape with a porch designed with conical ends. The central entrance has a transom with sidelights flanked by bay windows. The roof is accentuated with two hipped dormers. [Exceptional late 19th-century example.] (Courtesy Marshall Stith.)

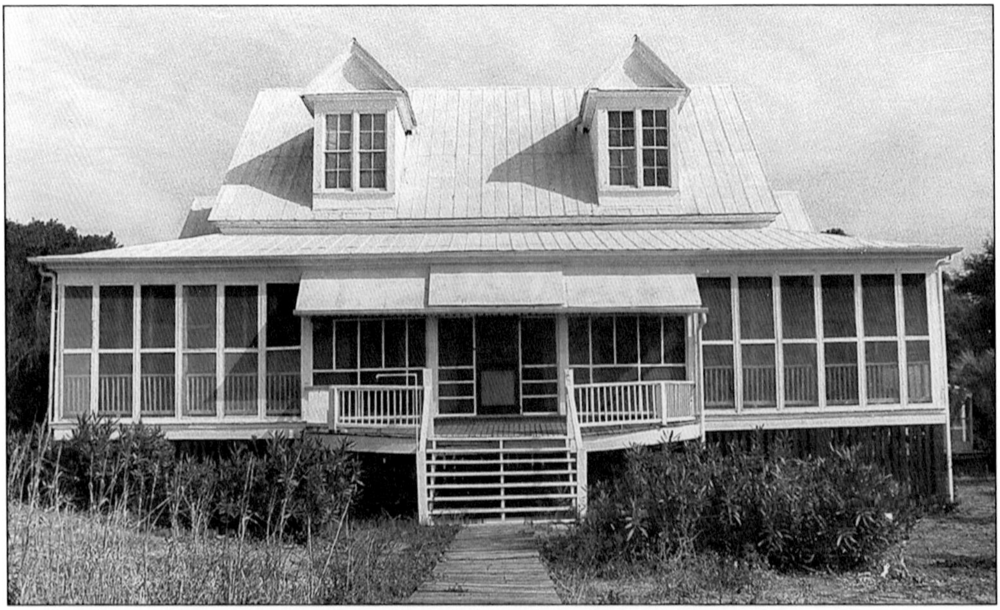

1103 MIDDLE STREET c. 1867. The Blake/Middleton/Brawley House was built as a summer residence for Judge William Hiram Brawley (1841–1916), congressman and federal judge, of Charleston. The rectangular structure has one-by-one bay wings to the east and west and two pedimented gable dormers with double four-by-four windows. Servant quarters have been attached to the northeast. [Exceptional 19th-century example.] (Courtesy Marshall Stith.)

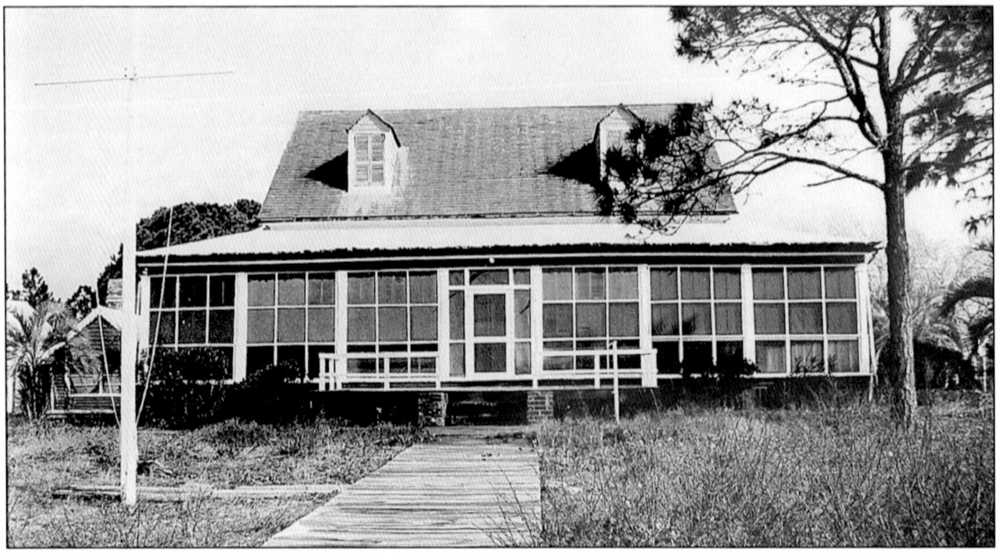

1109 MIDDLE STREET c. 1867. The Salmons-Lawson House was built by Judge Brawley as a summer residence for his daughter and son-in-law. Judge Brawley's granddaughter was born in this house. The property was bought in 1908 by the Waring family of Charleston and later transferred to their relatives, the Salmons family. The house has a central hall plan with four-panel doors and a wooden mantel and fireplace in the hall, although no chimney is visible. The rear elevation has a hipped porch with sawn trim and spindle work. What may have been a former kitchen building and servant's quarters are attached to the northeast and northwest elevations of the house. [Exceptional 19th-century example.] (Courtesy Marshall Stith.)

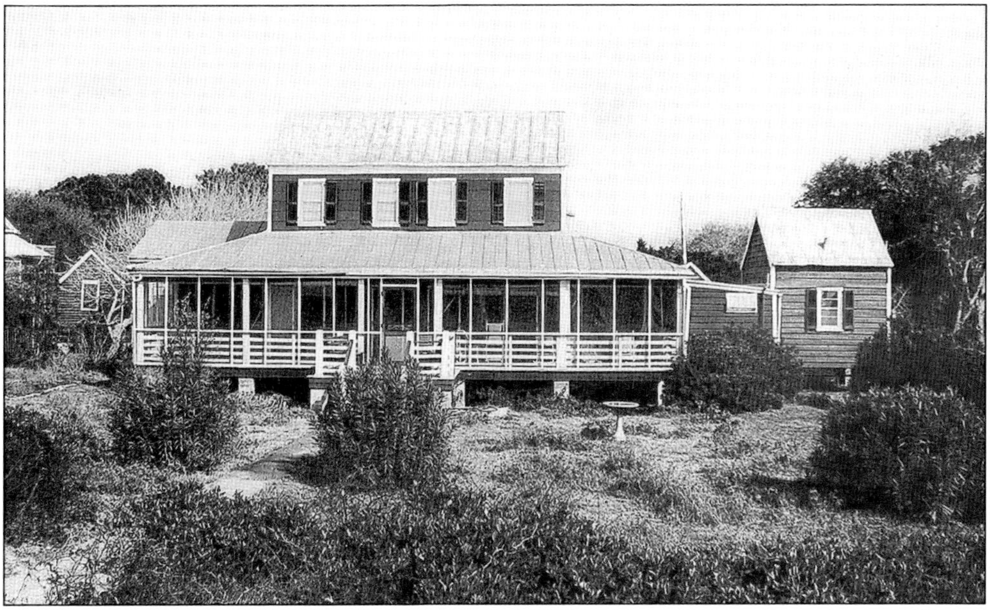

1111 Middle Street, 1830. Local tradition holds that the King House was used as officers' quarters during the Civil War. The structure is shown on the 1893 Sanborn Map of Sullivan's Island. The house is basically a rectangular block with wings to the east and west. [Exceptional 19th-century example.] (Courtesy Marshall Stith.)

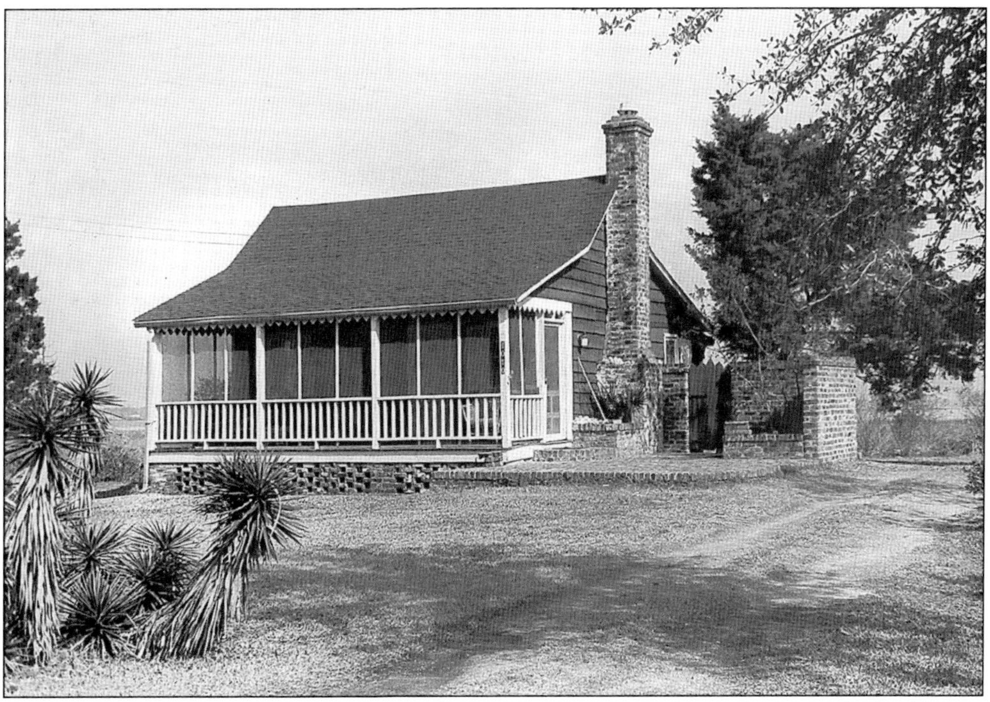

1010 Osceola Avenue, 1854. The Muller House is rectangular with a rear shed addition. The porch has decorative sawn trim (some is a recent replacement). [Representative of modest island residences built during the early 20th century.] (Courtesy Marshall Stith.)

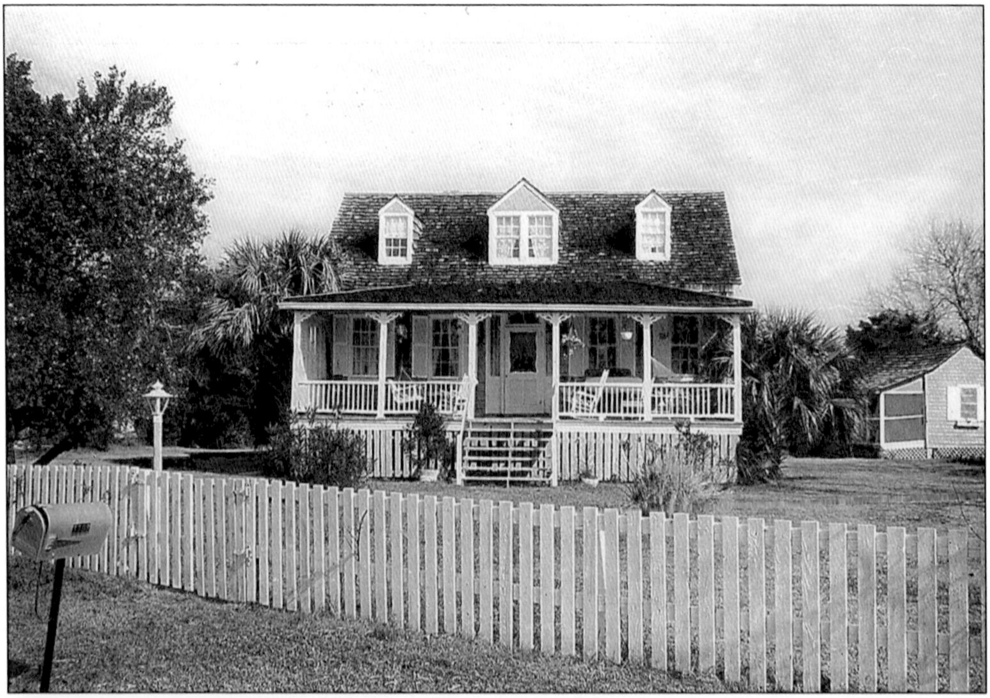

1102 Osceola Avenue. This classic Sullivan's Island home is the summer residence of the Stone Walker family, who live in Charleston on South Battery. (Courtesy Marshall Stith.)

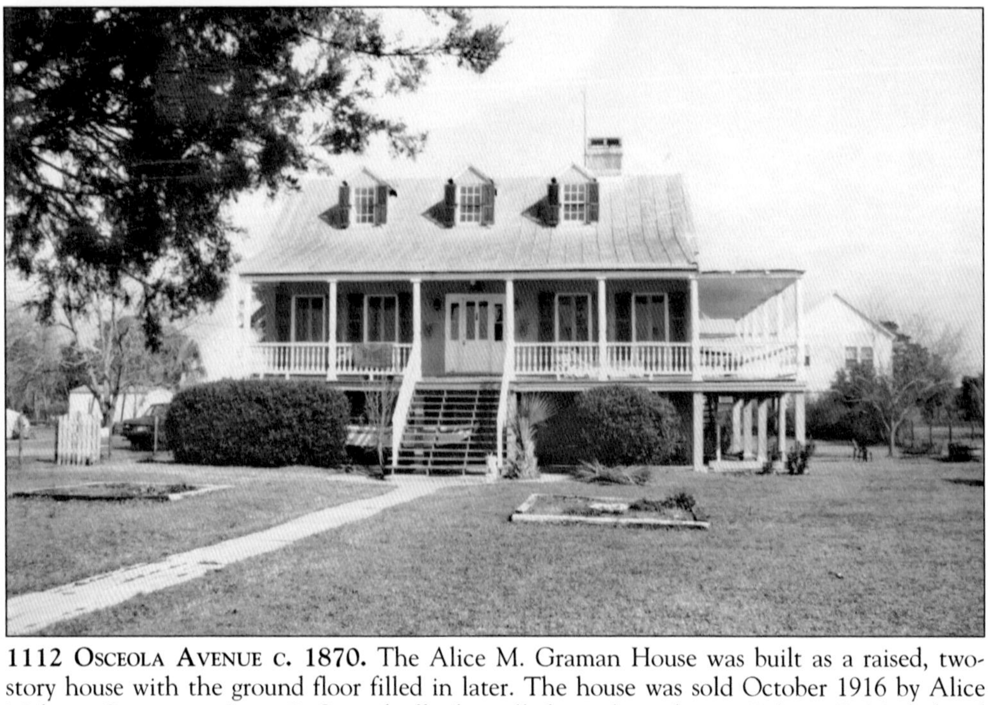

1112 Osceola Avenue c. 1870. The Alice M. Graman House was built as a raised, two-story house with the ground floor filled in later. The house was sold October 1916 by Alice Mahony Graman to Anna P. Ostendorff, who willed it to her relatives Sidonie D. Michel and H. St. Elmo Soubeyroux. Other former owners include Thomas Pollock and Letitia Galbraith. [Exceptional example of late 19th-century architecture.] (Courtesy Marshall Stith.)

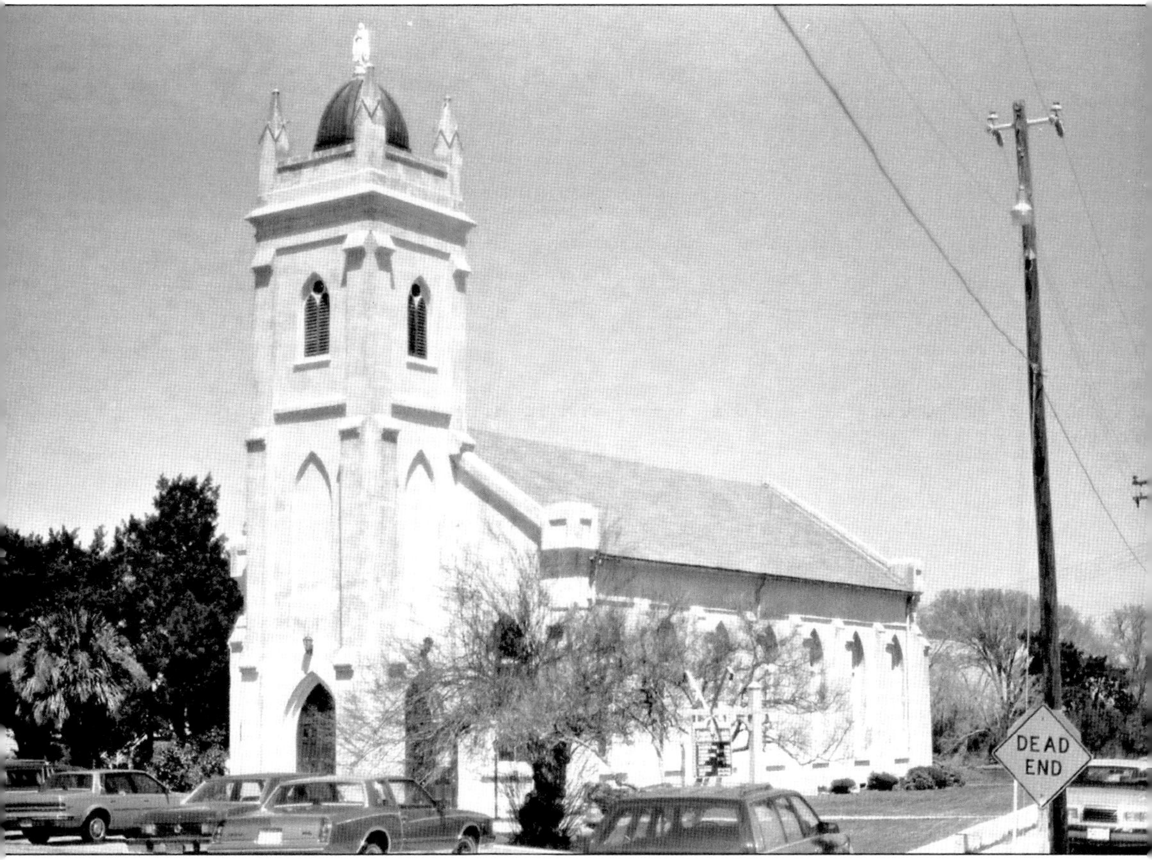

1204 Middle Street. Stella Maris Church ("Star of the Sea") is the second Catholic church on the island. It replaced the Church of St. John the Baptist, which was still in use until 1872 (and destroyed by a cyclone in 1885). The site for the present church was purchased in 1867; the cornerstone was set January 1, 1869, and the sanctuary completed in 1873. The current priest is Fr. Lawrence McInerny. According to tradition, Father Birmingham was given permission by the federal government to use loose bricks and stones from the debris around war-torn Fort Moultrie to build this church. This was stopped when the workers in their enthusiasm began to dismantle the fort's walls. John Henry Devereux (1840–1920), the noted Charleston architect, was a member of this congregation, and he and Father Birmingham together worked with their own hands on the foundations. Stained glass windows were installed in 1955 after the closing of Fort Moultrie. Until that time glass breakage was common due to the firing of the fort's guns. The interior of the church was filmed for the television series *North and South*. (Courtesy S.C. Department of Archives and History.)

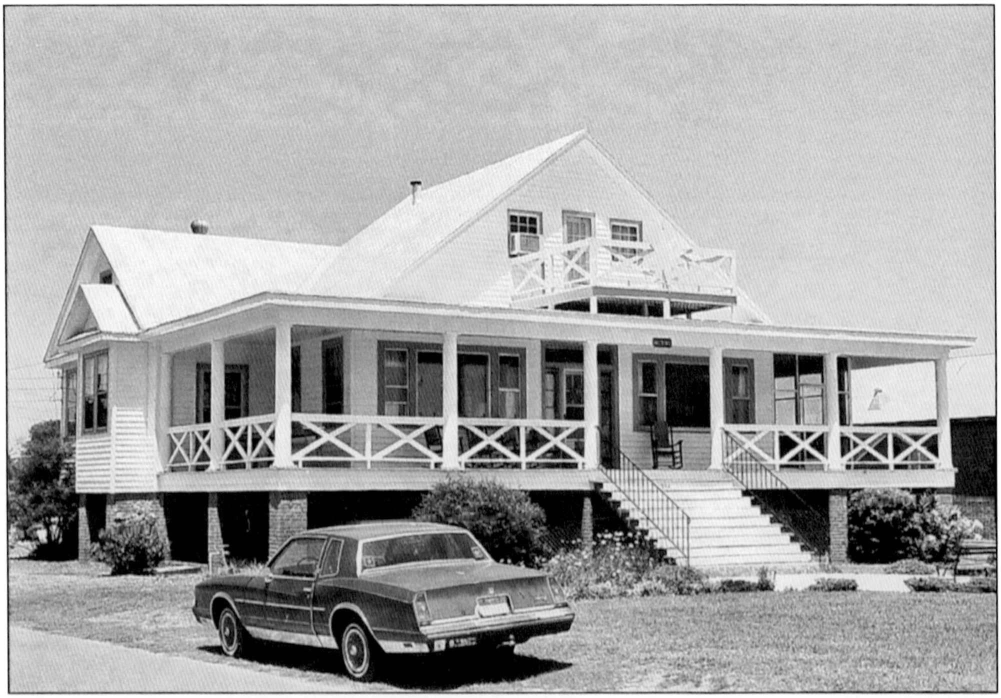

STELLA MARIS CATHOLIC CHURCH RECTORY C. 1930. Located on the northeast corner of Osceola Avenue and Middle Street, the rectory is said to have been built by a Mr. Dillon, a local carpenter. [Good example of early 20th-century architecture.] (Courtesy S.C. Department of Archives and History.)

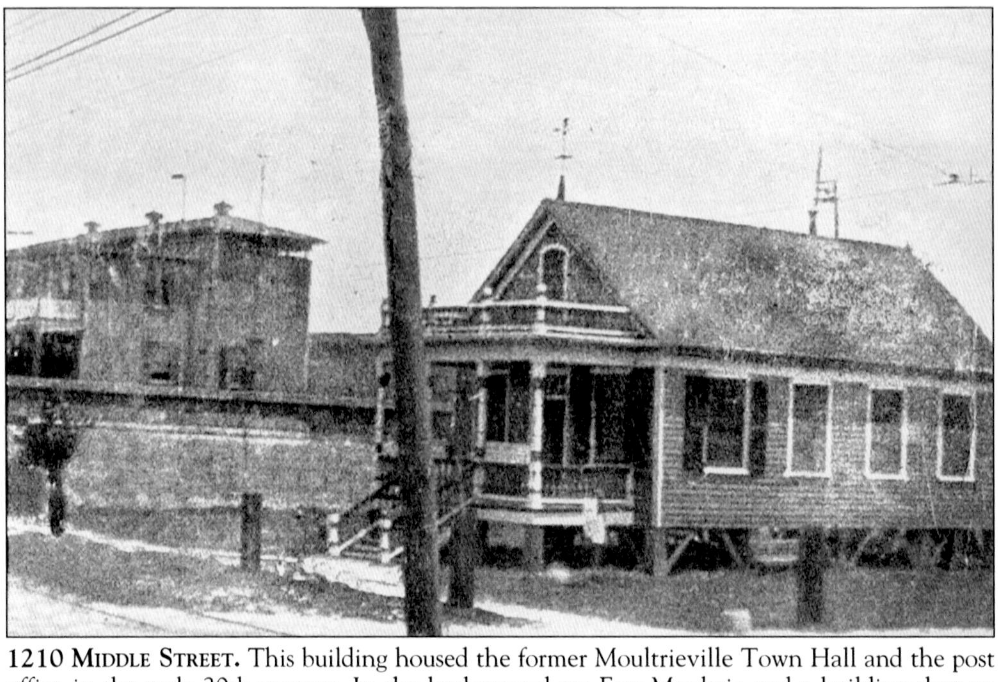

1210 MIDDLE STREET. This building housed the former Moultrieville Town Hall and the post office in the early 20th century. In the background are Fort Moultrie and a building that no longer exists. [Gone.] (Courtesy Marshall Stith.)

Two

FORT MOULTRIE

Stations 12–18

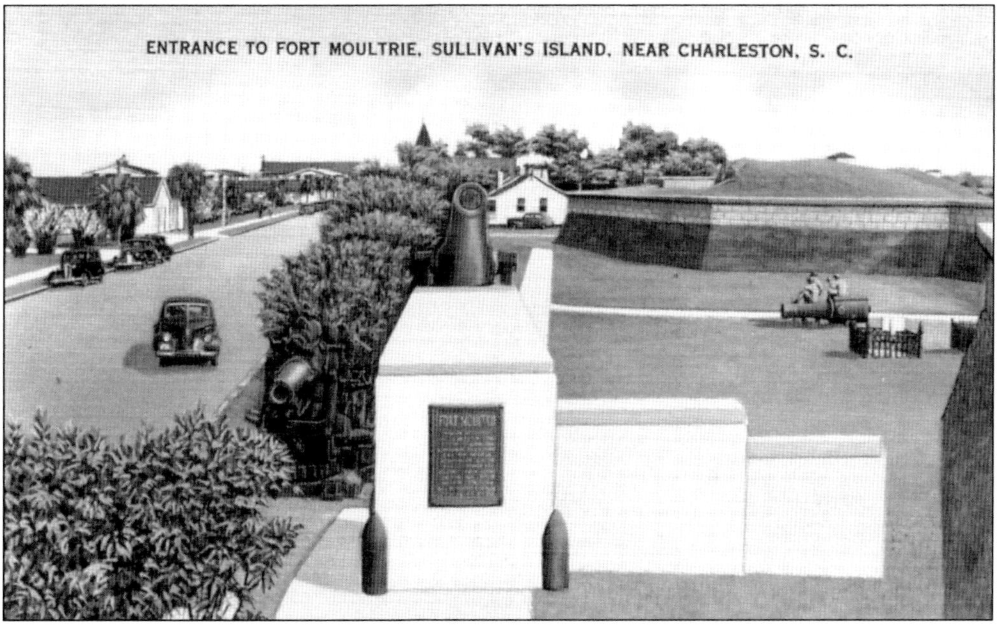

ENTRANCE TO FORT MOULTRIE. Today's Fort Moultrie is the third major military fortification located on this general site. The first, constructed in early 1776 under the command of Col. William Moultrie, successfully defended against an attack by the British in the Revolutionary War. The fort was later destroyed by the ocean tides. In 1796 the federal government erected a replacement, earthenwork fortification, which was destroyed in a heavy storm on October 1 and 2, 1803. Plans for a third Fort Moultrie were developed by Maj. Alexander McComb, U.S. Army Corps of Engineers, in 1809, and a new fort was completed by 1811. Additional work was completed between 1871 and 1876, and then the fort was all but abandoned until 1897, when tensions were growing between the United States and Spain. A major expansion in the late 19th and early 20th centuries took place as the United States sought to strengthen its coastal defenses. The Endicott System of coastal defenses—drawn up in 1885 by a board headed by William C. Endicott (then secretary of war)—called for the creation of 29 coastal defense locations armed with mortars, powerful rifles, numerous batteries, improvements to Batteries Jasper and Capron, the addition of numerous guns, and the mining of Charleston harbor. President Theodore Roosevelt was a firm believer in the importance of a strong mobile fleet, free from the necessity of defending the country's sea ports. (Courtesy Deborah Lofton.)

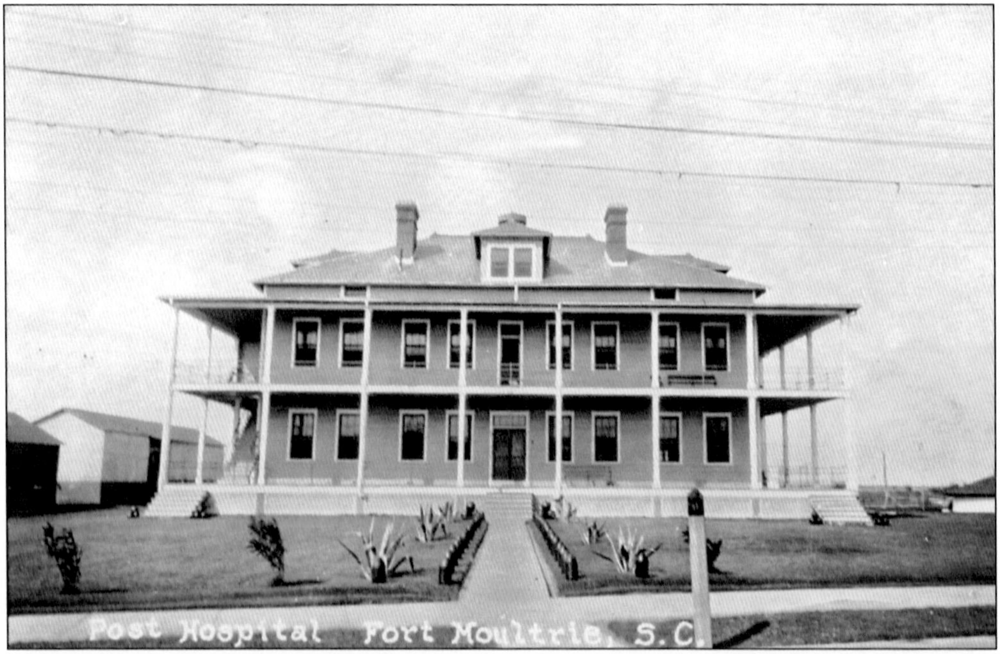

POST HOSPITAL, FORT MOULTRIE. The post hospital stood on the left after the entrance to Fort Moultrie. The main building and its supporting units no longer stand. The site today is occupied by the Fort Sumter/Fort Moultrie Visiting Information Center. In 1902 the government took much of the land between stations 12 and 18 for the fort's expansion. Eventually the fort was de-activated in 1947, and the National Park Service acquired the property in 1960. (Courtesy Deborah Lofton.)

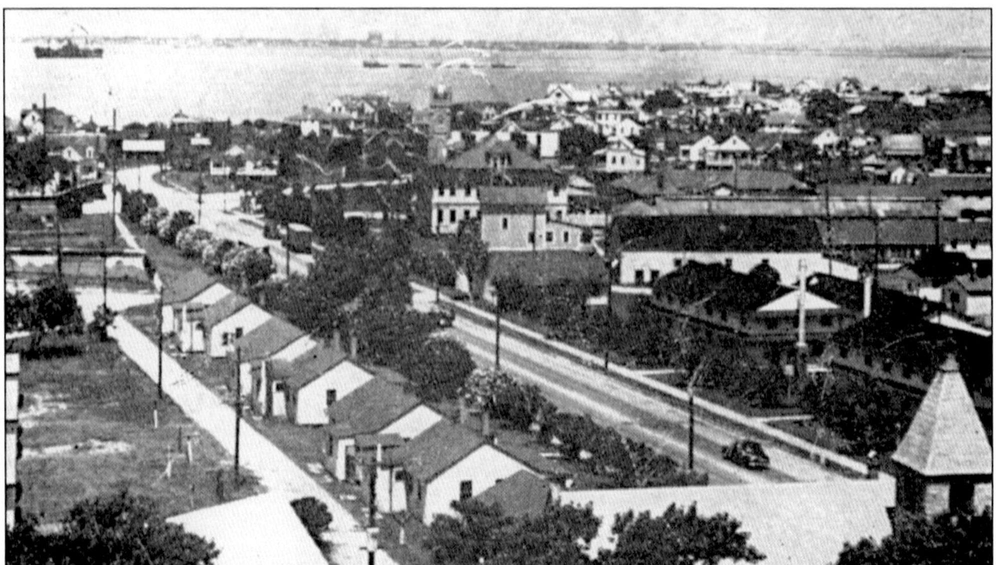

FORT MOULTRIE 1947. This view of Fort Moultrie looks westward from the Post Chapel and shows the non-commissioned officer's quarters and the Post Hospital. Stella Maris Church and Charleston Harbor are seen in the background. (Courtesy Virginia Damewood Chasteen.)

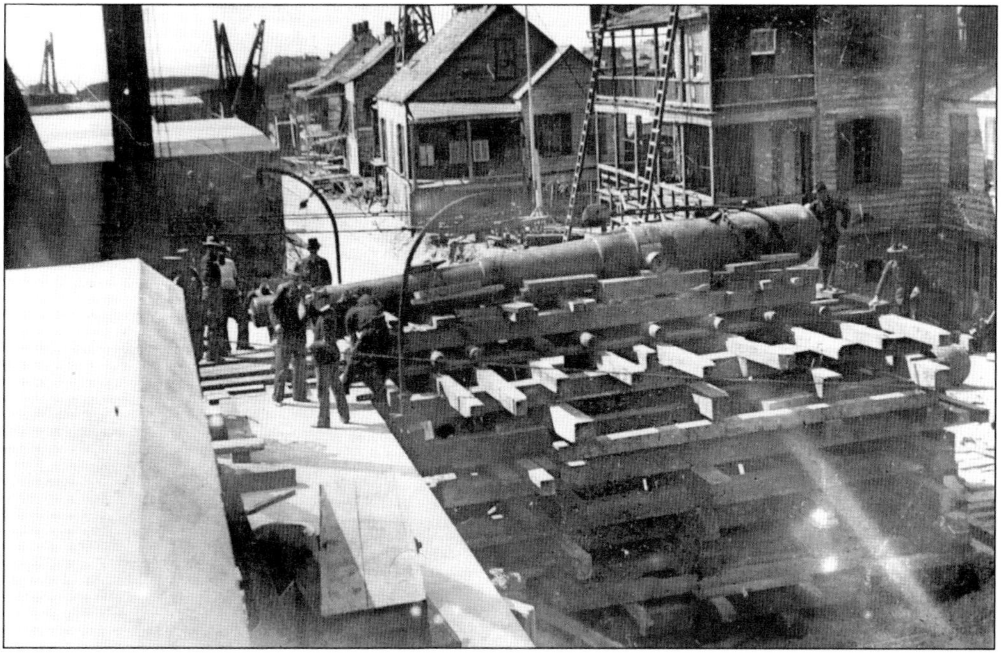

Mounting 10-Inch Sea Coast Gun, Battery Jasper c. 1898. The foundation work for Battery Jasper was laid in the early spring of 1897. This was a four-gun battery with 10-inch pieces mounted on disappearing carriages, hydraulically and electrically operated with a range of about nine miles. This work was completed in 1898 with a total expenditure of $235,000. The houses in the background were either moved or destroyed. The battery was named in honor of Sgt. William Jasper, who, during the attack by the British Fleet on June 28, 1776, restored to Fort Moultrie the flag that had been shot away. (Courtesy Col. Johnson Hagood.)

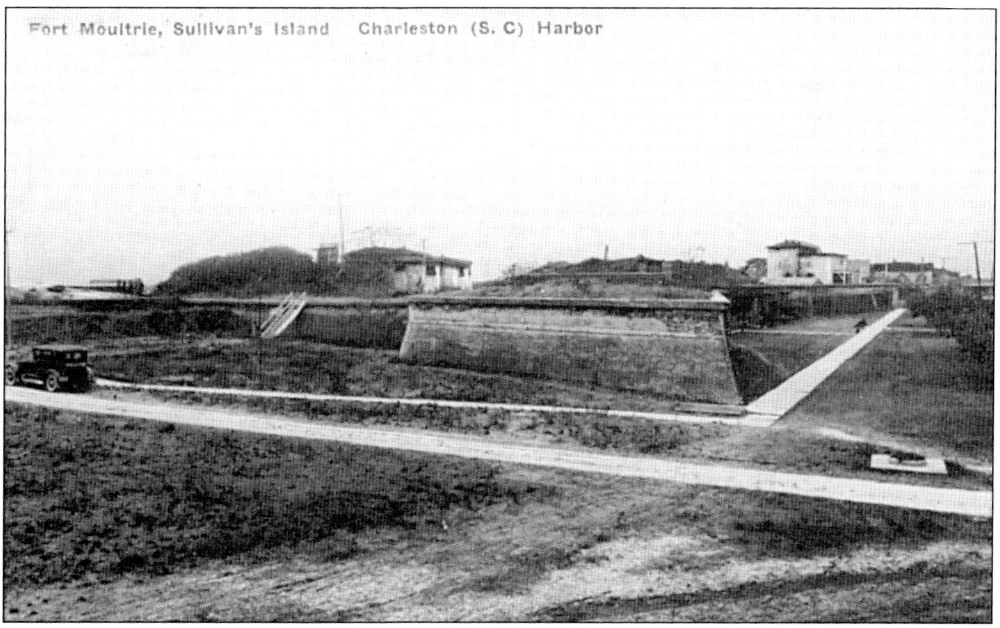

Fort Moultrie. This old view of the fort shows several buildings that were later removed. (Courtesy Deborah Lofton.)

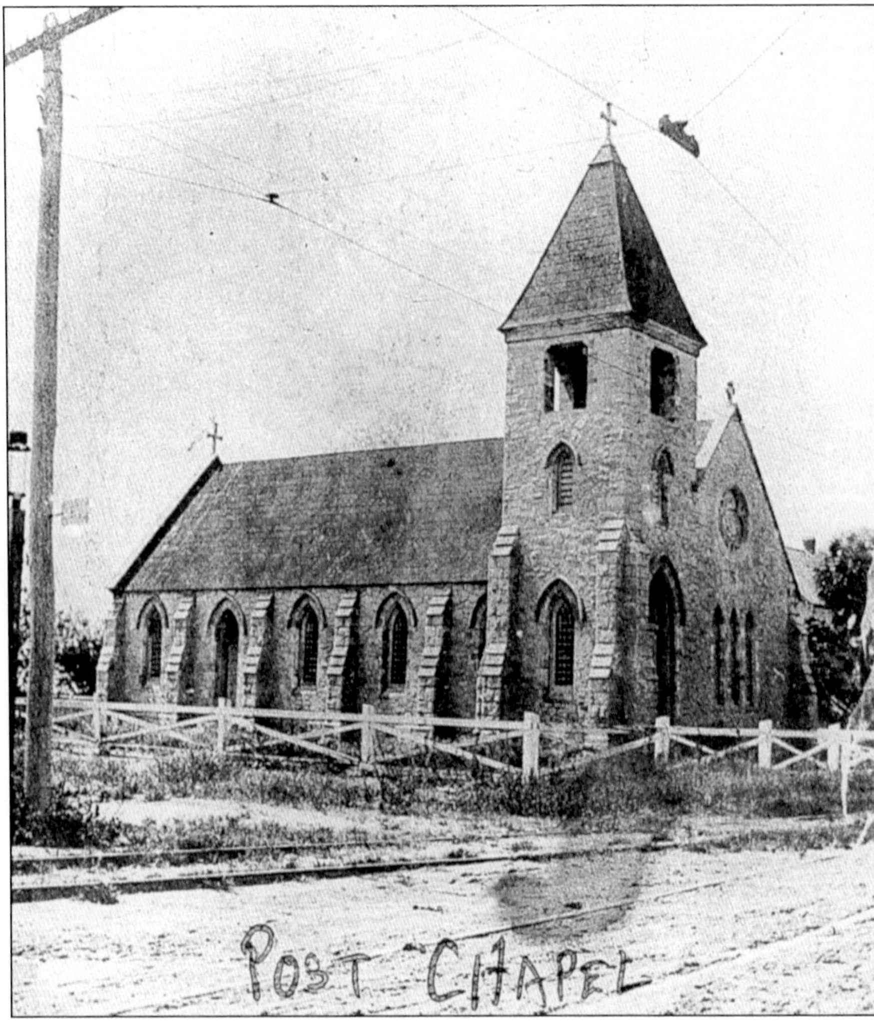

1401 Middle Street, Post Chapel/Holy Cross Episcopal Chapel. In 1813 Grace Episcopal Church was established for summer residents. It was disbanded in 1861 and sold in 1879; the proceeds were used to purchase this lot, on which the Chapel of the Holy Cross was built by Robert McCarrell and designed by W.W. Deveaux of New York, formerly of Charleston. The cornerstone was laid on September 12, 1891, and the first service as held on July 10, 1892. The total cost of construction was slightly over $6,000. The bell was dedicated in 1895, and the roof was badly damaged by a storm in September 1896. In 1902, with the expansion of Fort Moultrie, the site was condemned by the federal government and used as a post chapel from 1907 to 1947. The congregation sold the building to the government, removed the memorial window, bell, and chancel, and incorporated them into a new Chapel of the Holy Cross built at 2520 Middle Street. Upon the deactivation of Fort Moultrie in 1947, the building was bought by J.C.W. Bischoff for $2,600 from the War Assets Administration and presented to the Town of Sullivan's Island. After several years of disuse the structure was given by the town to the South Carolina Lutheran Synod, to be used by a newly formed congregation as St. Marks Lutheran Church. This church later moved to the Isle of Palms; the building was sold and converted for use as a private residence. [Exceptional structure; significant as an example of early vernacular 20th-century church architecture and for its historical associations with Fort Moultrie from 1904 to 1947.] (Courtesy Mrs. Fromberger.)

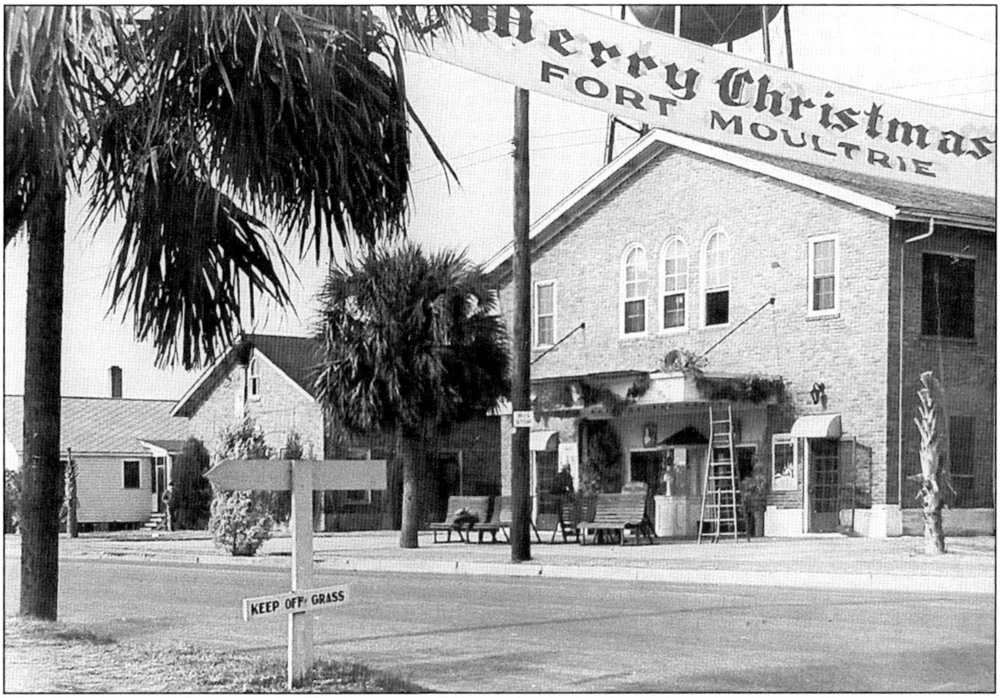

1454 Middle Street c. 1930. The Fort Moultrie Post Theatre was constructed as a motion picture theatre for Fort Moultrie families. It was sold by the government in the early 1950s and was converted for use as a warehouse c. 1975. This building served as the fort's primary entertainment facility until 1947, when the fort was deactivated and most of its property sold to private individuals or turned over to the State of South Carolina. [Part of a significant grouping of military structures associated with the expansion of Fort Moultrie between 1897 and 1935. It is important as an example of early 20th-century military architecture.] (Courtesy Marshall Stith.)

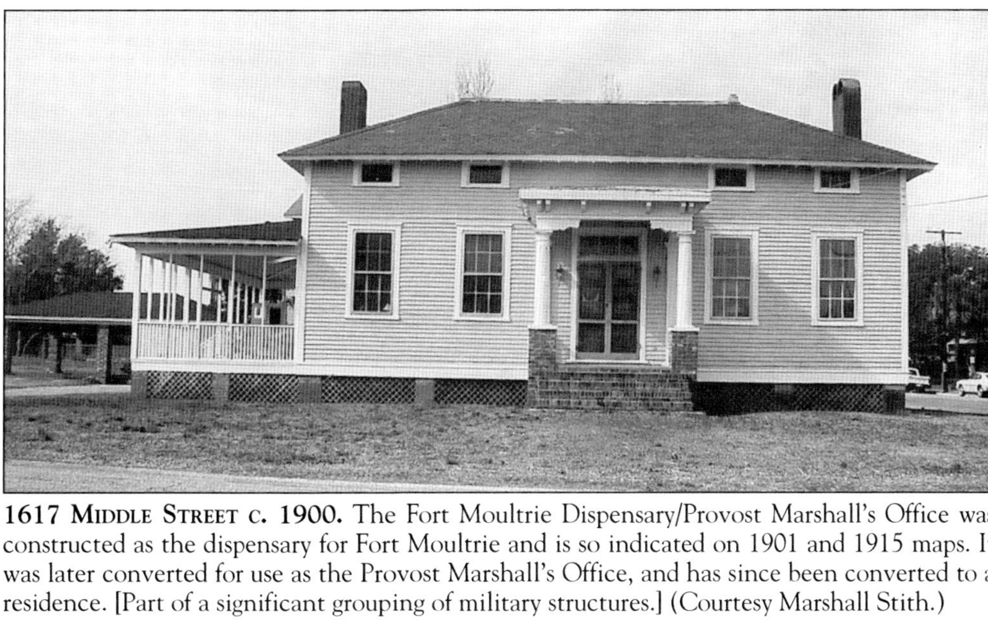

1617 Middle Street c. 1900. The Fort Moultrie Dispensary/Provost Marshall's Office was constructed as the dispensary for Fort Moultrie and is so indicated on 1901 and 1915 maps. It was later converted for use as the Provost Marshall's Office, and has since been converted to a residence. [Part of a significant grouping of military structures.] (Courtesy Marshall Stith.)

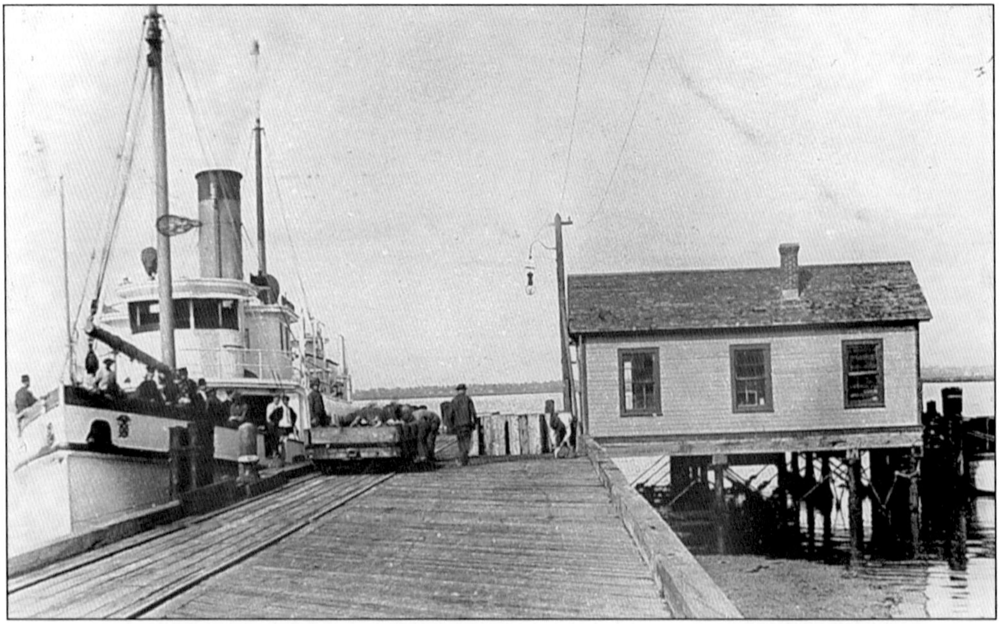

North End of Station 16 c. 1915. Shown here is the Fort Moultrie Quartermaster's Dock. A dock appeared at this location as early as 1901 as "the Store House Wharf," according to a map of Fort Moultrie. It is uncertain whether this dock and building are the remnants of that wharf or a replacement. A wharf of similar shape is shown for the first time on a 1921 fort map but is referred to as the "Q.M." (Quartermaster) Dock on a 1945 fort map. The boat *Sprig Carroll* is at the dock. [The structure remains as the only substantially intact historic dock on the island.] (Courtesy Marshall Sith.)

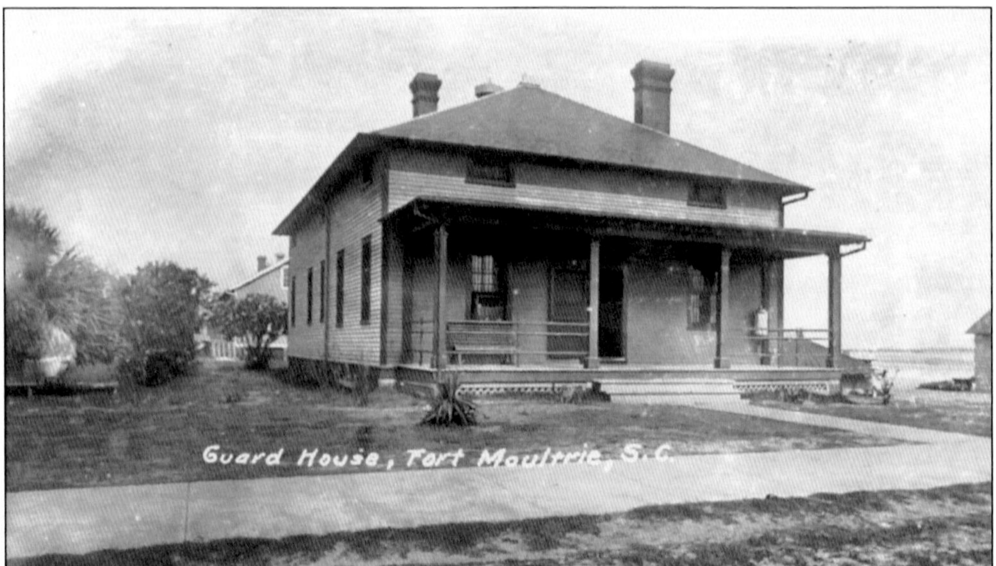

Guard House, Fort Moultrie. This building was located across the street from the Fort Moultrie Dispensary. According to a postcard written by a soldier to his girlfriend, "This is where you go if don't behave yourself. I am going to sleep there tomorrow night while I am on guard." (Courtesy Deborah Lofton.)

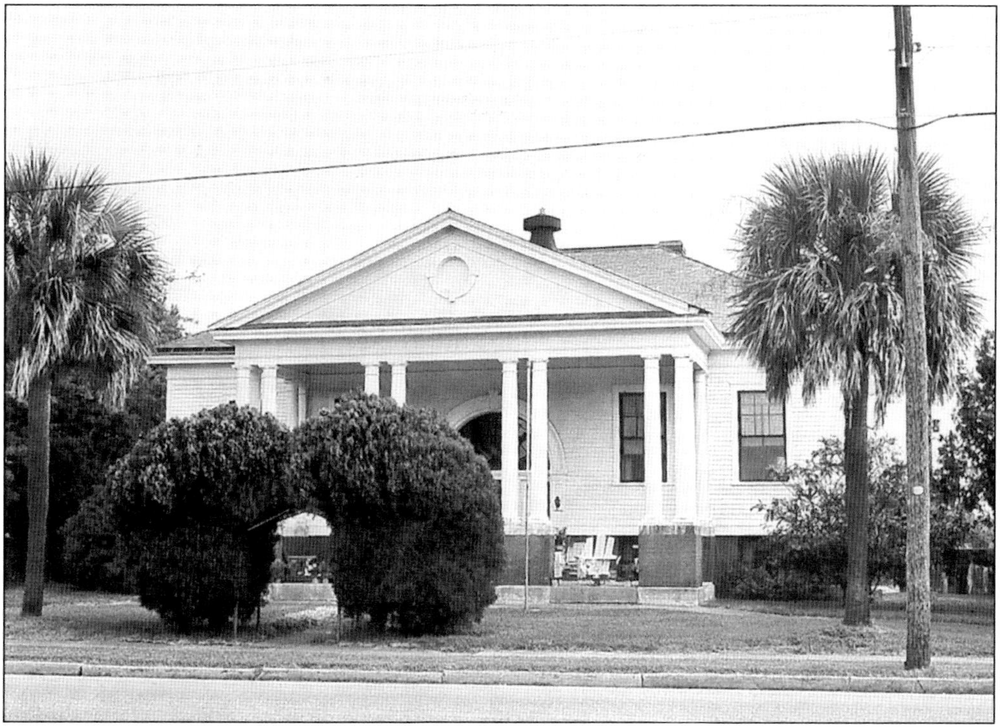

1714 Middle Street, 1906. Fort Moultrie Post Engineer's Headquarters was constructed as the Post Exchange and Gymnasium for Fort Moultrie. It was converted for use as the Post Engineer's Office by 1945 and sold in 1954 to the Broome family, who converted it for use as a residence. The rear wing is a large, open gymnasium with a pressed metal ceiling. The T-shaped, monumental, front-facing pedimented gable portico has a round window, boxed cornice, and tile ridge caps on a slate roof. The front of the building retains some historic trim, doors, and lighting fixtures. The picture at right shows the principal entrance with an elaborate surround with oversized fan light and side lights. [Part of a significant grouping of military structures.] (Courtesy S.C. Department of Archives and History.)

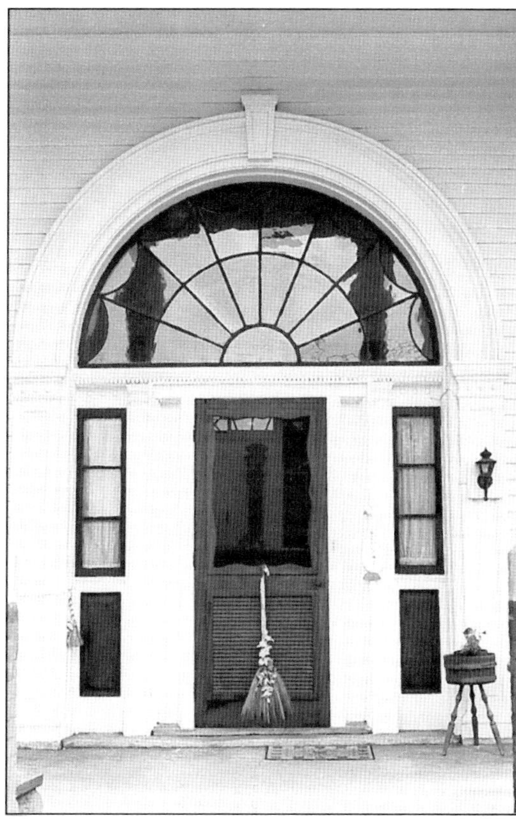

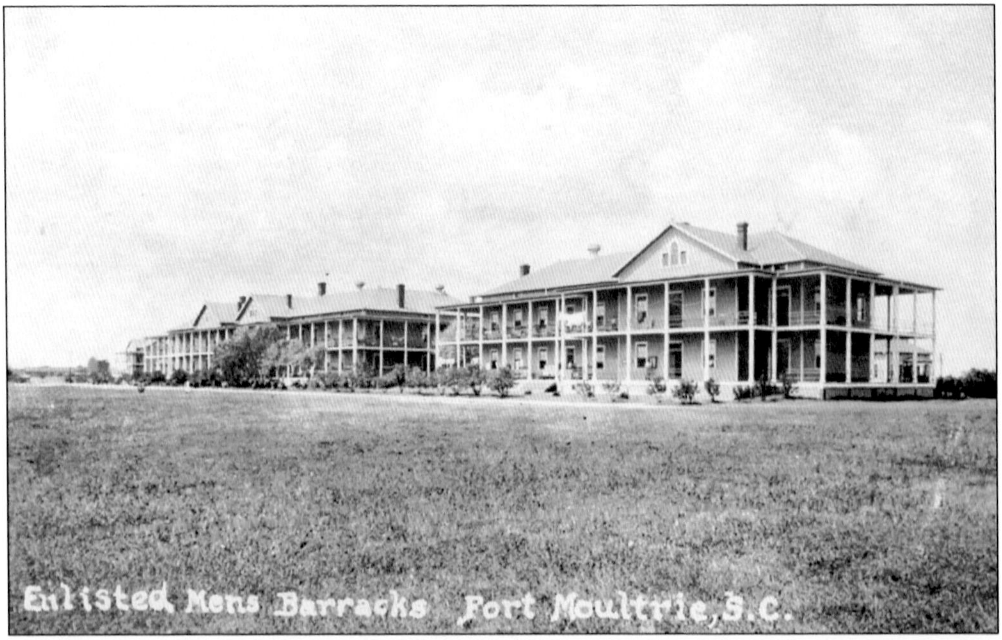

ENLISTED MEN'S BARRACKS, FORT MOULTRIE. This series of two-and-a-half story structures for enlisted men no longer stands. They were adjacent to the Fort Moultrie Dispensary/Provost Office. [Gone.] (Courtesy Deborah Lofton.)

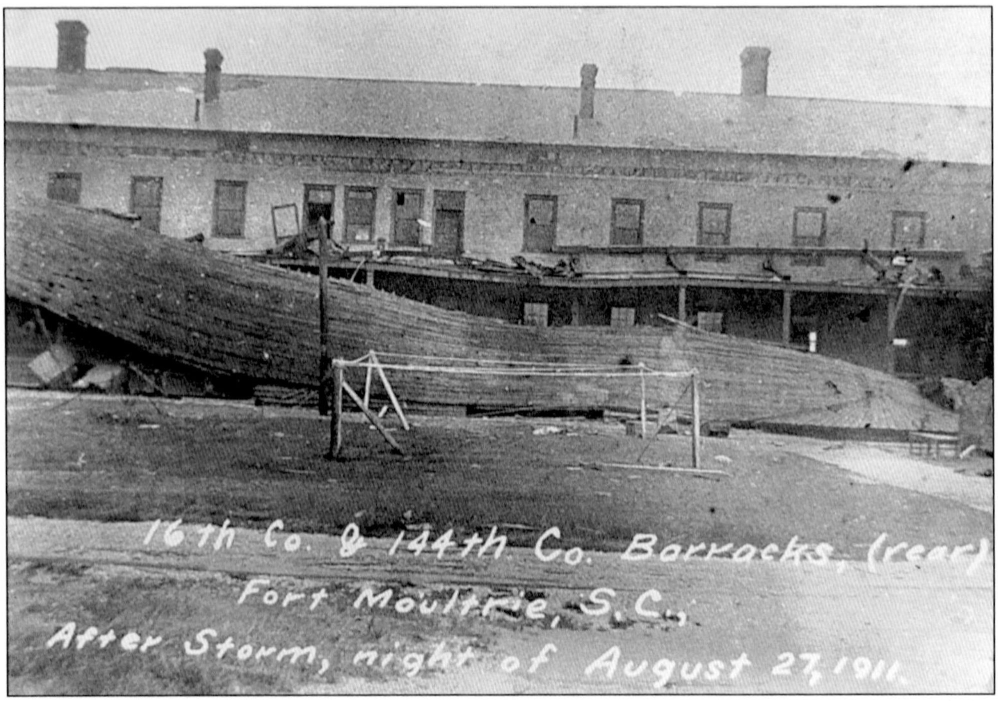

BARRACKS OF THE 16TH COMPANY AND THE 144TH COMPANY. This is a rare view of the barracks with the collapsed porches, taken after the hurricane of August 27, 1911. (Courtesy Marshall Stith.)

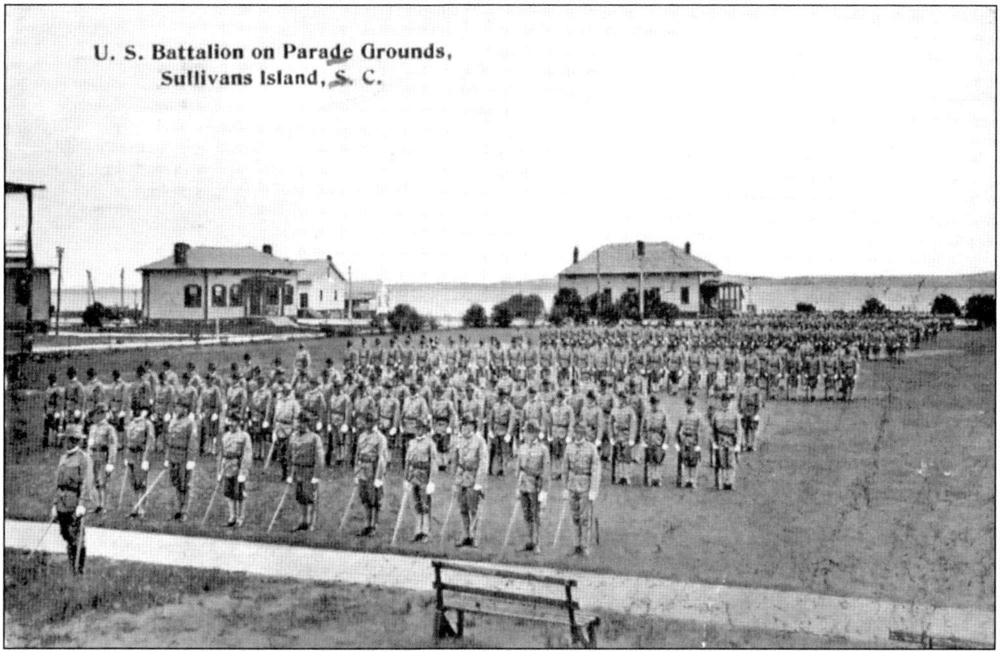

U.S. BATTALION ON PARADE GROUNDS, FORT MOULTRIE. The picture shows the Fort Moultrie Dispenser and the Guard House with Cove Inlet in the background. The postcard writer commented "fine weather down here" to a resident of South Orange, New Jersey, on March 13, 1913. (Courtesy Deborah Lofton.)

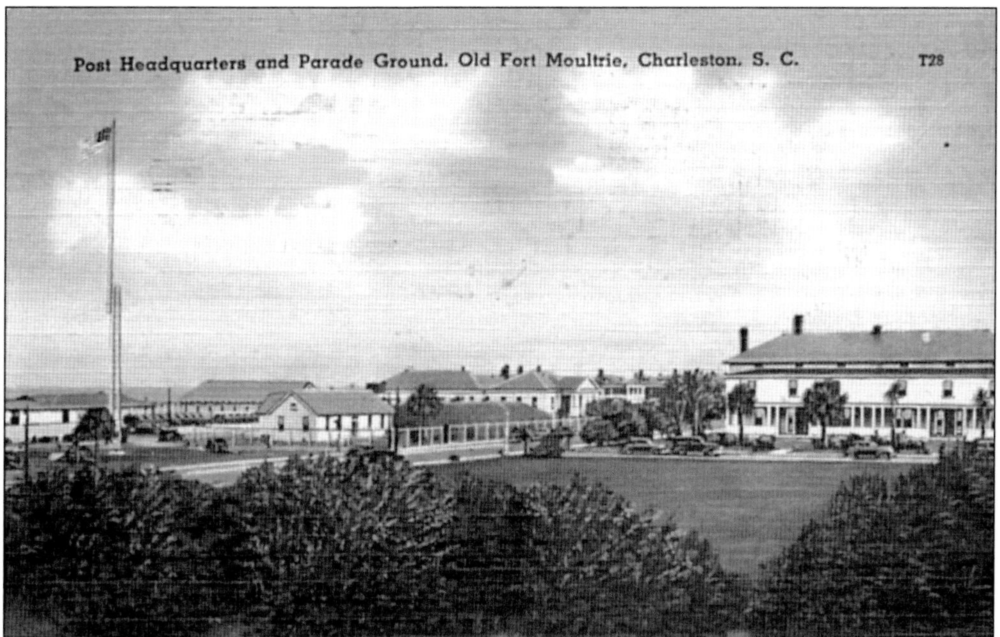

POST HEADQUARTERS AND PARADE GROUND, FORT MOULTRIE. Both the Post Headquarters and the Post Engineer's Headquarters are still standing. The parade ground was divided into building lots and today is covered with houses. (Courtesy Deborah Lofton.)

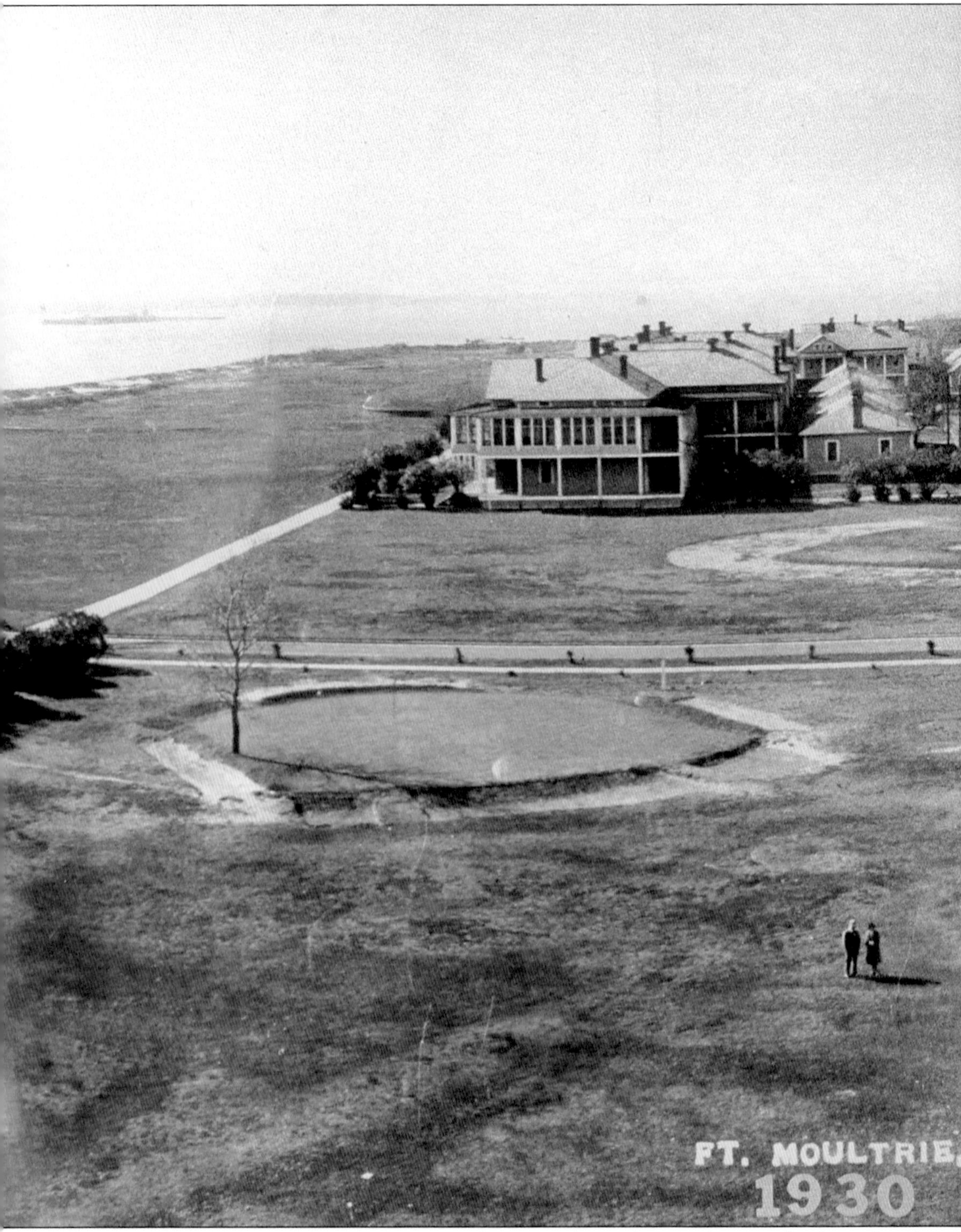

Aerial View of Fort Moultrie, 1930. This view shows the parade grounds, the enlisted men's barracks, Fort Sumter to the left, Cove Inlet to the right, and Stella Maris Catholic

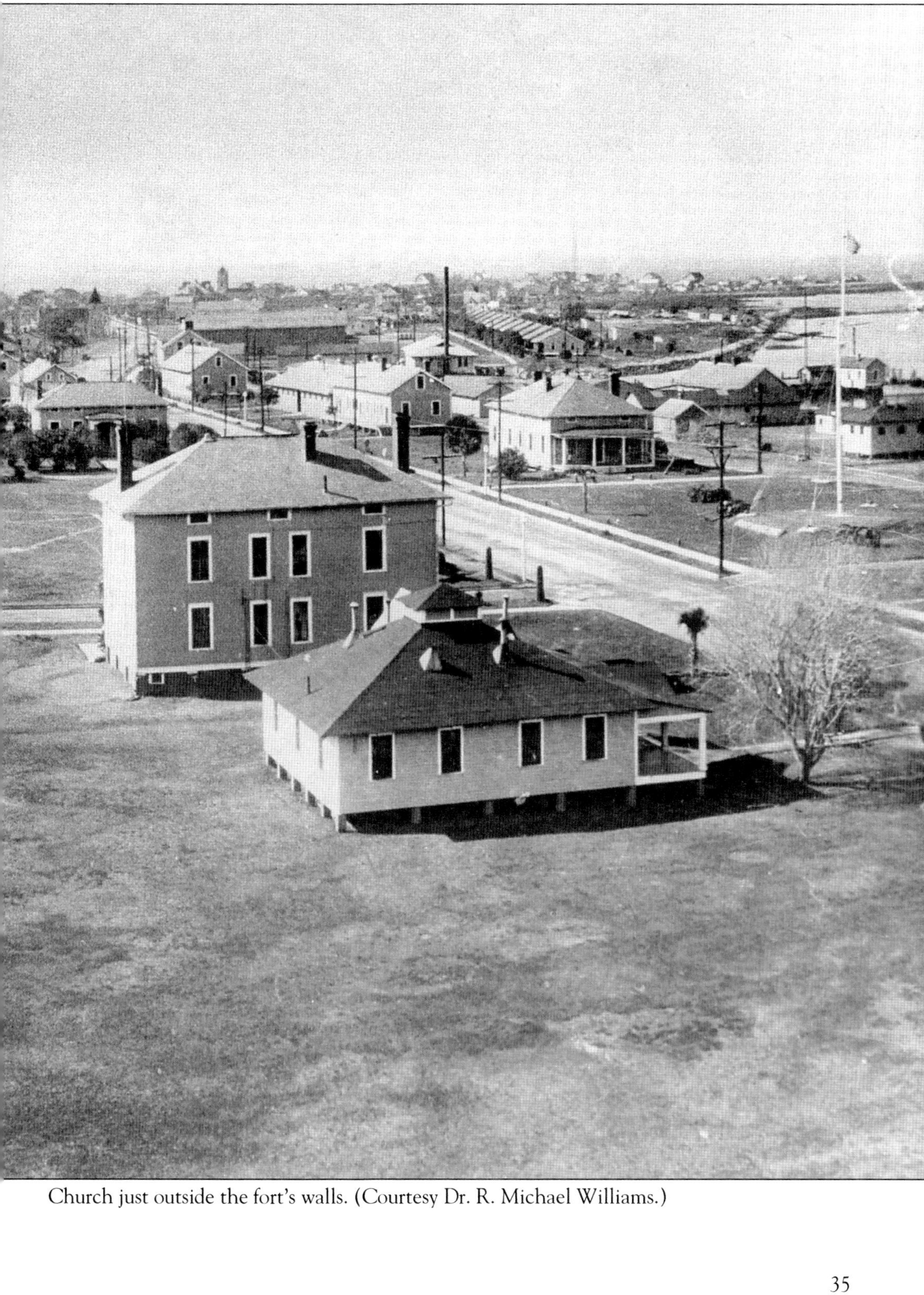

Church just outside the fort's walls. (Courtesy Dr. R. Michael Williams.)

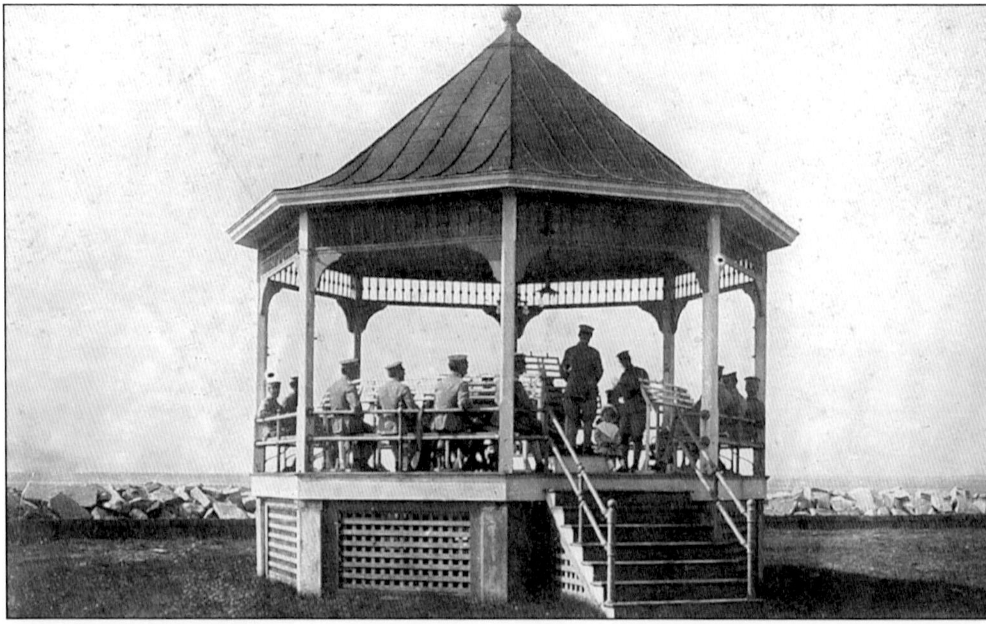

Bandstand, Fort Moultrie c. 1905. This building was constructed as the bandstand for Fort Moultrie. John Philip Sousa is said to have conducted from this bandstand. It was sold by the government in the early 1950s and moved to 1462 Thompson Avenue, where Miss Betty Lemon converted it for use as a residence. [Part of a significant grouping of military structures.] (Courtesy Marshall Stith.)

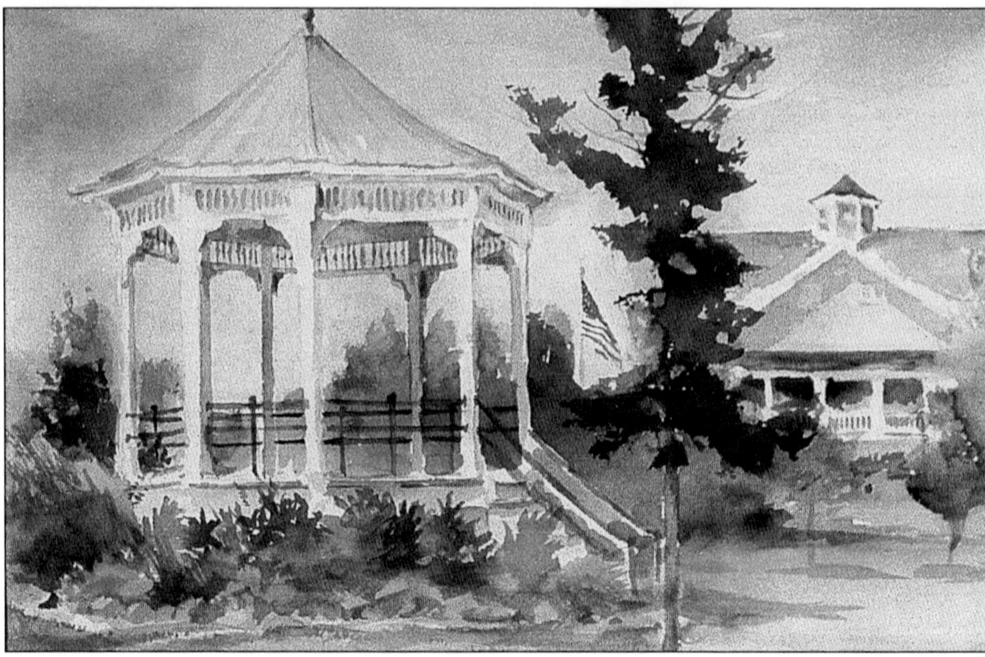

Bandstand, Play Ground, Station 21. The bandstand was eventually moved during the 1980s to the Sullivan's Island Play Ground next to the fire department and has reverted to its original use. [Part of a significant grouping of military structures.] (Photo of painting by Jim Darlington.)

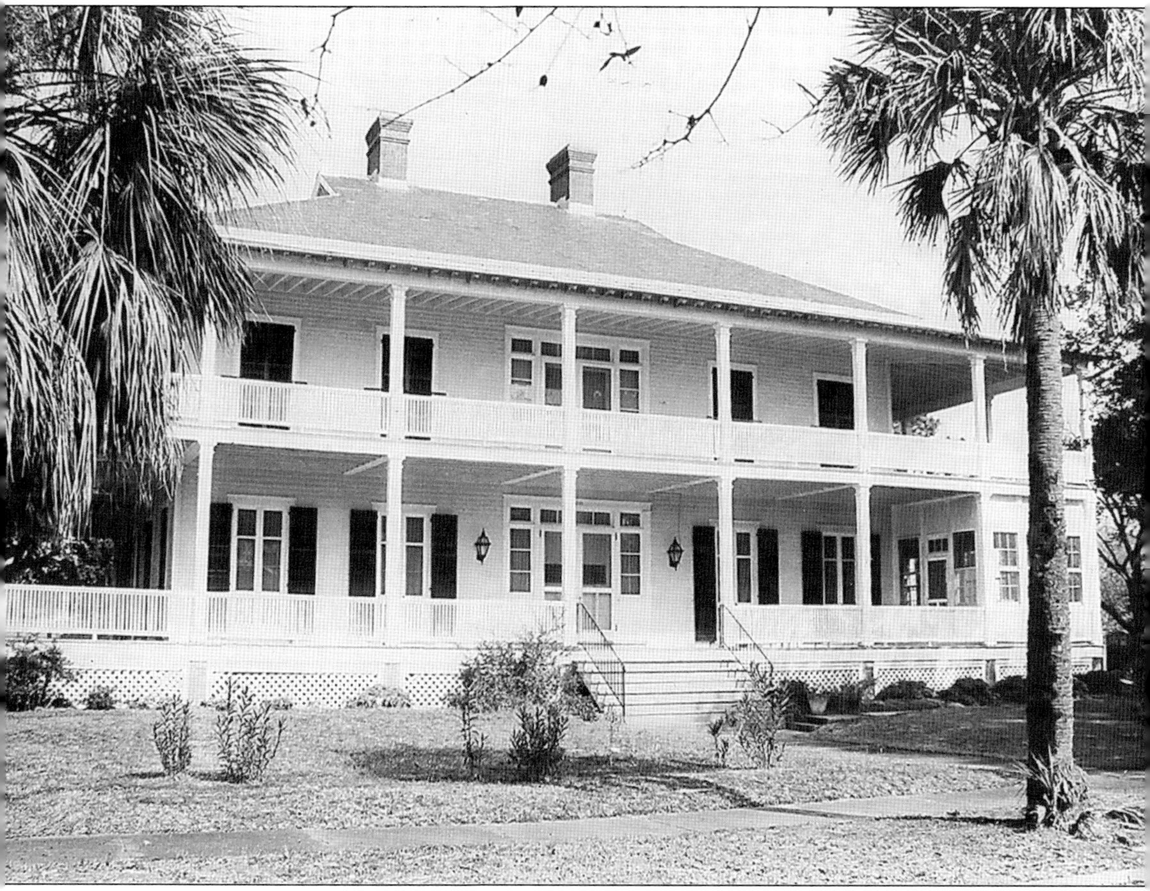

1702 I'ON AVENUE C. 1905. This house, the base commandant's quarters, is the largest and most elaborate of a row of 10 similar surviving buildings that were constructed as senior officer's quarters for Fort Moultrie. George C. Marshall, later to become army chief of staff during World War II, resided here for several months in 1933. According to one local wag, the Marshalls were only here long enough for Mrs. Marshall to put up the curtains and take them down again. This structure was one of many constructed to house the rapidly increasing garrison at the fort. The house was sold and converted for use as a private residence in the early 1950s. [Part of a significant grouping of military structures associated with the expansion of Fort Moultrie.] (Courtesy Marshall Stith.)

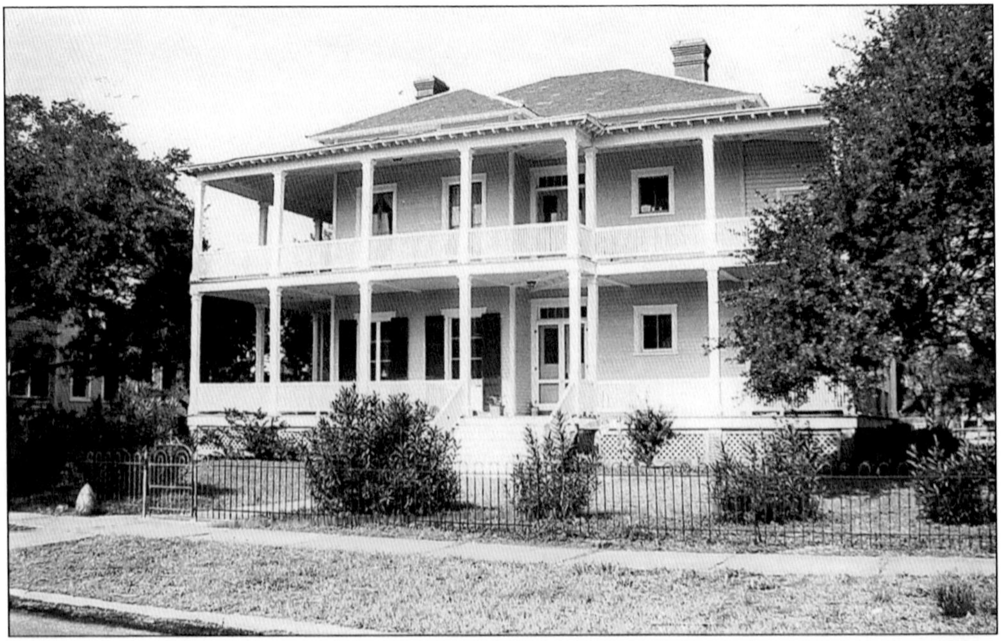

1738 I'on Avenue c. 1905. This is one of the senior officer's houses at Fort Moultrie along I'on Avenue. Interior features include pressed metal ceilings, mantelpieces with mirrors over mantels, and paneled doors. [Part of a significant grouping of military structures.] (Courtesy Marshall Stith.)

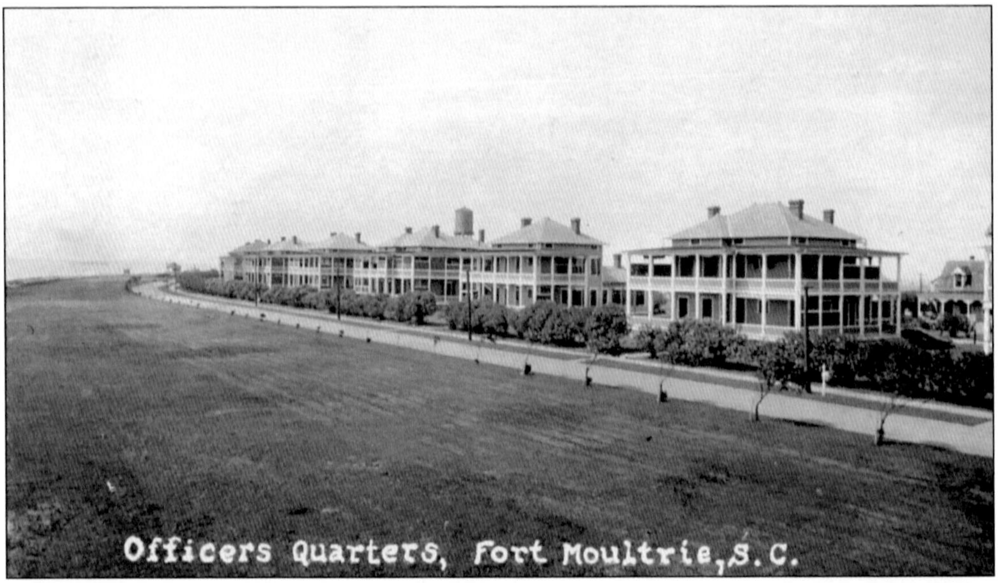

1710, 1718, 1724, 1728, 1734, 1738, 1744, 1750, and 1754 I'on Avenue c. 1905. These houses are part of a row of nine similar surviving buildings that were constructed as senior officers' quarters for Fort Moultrie. These houses were sold and converted for use as private residences in the early 1950s. Several of the houses have been slightly altered, and 1710 was rebuilt after a devastating fire. These former waterfront houses now have two rows of dwellings between them and the ocean. [Part of a significant grouping of military structures.] (Photograph courtesy of Marshall Stith.)

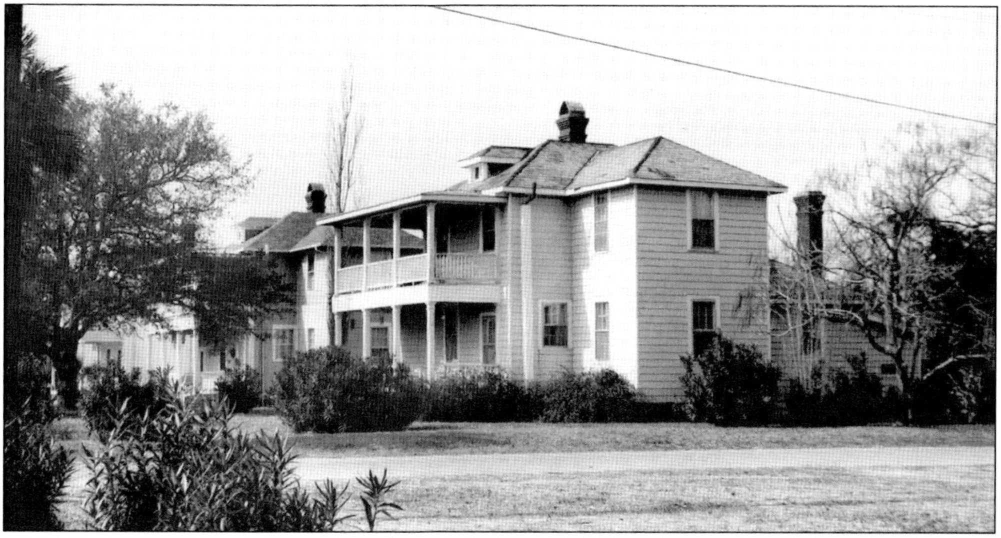

1754 Central Avenue, c. 1905. This house is part of a row of 11 similar buildings that were constructed on Central Avenue and Middle Street as junior grade officers' quarters for Fort Moultrie. These structures, built to house the rapidly increasing garrison at the fort, were sold and converted for use as private residences in the early 1950s. Mr. and Mrs. Jamie L. Nettles live at 1754 Central Avenue. [Part of a significant grouping of military structures associated with the expansion of Fort Moultrie.]

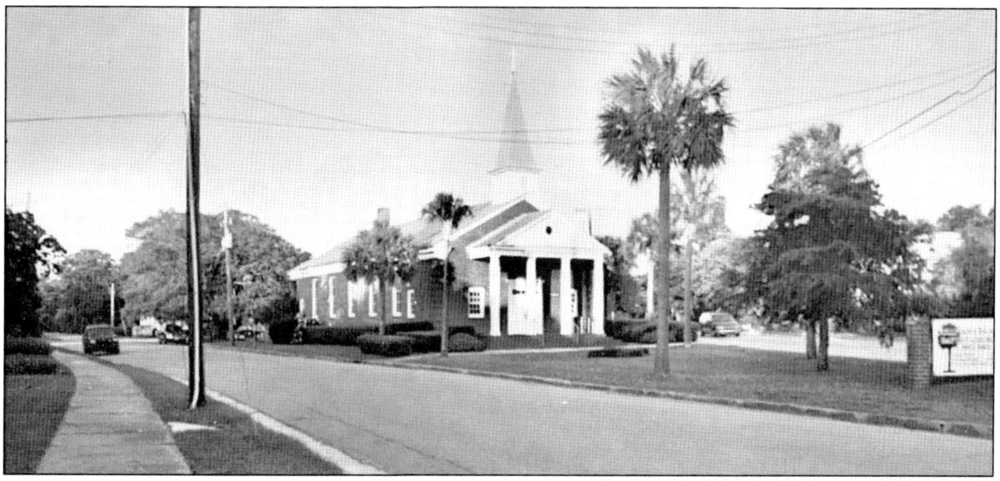

1753 Central Avenue c. 1914. The Sullivan's Island Baptist Church, a frame building with asbestos siding, was originally constructed as a new base chapel for Fort Moultrie. The War Assets Administration gave permission to the church and its 75 members in 1948 to rent the building, and the group bought it in late 1949 for $4,500. At 1739 Middle Street was the army nurses' barracks—a building constructed of two long wings. One of the wings was relocated across the street and attached to the church for a Sunday school building. (The other wing was turned on its axis, added to, and is now a residence.) In 1953 the large, 50,000-gallon cistern behind the church was connected to it and converted for office space. The interior was completely reworked again in 1975, and in 1985 six new rooms were built on top of the cistern. The Church also bought the nearby Keros property in 1950 for use as a youth department. The current pastor is the Reverend Alan M. Wilson. [Part of a significant grouping of military structures put to another use.] (Courtesy Bonnie A. Williams.)

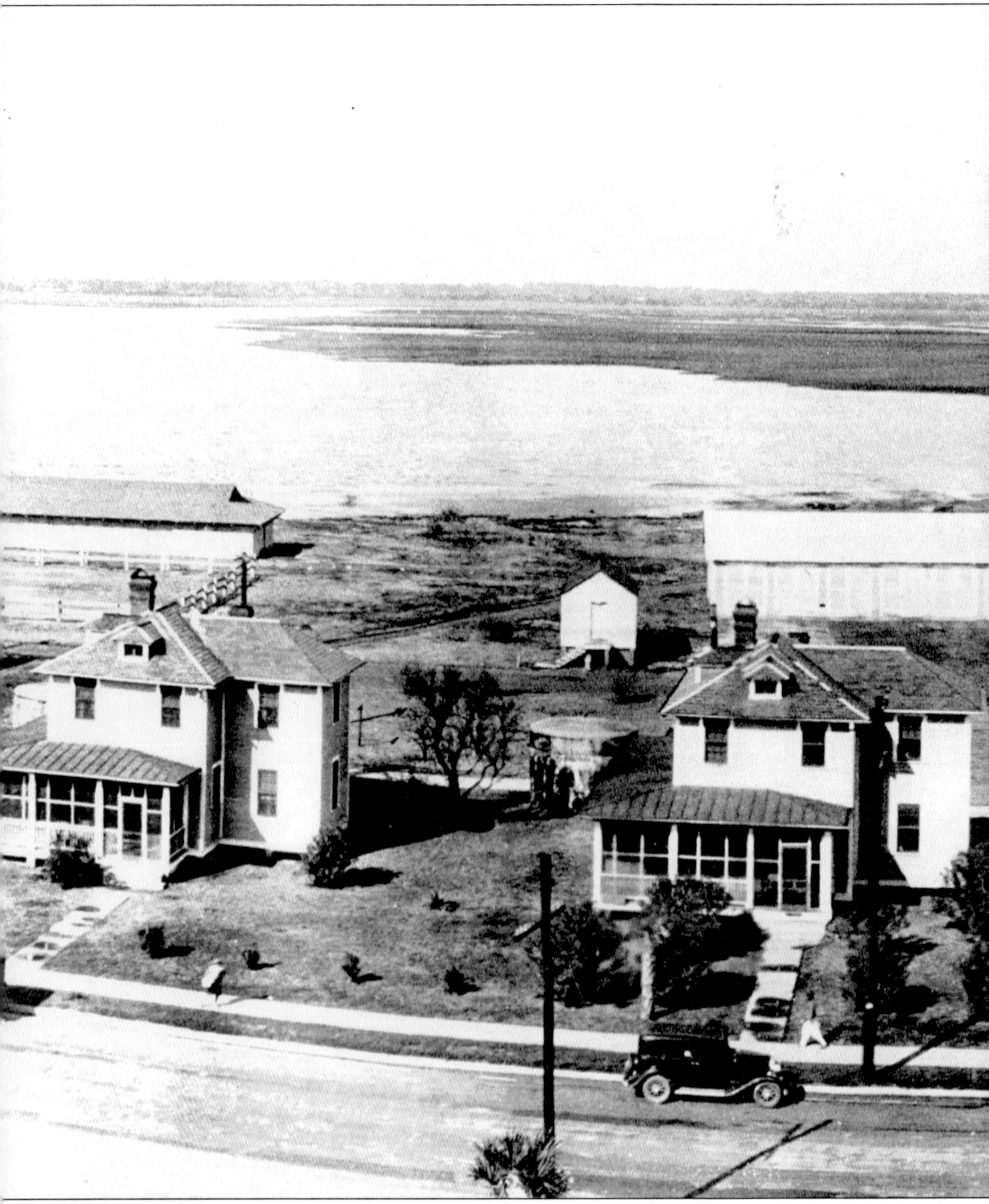

Aerial view of the Junior Officers' Quarter, Fort Moultrie, 1930. Today behind this row of Junior Officers' Quarters are houses. Notice the cisterns beside each house in the picture. In the background is Mount Pleasant, which today would show much development. In

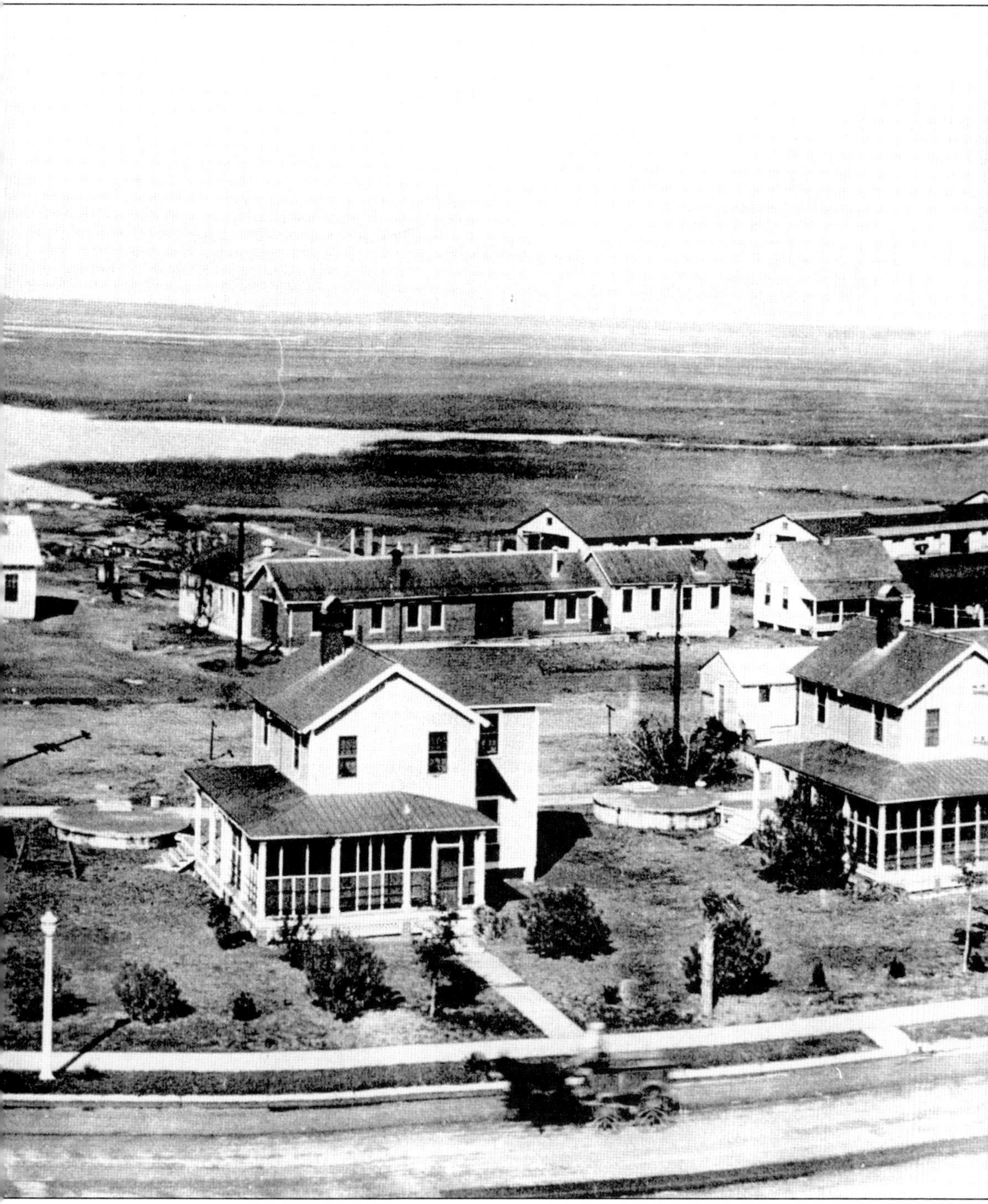

the middle of this picture is one of the stone lamp posts that were found at Fort Moultrie when the fort was active. (Courtesy Dr. R. Michael Williams.)

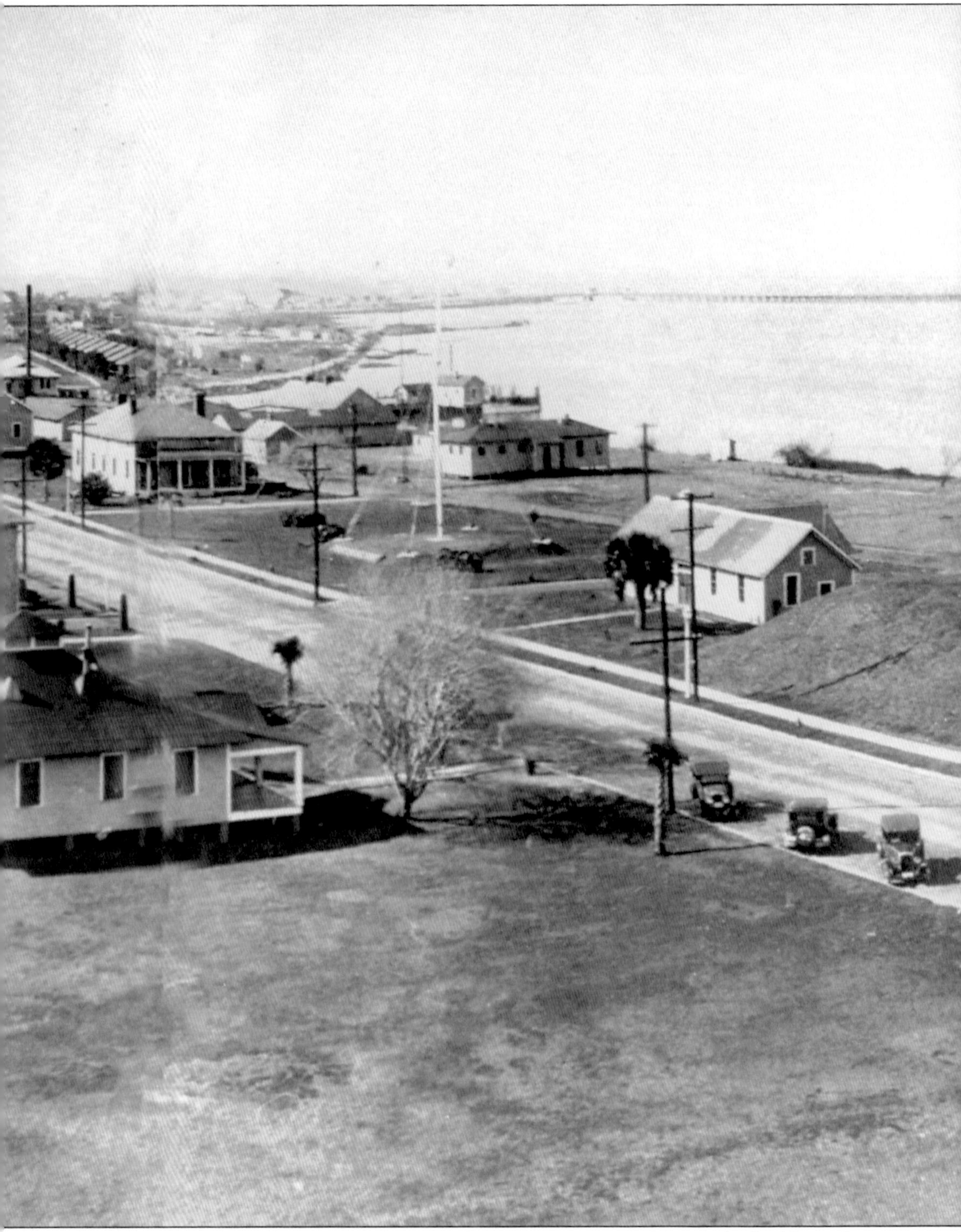

AERIAL VIEW OF FORT MOULTRIE AROUND STATION 17, 1930. Among the buildings shown in this photograph are the Guard House, Fort Moultrie Post Engineer's Headquarters, and married enlisted men's quarters on Thompson Avenue. In the distance is the Cove Island Bridge.

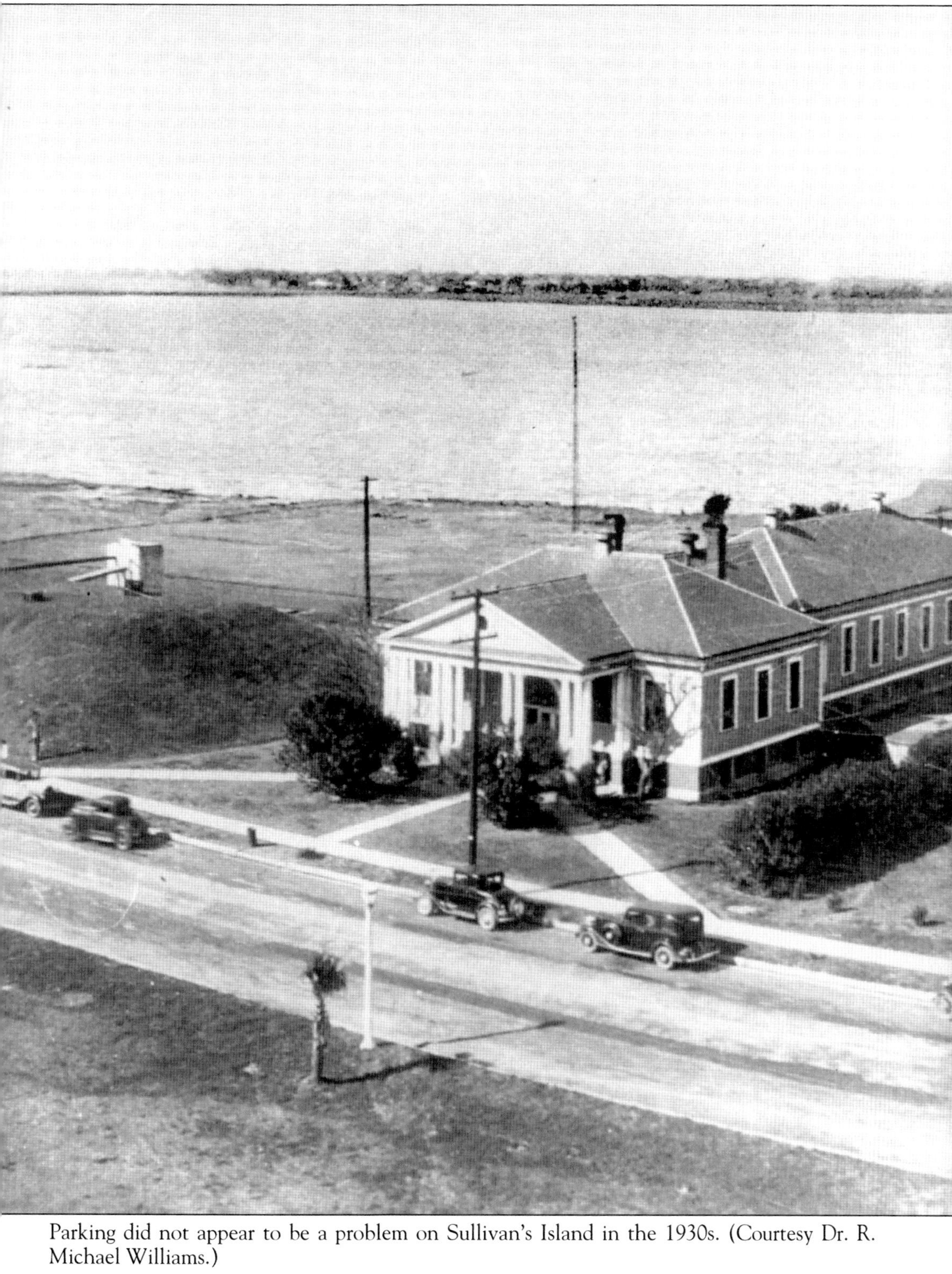

Parking did not appear to be a problem on Sullivan's Island in the 1930s. (Courtesy Dr. R. Michael Williams.)

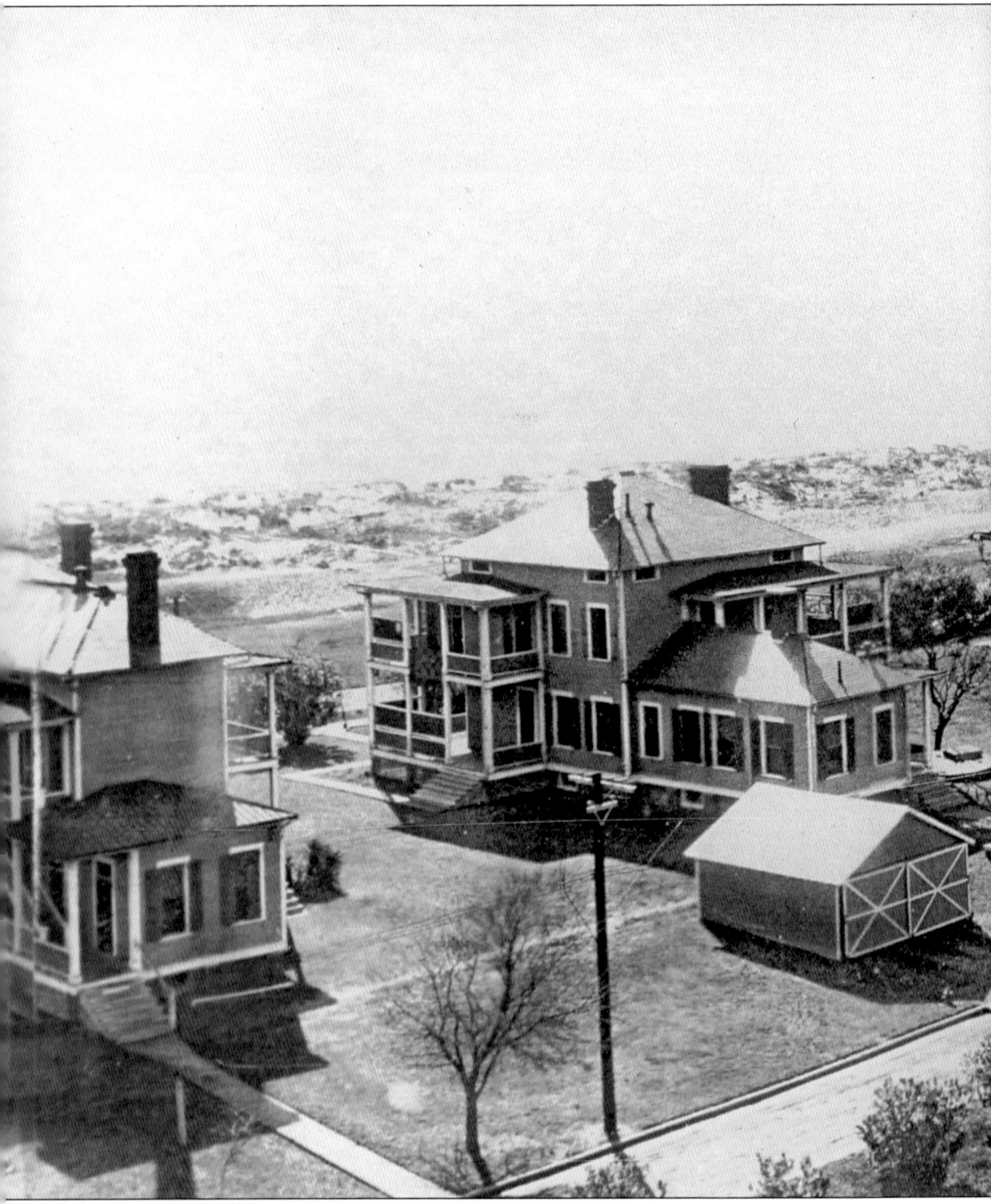

AERIAL VIEW OF FORT MOULTRIE BASE COMMANDER'S QUARTERS, SENIOR OFFICERS ROW, AND PARADE GROUND, 1930. This picture shows how close the ocean was before the land in front of I'on Street accreted. Today there are houses in front of the Senior Officers Row, as well as

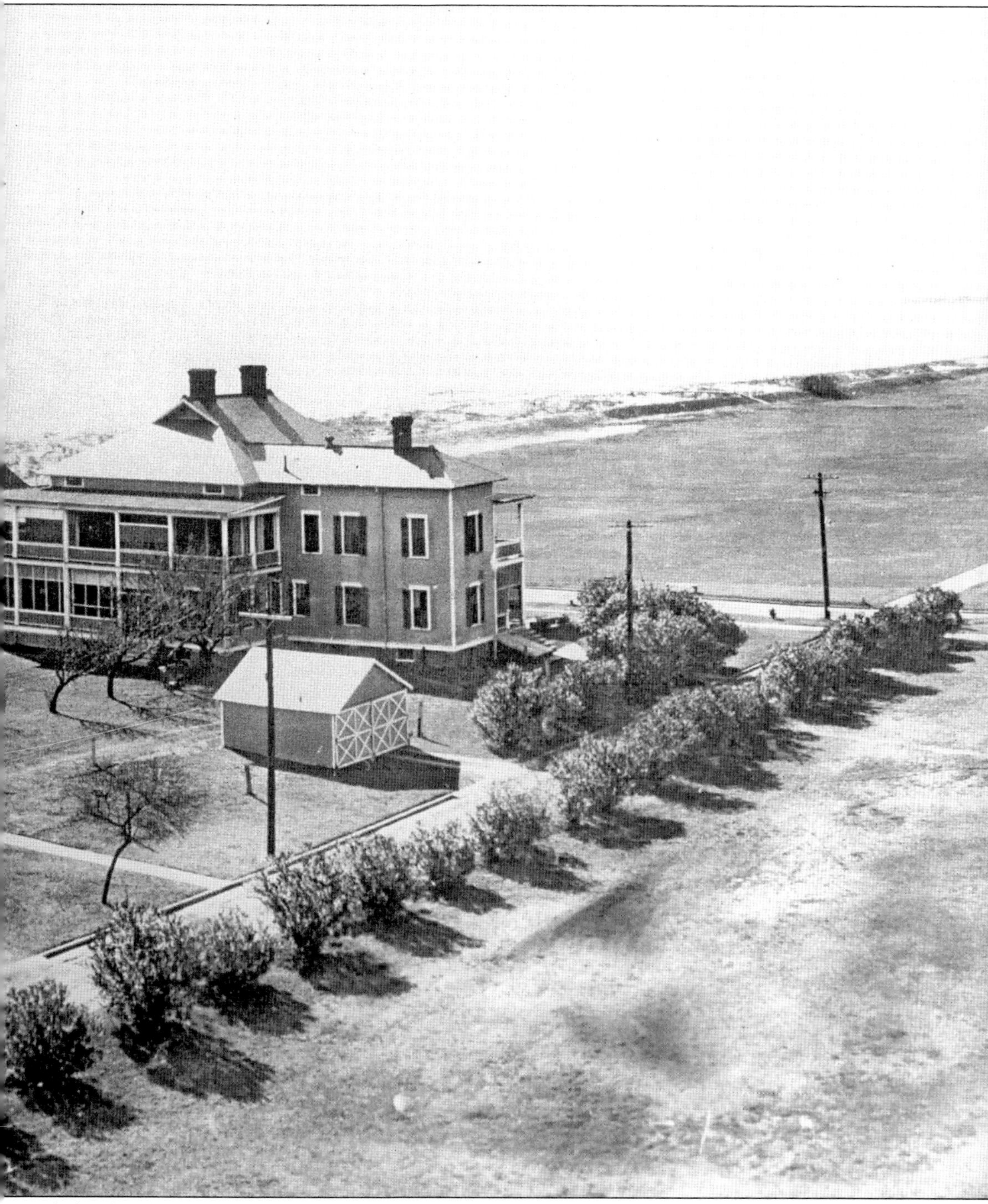

behind and to the east, where the parade ground use to be. Notice the tip of the roof of the Fort Moultrie Band Stand adjacent to the Fort Moultrie Base Commander's Quarters. Fort Sumter is barely visible at the right side of the picture. (Courtesy Dr. R. Michael Williams.)

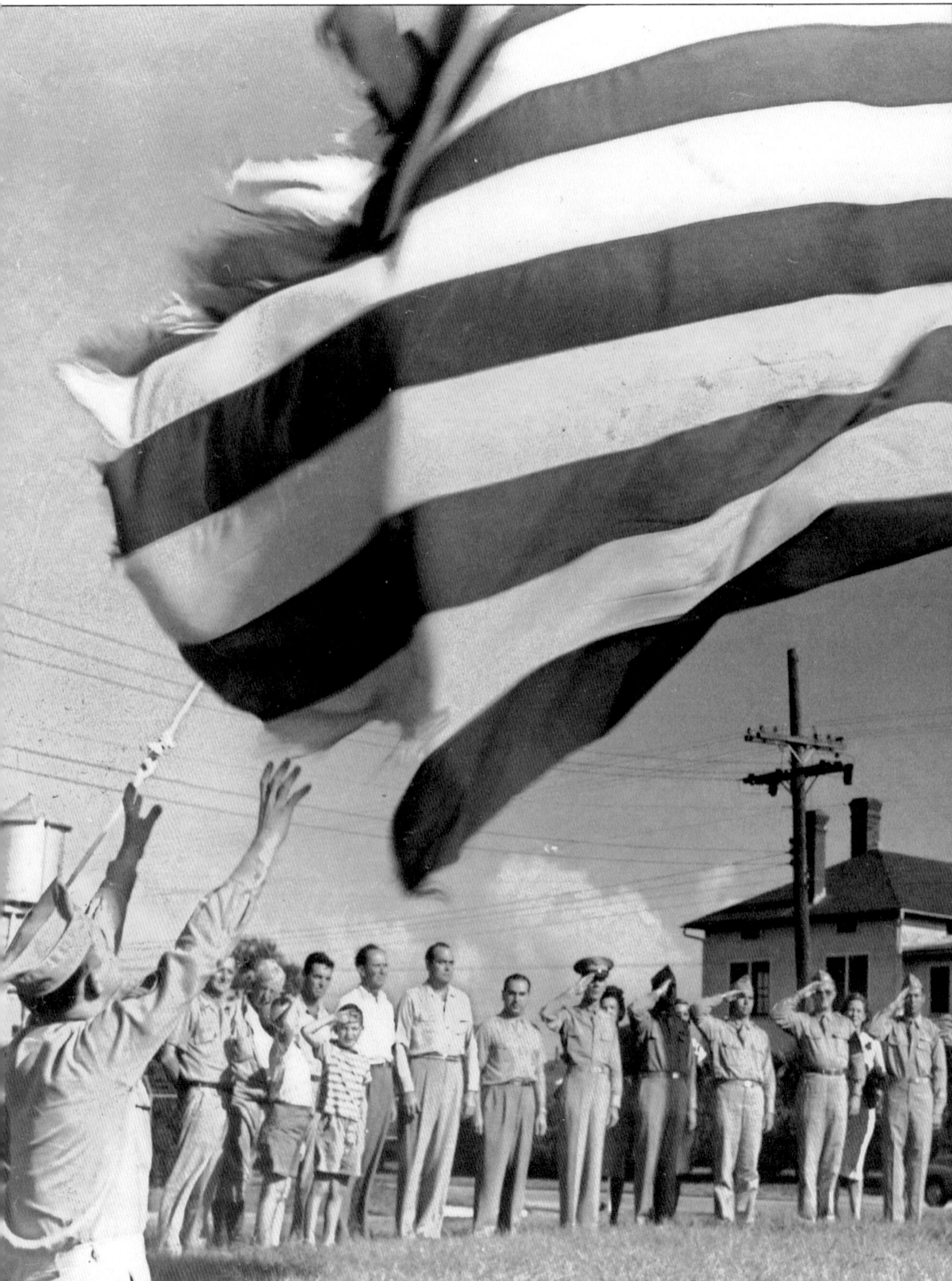

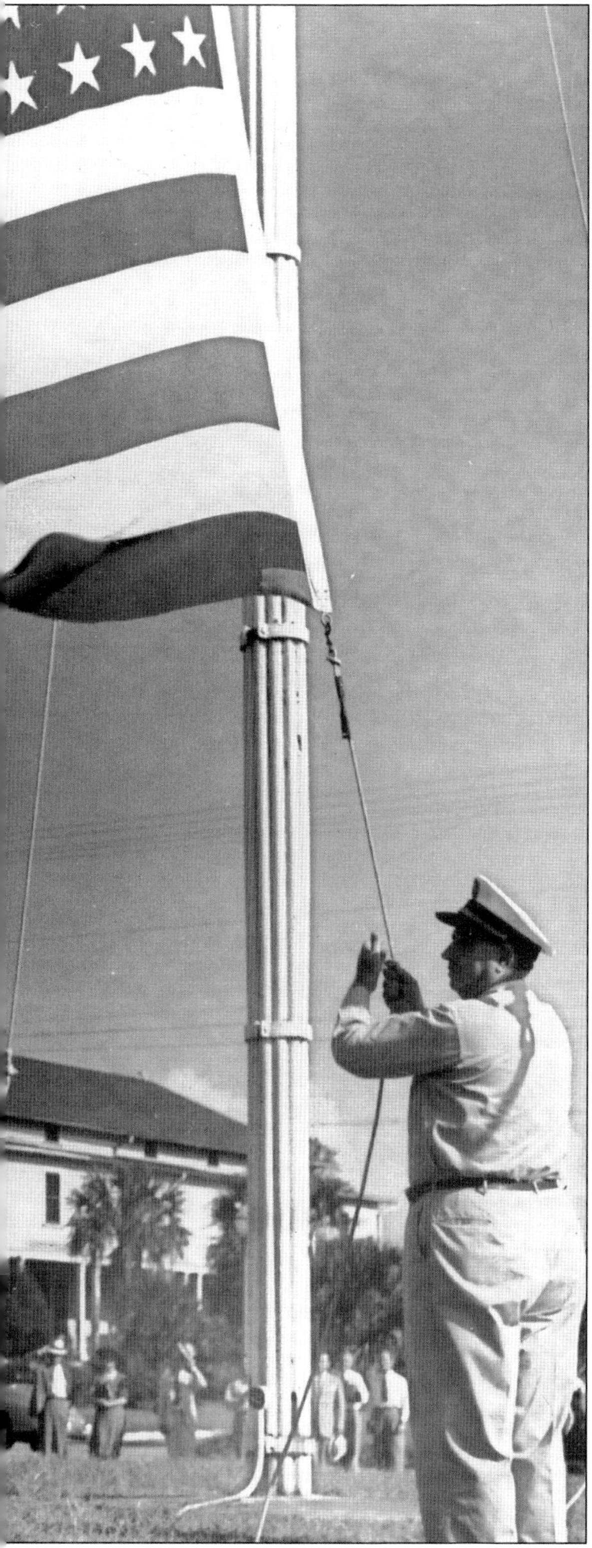

OFFICIAL CLOSING OF FORT MOULTRIE. The lowering of the flag for the last time on August 15, 1947, marked the final closing of an era in the history of Fort Moultrie. The closing of the fort posed an economic challenge for many island residents whose livelihoods depended on jobs created by the army operations at Fort Moultrie. The fort had also provided support services for many island residents. (Courtesy Marshall Stith.)

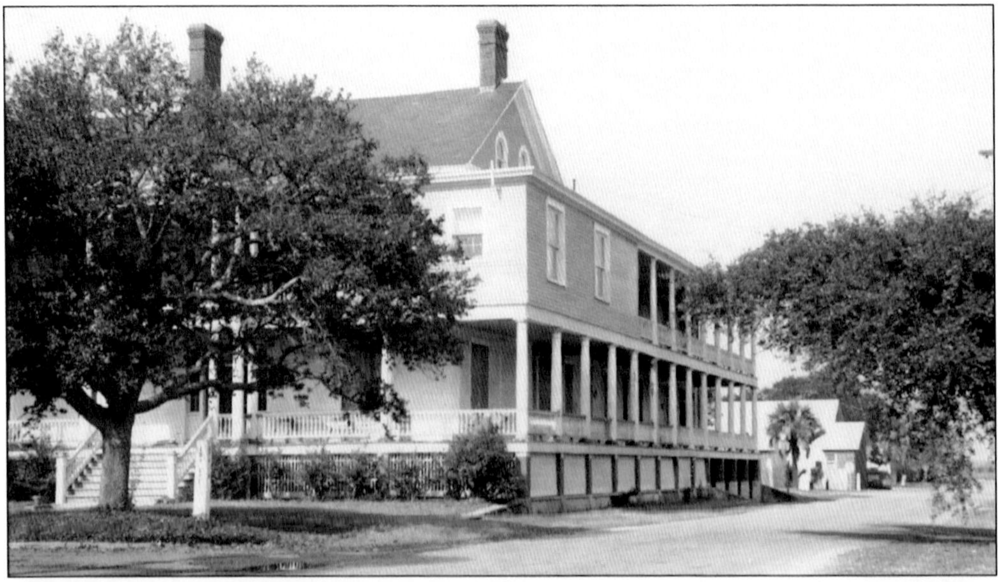

1766 I'on Avenue c. 1900. The Bachelor Officers' Quarters are L-shaped with porches at the south façade and the east elevation. The foundation is brick pier to the south end and brick over sandstone on concrete to the north. The principal entrances have transoms and sidelights, and the west section is the oldest portion. The extension to the north was added after 1925. Fort Moultrie Bachelor Officers' Quarters have been converted for use as residential apartments. [Important as an example of early 20th-century military architecture.] (Courtesy Marshall Stith.)

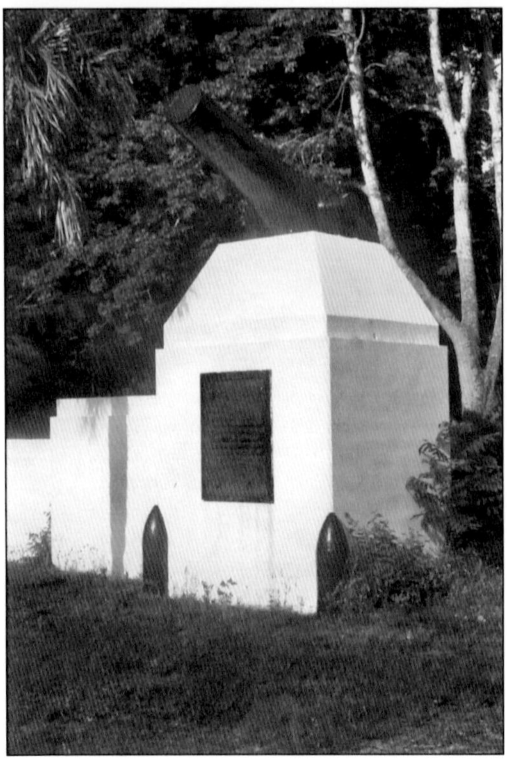

Fort Moultrie Rear Entrance Gates. This is one of a pair of gates to Fort Moultrie that was constructed c. 1920. The two masonry monuments flank Middle Street to the west of Station 18. Each is a square with a shaped cap and short, low-profile, flanking masonry wall. Artillery shells are embedded at each corner of the base as a decorative element, and each monument has a bronze plaque. [Part of a significant grouping of military structures.] (Courtesy S.C. Department of Archives and History.)

Three

MOULTRIEVILLE

Stations 18–22

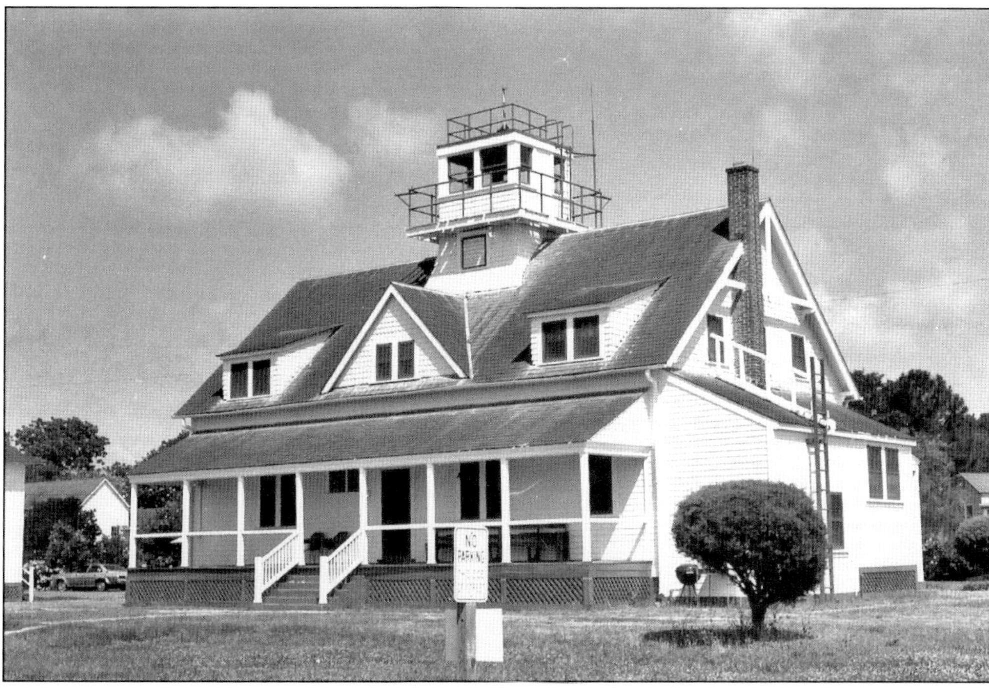

U.S. COAST GUARD HISTORIC DISTRICT. This building is an outstanding example of East Lake architecture built in 1891. It is located on a five-acre rectangular plot with two other buildings—a one-story, rectangular frame boat house and a one-story, rectangular frame garage, both with board and batten siding, and both also built in 1891. There are also two other structures, a historic earthen bunker constructed in 1898 and a concrete lighthouse constructed in 1962. The U.S. Coast Guard Station on Sullivan's is the oldest extant life saving station on the South Carolina coast. The town of Moultrieville deeded five acres of land to the federal government in 1891 for the establishment of a life saving station. Additional land was donated in 1896 to compensate for land lost to erosion. [Listed on the National Register of Historic Places.] (Courtesy S.C. Department of Archives and History.)

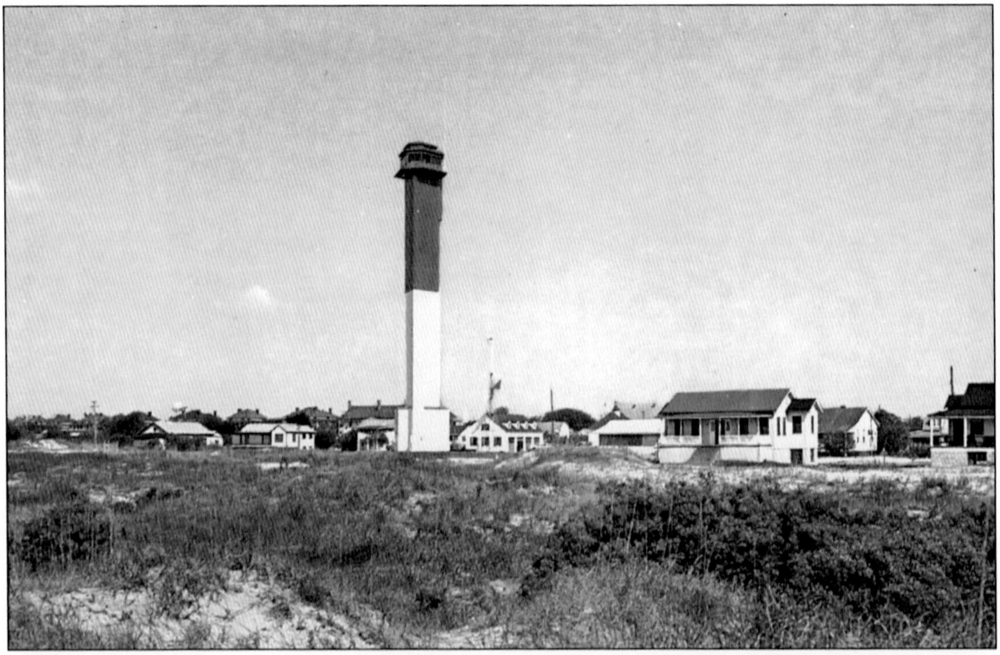

SULLIVAN'S ISLAND LIGHTHOUSE. The lighthouse is the most notable feature of the coast guard complex. The triangular-shaped structure is 173 feet tall and operates at 28 million candle power at high intensity. It is said to be the second most powerful light in the world. (Courtesy Deborah Lofton.)

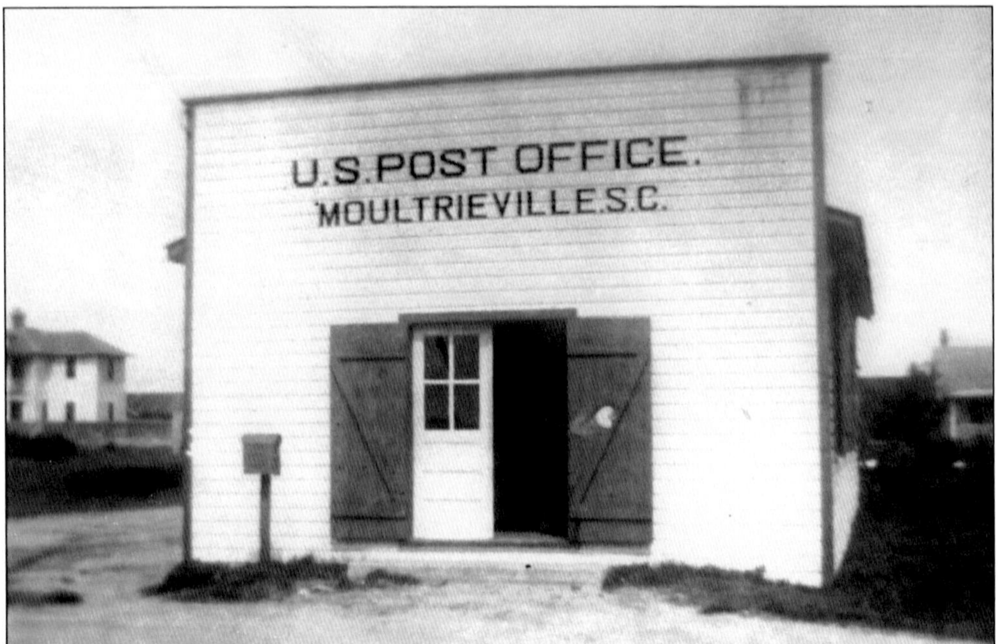

U.S. POST OFFICE, MOULTRIEVILLE. This was the Moultrieville Post Office in the 1940s. It was located just outside the fort and next door to the Mazyck House. The post office has had many locations over the years. [Gone.] (Courtesy of Marshall Stith.)

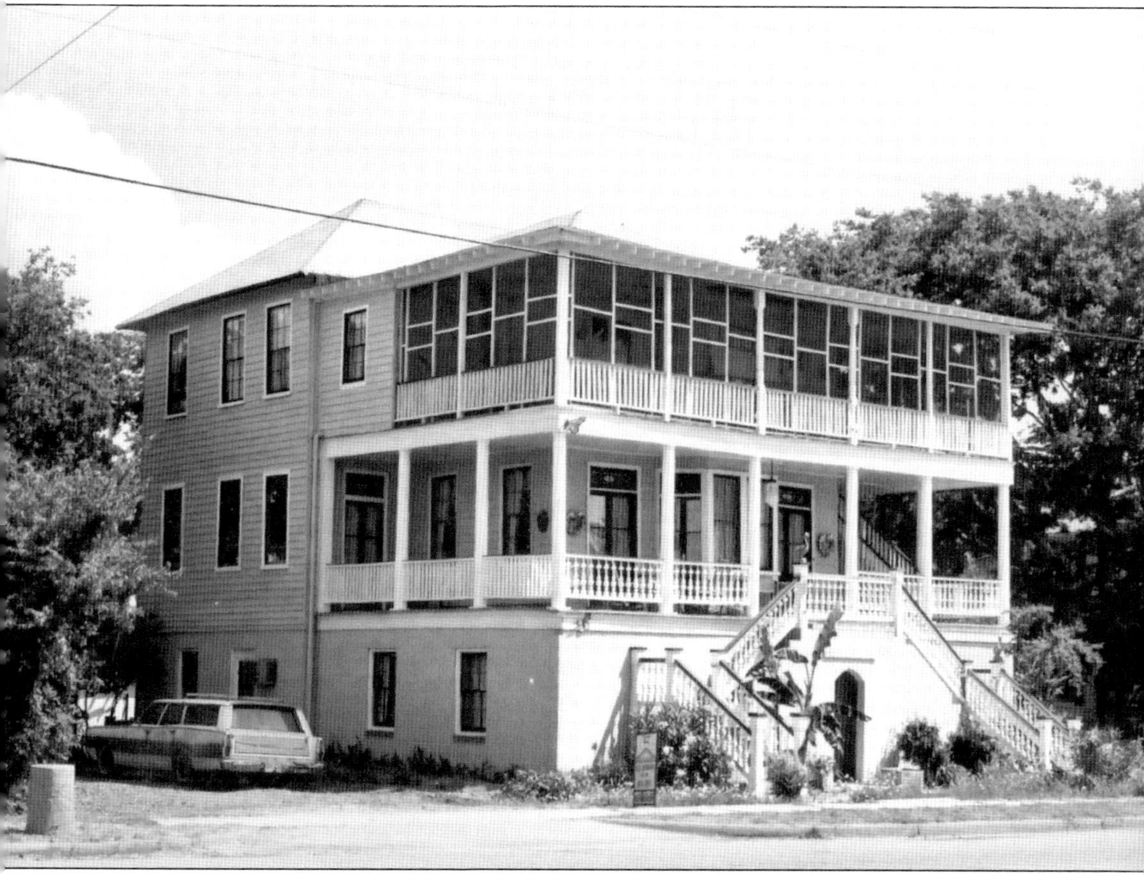

1808 Middle Street c. 1911. The first Mazyck house, a 22-room dwelling built by William Gaillard Mazyck (1845–1942), burned in 1904, but a new summer home was rebuilt by 1911. Mr. Mazyck was an internationally known conchologist who lived at 56-A Montagu Street in Charleston and was vice president of the Equitable Fire Insurance Company at Broad and Church Street. Mr. Mazyck had grown up at Fairlawn Plantation, but his family spent their summers on Sullivan's Island. His interest in shells dated back to those days when, at the age of eight, Dr. Edmund Ravenel, a pioneer in conchology, noticed Mazyck's interest in shells gathered along the strand and showed him his collection. Mazyck's collection eventually grew to 160,000 shells, said to have been the largest collection in the world at the time of his death. What he considered his most interesting find was made near the lifesaving station on Sullivan's Island where he discovered Cochicella Ventricosa, which neither before nor since has been found on this side of the Atlantic. Another shell, the only one of its kind, found at a phosphate works near Cainhoy was named Scalario Mazykii in his honor. His shell collection is housed at the Charleston Museum. [Very good example of early 20th-century island architecture.] (Courtesy S.C. Department of Archives and History.)

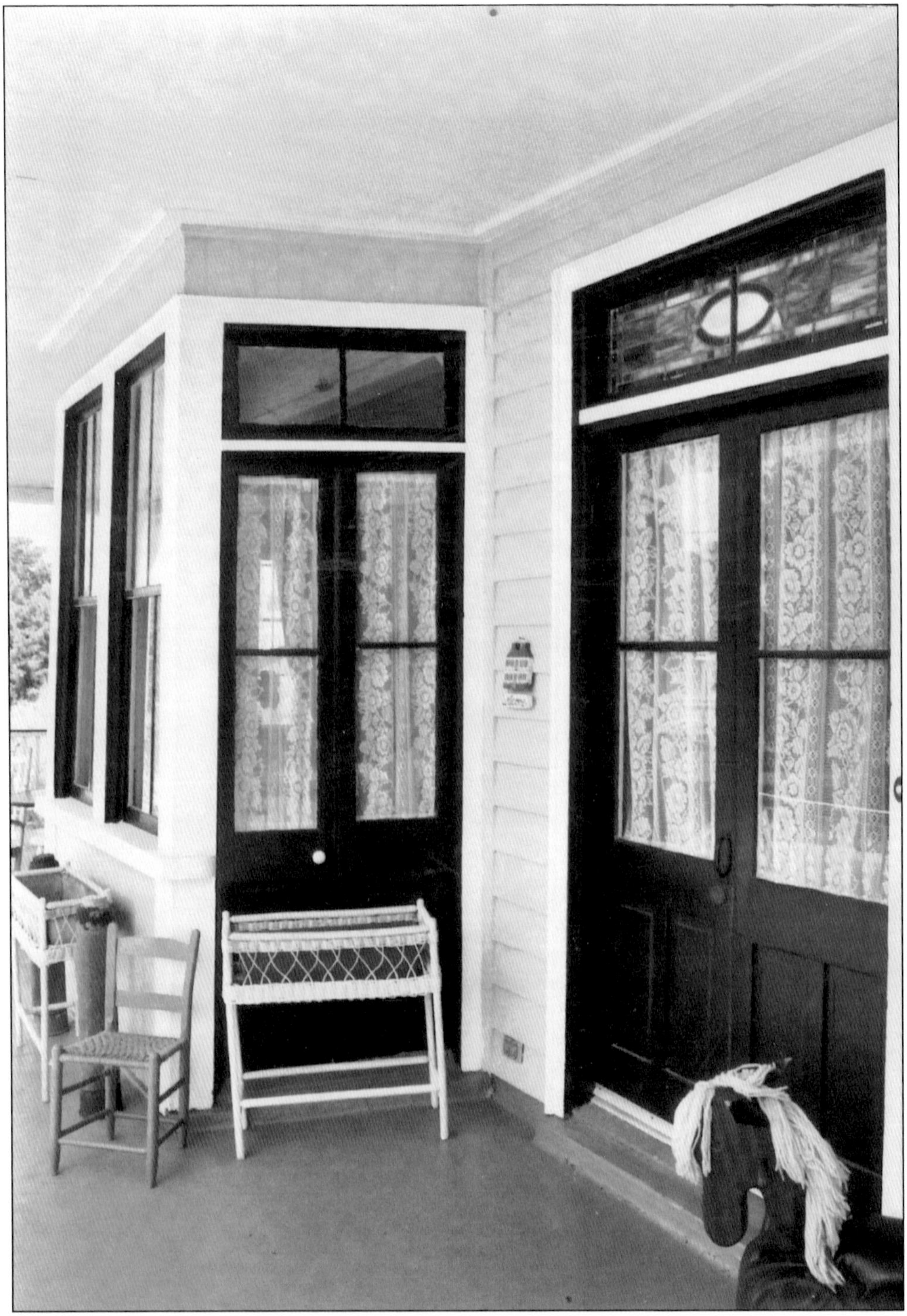

MAZYCK HOUSE DETAILS. The first story of this piazza has turned balustrades, and the second level has wood columns. The main level has a central projecting octagonal bay with double windows to the south and French doors to the east and west flanked by French doors with stained-glass transoms. (Courtesy S.C. Department of Archives and History.)

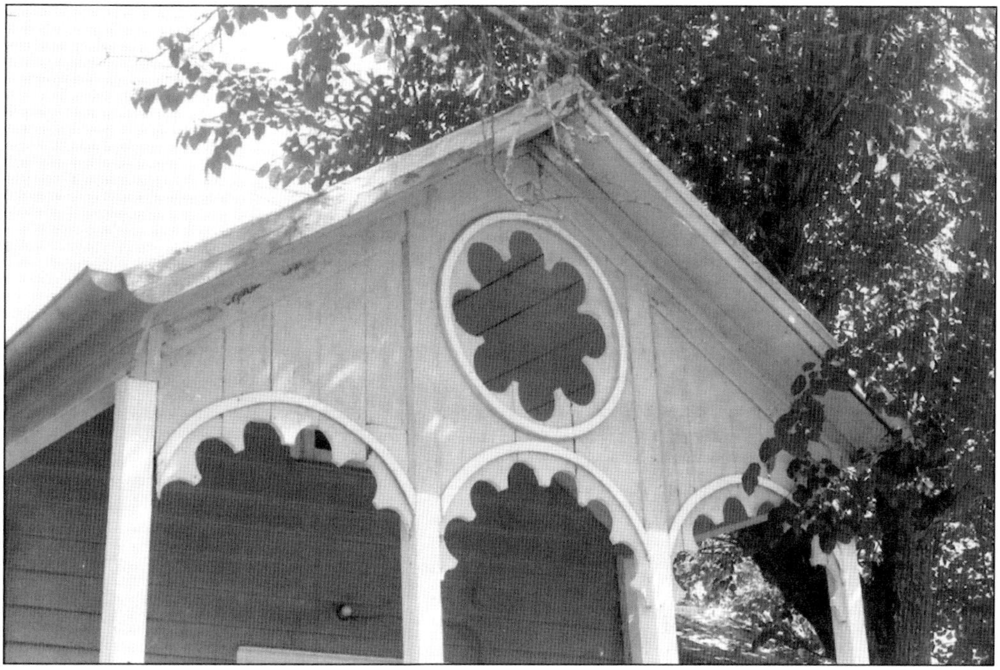

1813 Middle Street c. 1845. The irregularly shaped block of the main house has one-by-one bay wings to the northeast and northwest and a shed addition to the rear. The front facing gable over the porch has a decorative sawn screen. [Exceptional example of 19th-century island architecture.] (Courtesy S.C. Department of Archives and History.)

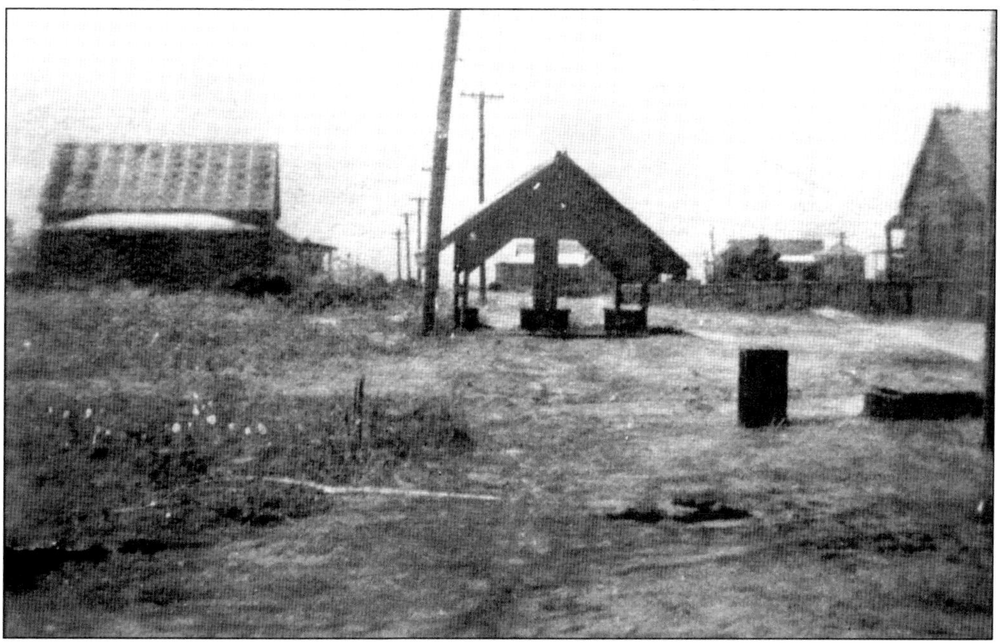

Trolley Car Shed. The trolley ran from Mount Pleasant to the Long Island (Isle of Palms). On Sullivan's Island the trolley ran east on Central Avenue, turning south at the corner beyond 1820 Middle Street, on what was then Patrick Street and is now Station 18 1/2 Street, and continued east on Middle Street. [Gone.] (Courtesy of Marshall Stith.)

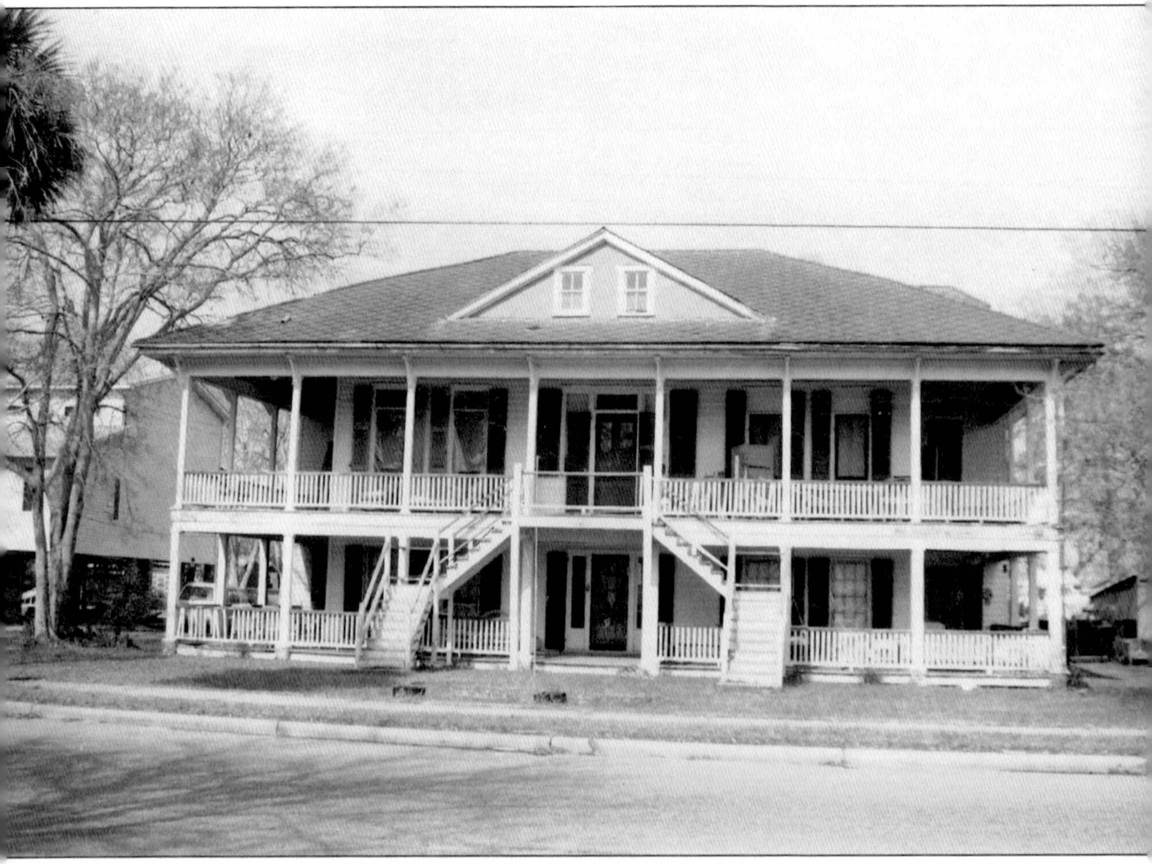

1820 Middle Street c. 1870. The Dr. John B. Patrick House, built of cypress as a front beach summer retreat, is a two and one-half story residence with a symmetrical plan on all but the rear elevation. It has a two-tiered integral piazza that wraps onto the east and west elevations and terminates with flanking wings. The main floor's entrance is flanked by four double-leaf, glazed and paneled doors with leaded stained- and clear-glass transoms depicting the phases of the moon. The property originally reached to the ocean, but as the land accreted, a street was added and part of the property came into the possession of the U.S. Coast Guard, which built a station and lighthouse. Classical Revival in style with Victorian touches, the house is constructed in a post-and-beam manner of heart pine beams and joists. The beams contain Roman numerals and are mortised, tenoned, and pegged together, indicating the wood was probably cut at a mill in Charleston and shipped to Sullivan's Island, where the house was assembled. Dr. Patrick (1822–1903) was a Charleston dentist who, near the end of the Civil War, patented a piece of dental equipment that was first widely used in Europe and then in the United States. Dr. Patrick's Charleston home and office were at 82 Society Street. He and his wife Sarah Aukland had eight children—five boys and three girls. Dr. Patrick built the house, now across the street (1820 I'on), as a card house and cottage for him and his sons in which to play cards away from the women of the family. Dr. Patrick was elected intendent (mayor) of Moultrieville in 1872. The current owner is John B. Geer of Charlotte, North Carolina. [On the National Register of Historic Places, exceptional example of late 19th-century island residential architecture.] (Courtesy Marshall Stith.)

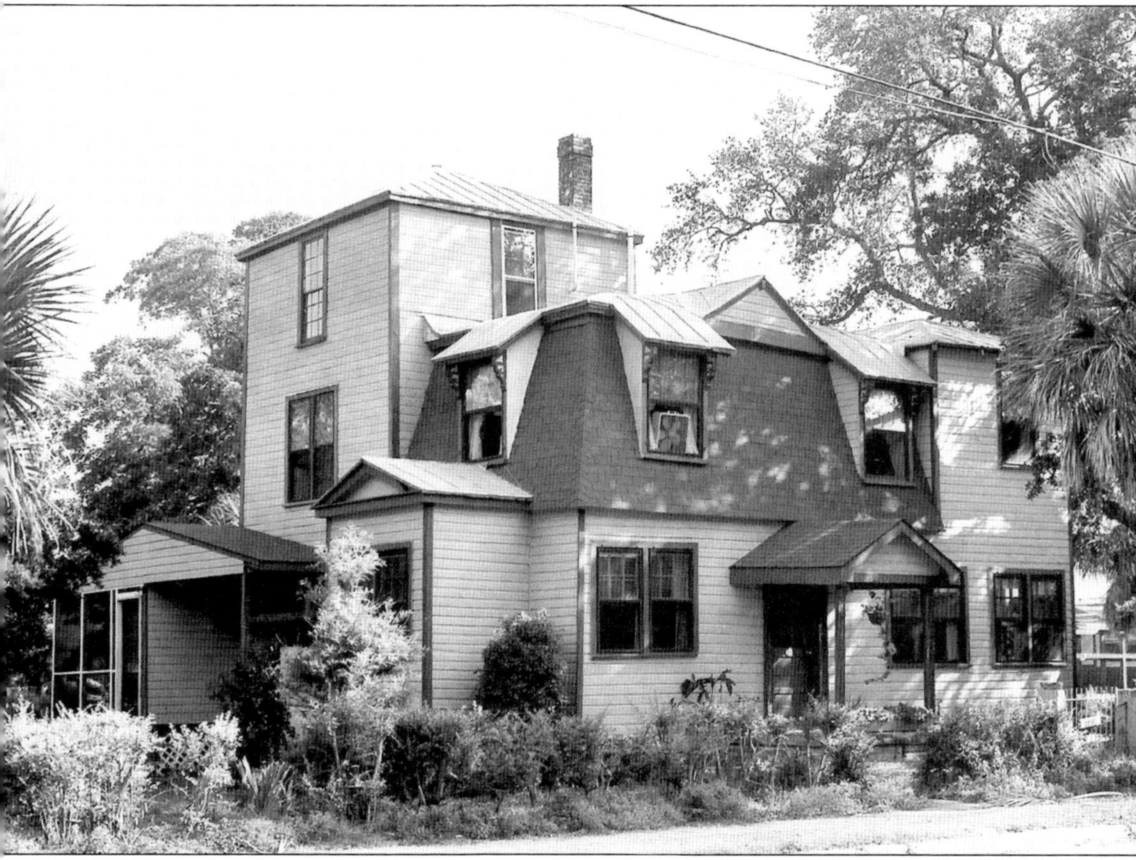

1914 Middle Street, Gate House c. 1875. The Devereux Mansion Gate House was built as the entrance to John Henry Devereux's Sullivan's Island home. It originally had a two-story entrance portico. The upper level was destroyed by a hurricane. The mansard roof is original, but the two-story block to the north is an addition. The basic house plan is irregular; the dormers have shed roofs and decorative craved brackets. There are pedimented gable ends at the stoop and wings. The house has a latticed foundation, and the gate posts are original to the property. Former owners include the Ward family and poet Marjorie Wentworth and her family. [Although altered, the building is an exceptional example of 19th-century island residential architecture; significant due to its association with J.H. Devereux.] (Courtesy S.C. Department of Archives and History.)

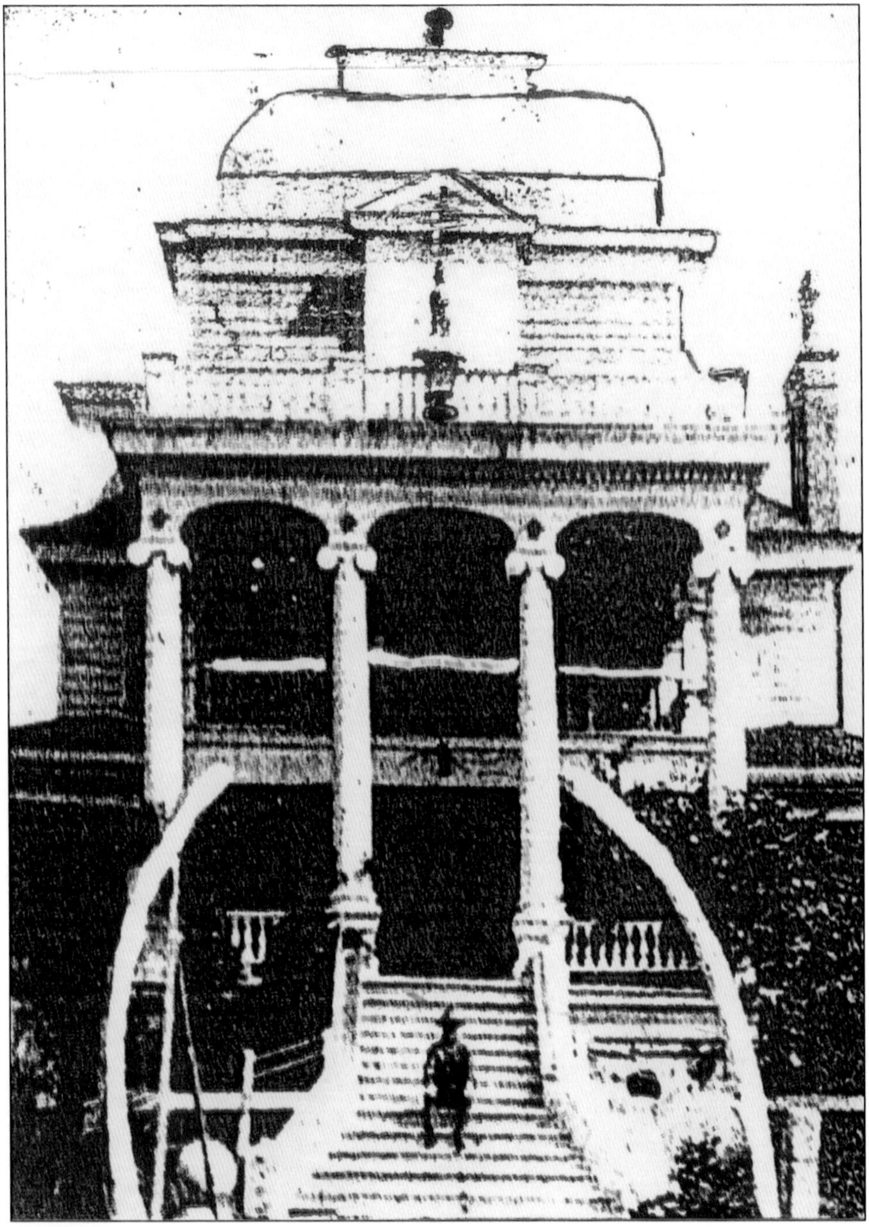

1914 MIDDLE STREET c. 1875. The Devereux Mansion, built by Charleston architect John Henry Deveraux, was called "Elysium." An elaborate architectural composition, the structure featured an entrance flanked by two 10-foot whale jaw bones taken from a whale that had beached itself on Sullivan's Island. One island resident said it took weeks to get rid of the whale. Devereux practiced architecture from 1865 into the early 20th century. He was a student of Edward C. Jones, one of Charleston's finest antebellum architects. Devereux's works include St. Mathew's Lutheran Church (1867–1872), the Academy of Music (1869), and the Charleston Post Office, as well as other prominent commercial buildings throughout the city and country. In 1885 Devereux served the Treasury Department as superintendent of construction and repairs and as traveling inspector of public buildings. Mr. Devereux was born in Wexford, Ireland. [Gone.]

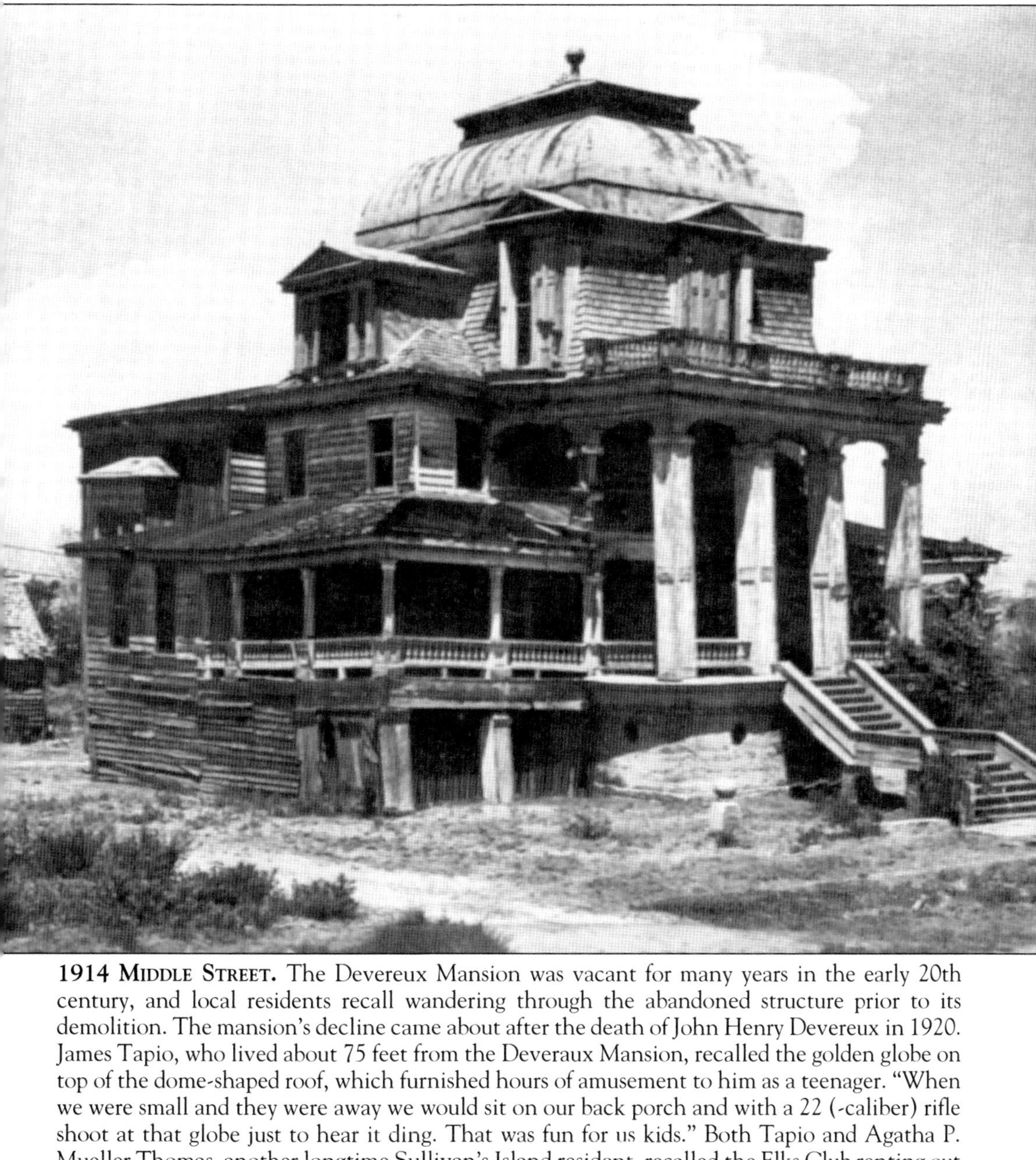

1914 Middle Street. The Devereux Mansion was vacant for many years in the early 20th century, and local residents recall wandering through the abandoned structure prior to its demolition. The mansion's decline came about after the death of John Henry Devereux in 1920. James Tapio, who lived about 75 feet from the Deveraux Mansion, recalled the golden globe on top of the dome-shaped roof, which furnished hours of amusement to him as a teenager. "When we were small and they were away we would sit on our back porch and with a 22 (-caliber) rifle shoot at that globe just to hear it ding. That was fun for us kids." Both Tapio and Agatha P. Mueller Thomas, another longtime Sullivan's Island resident, recalled the Elks Club renting out the Devereux house for dances and the lighted B.P.O.E. (Benevolent Protective Order of the Elks) sign on the home. Mrs. Thomas also remembered that soldiers would rent out the dining room for dances. She recalled walking across the dining room floor, which had started to slant as the house deteriorated. Tapio left for military service in World War II in 1944. When he returned the Devereux Mansion had been torn down. (Courtesy Mrs. Charles Liebenrood II.)

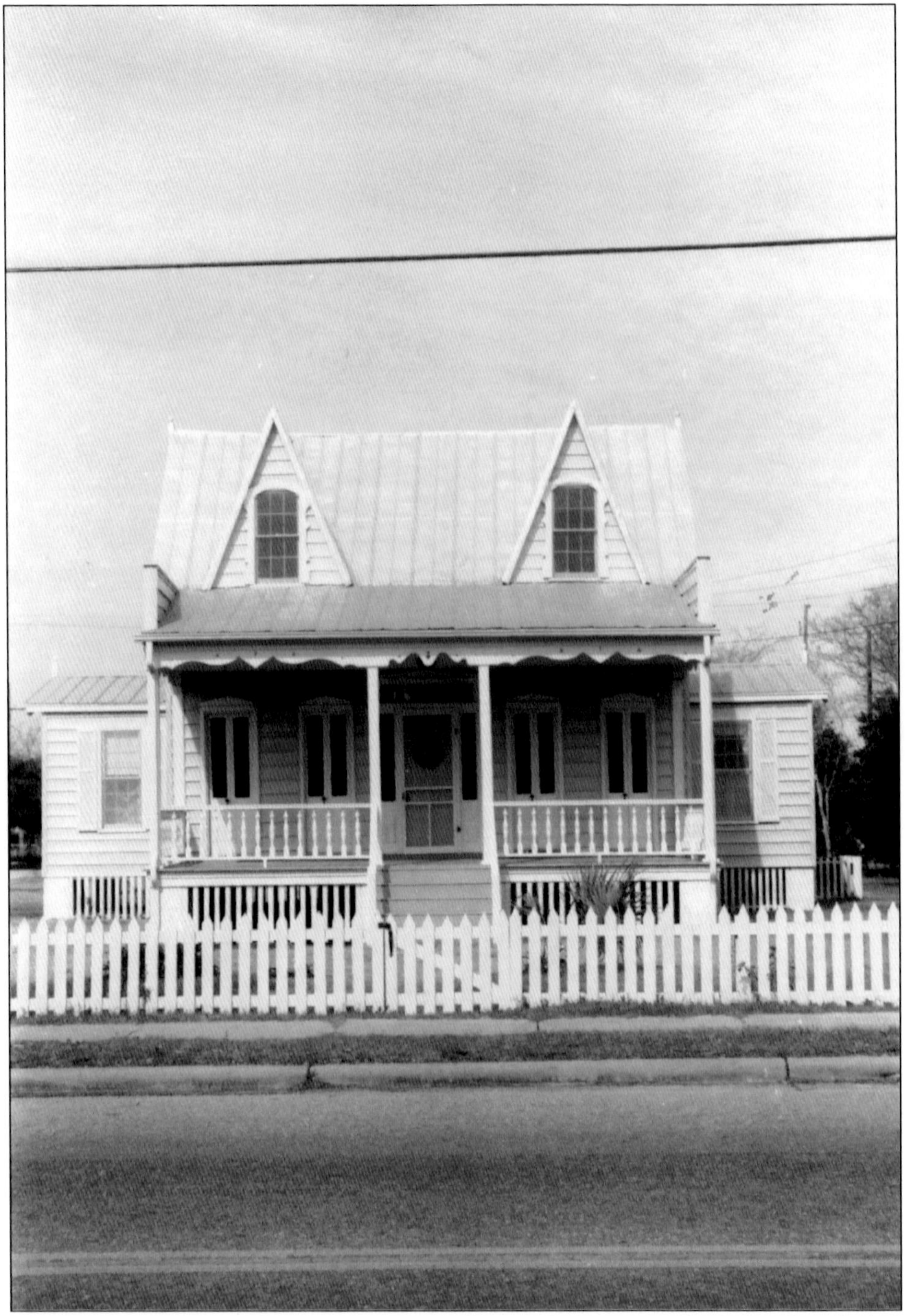

2002 Middle Street c. 1885. This was the home of the McGoldrick family, which had one of the two ice supply companies on the island. (The competing firm belonged to the Truesdale family). The McGoldricks are said to have bought the house from the Schachte family when the expansion of Fort Moultrie forced the McGoldricks to move. [Although altered, the building is a good example of 19th-century island residential architecture.] (Courtesy Marshall Stith.)

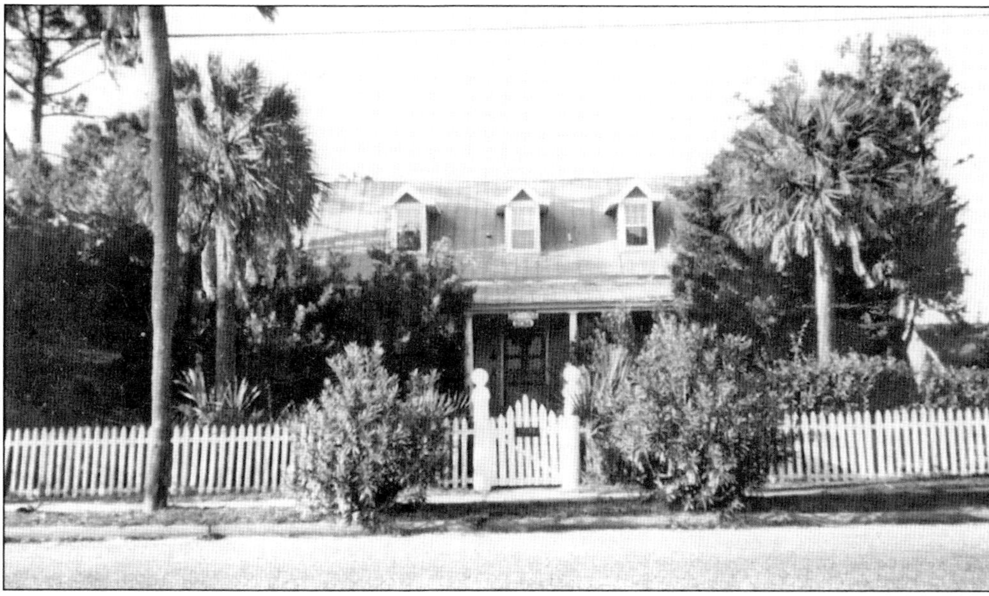

2014 Middle Street c. 1895. This property (The Palmettos) was purchased c. 1920 by Bart Buckley, operator of a horse cart business from the ferry landing, after his house at Station 18 1/2 burned. Much of the historic interior was lost in a fire in the late 1960s; it was rehabilitated c. 1947 but burned again and was repaired c. 1981. Mr. Buckley was the last mayor of Moultrieville, holding that office when the town charter was revoked in 1906. Buckley's daughter managed the post office, located next door at 2018 Middle Street, until 1928. The Palmettos was owned by the Buckley family until 1947. [Good example.] (Courtesy Jeri England.)

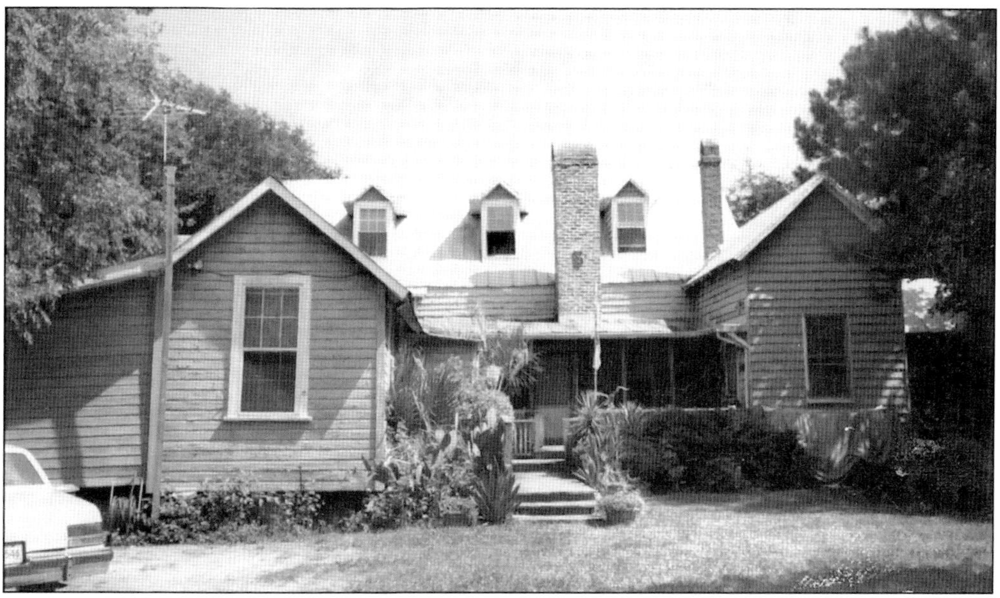

2014 Middle Street (rear view). The maid's quarters of the main house infilled before 1917. The double-shouldered rear chimney, built of brick from an old mill in Orangeburg County, was added c. 1974. The cistern, built of old brick, remains under the front porch. (Courtesy Jeri England.)

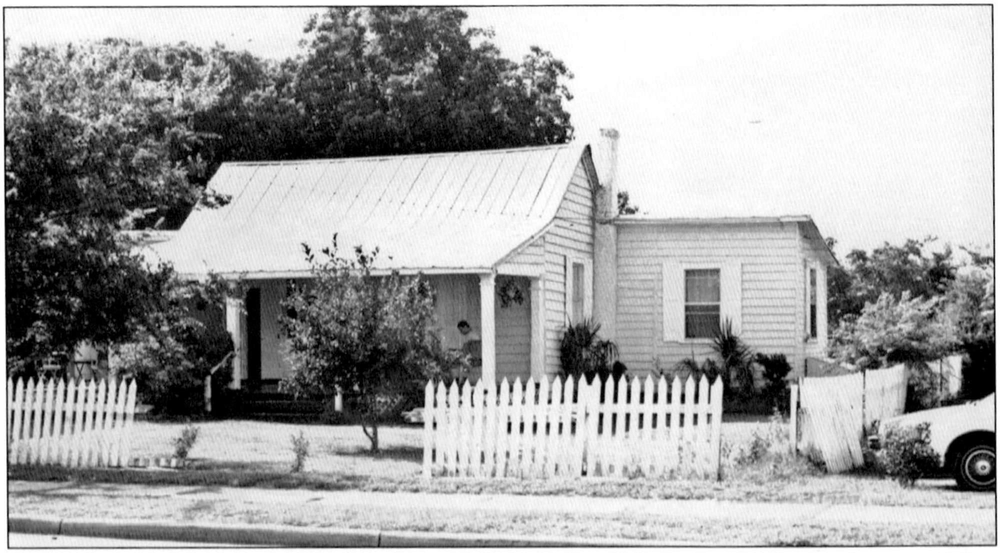

2018 Middle Street c. 1890. The Anthony House served as the Moultrieville Post Office from shortly before 1920 until 1928. The post office was operated by one of two Buckley sisters who were living next door at 2014 Middle Street. Their brother, Fr. Anthony Buckley, also lived at the property; thus the name. The house is rectangular with a one-by-one bay wing to the northeast and a shed addition to the rear. The western entrance of the south façade has a transom and sidelights. [Good example of late 19th-century island architecture.] (Courtesy Nita Byrum.)

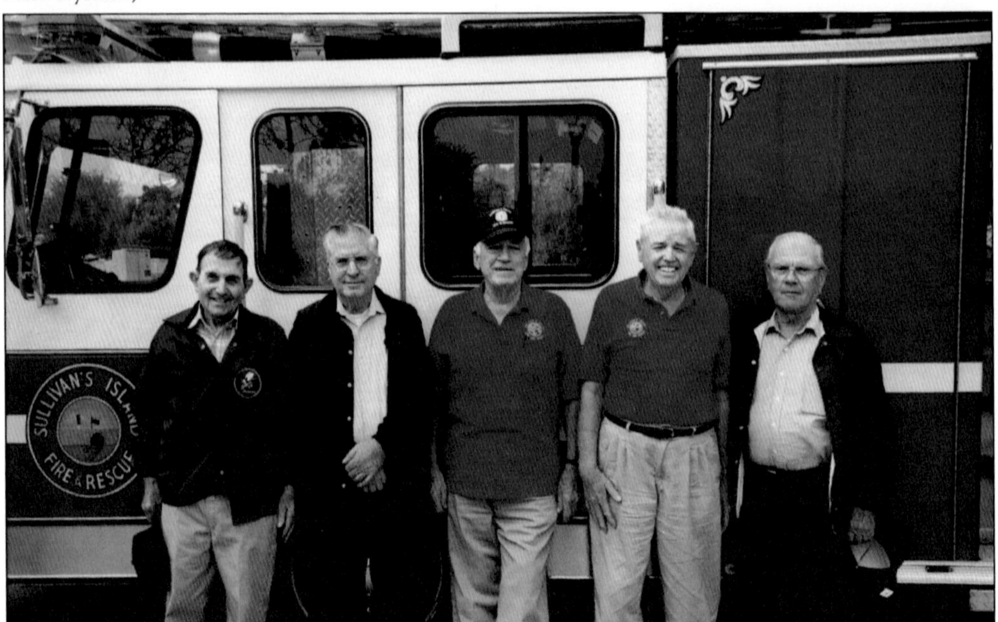

Volunteer Fire Department, Station 20. The Volunteer Fire Department is one of Sullivan's Island's best examples of volunteer citizens' involvement at the local, grassroots level. They work in conjunction with the Sullivan's Island Fire Department at Station 20. The original volunteer fire department members, from left to right, are Joe Rowland, Leo Truesdell, Louis Stith, Red Wood, and Arc Chiola. (Courtesy of George Kablick.)

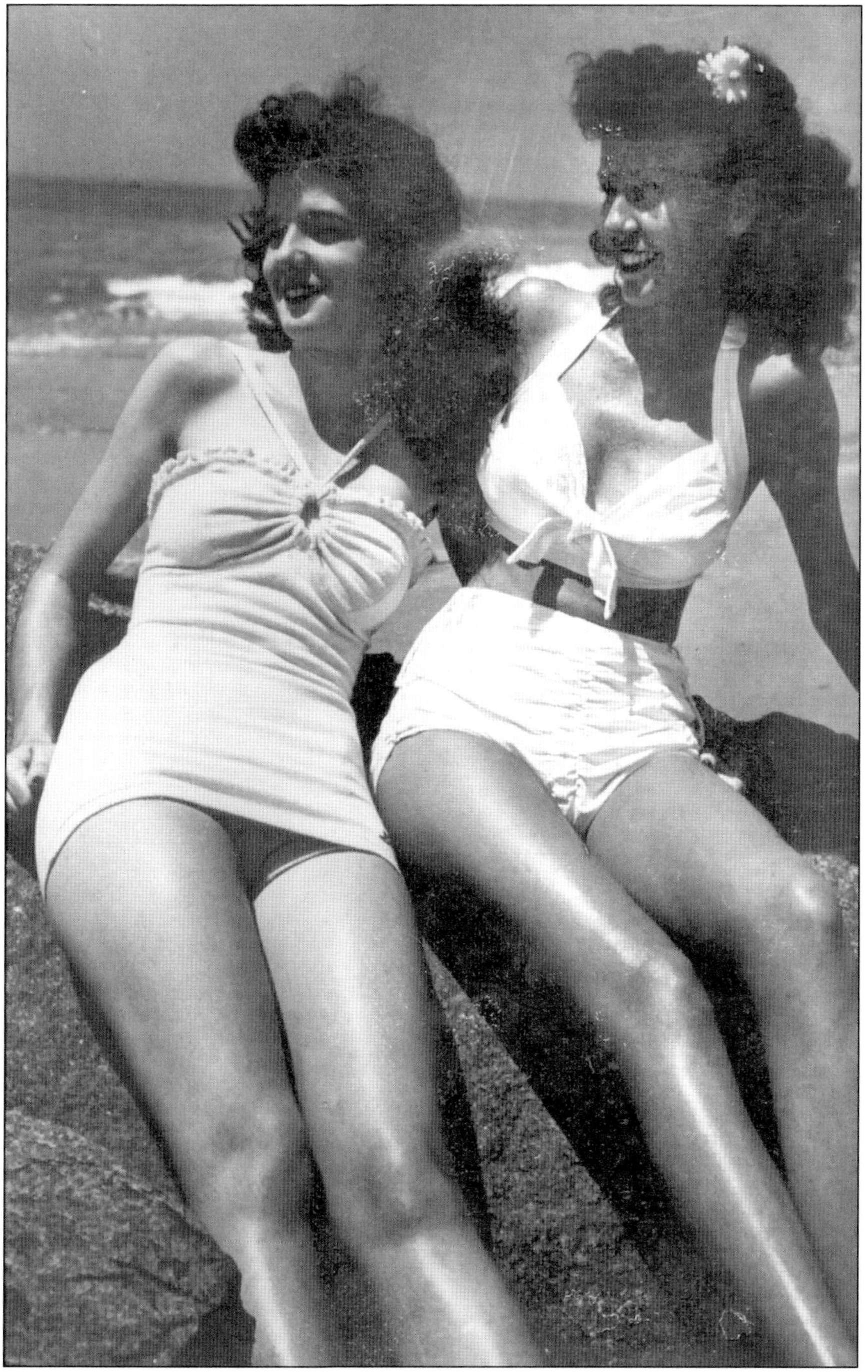

TWO LADIES ON THE BEACH. These two young ladies were photographed in the late 1940s on the beach not far from Station 21. They are Rose Strickland Teske (left) and her sister Marguerite Strickland Stith; Rose's husband, Frank Teske, took the picture. Marguerite Stith's husband was Judge Louis Stith, and one of her sons, Marshall, became mayor of Sullivan's Island. Another son, Anthony, became Sullivan's Island's fire chief. The Stith family has lived on Sullivan's Island for generations. (Courtesy Marshall Stith.)

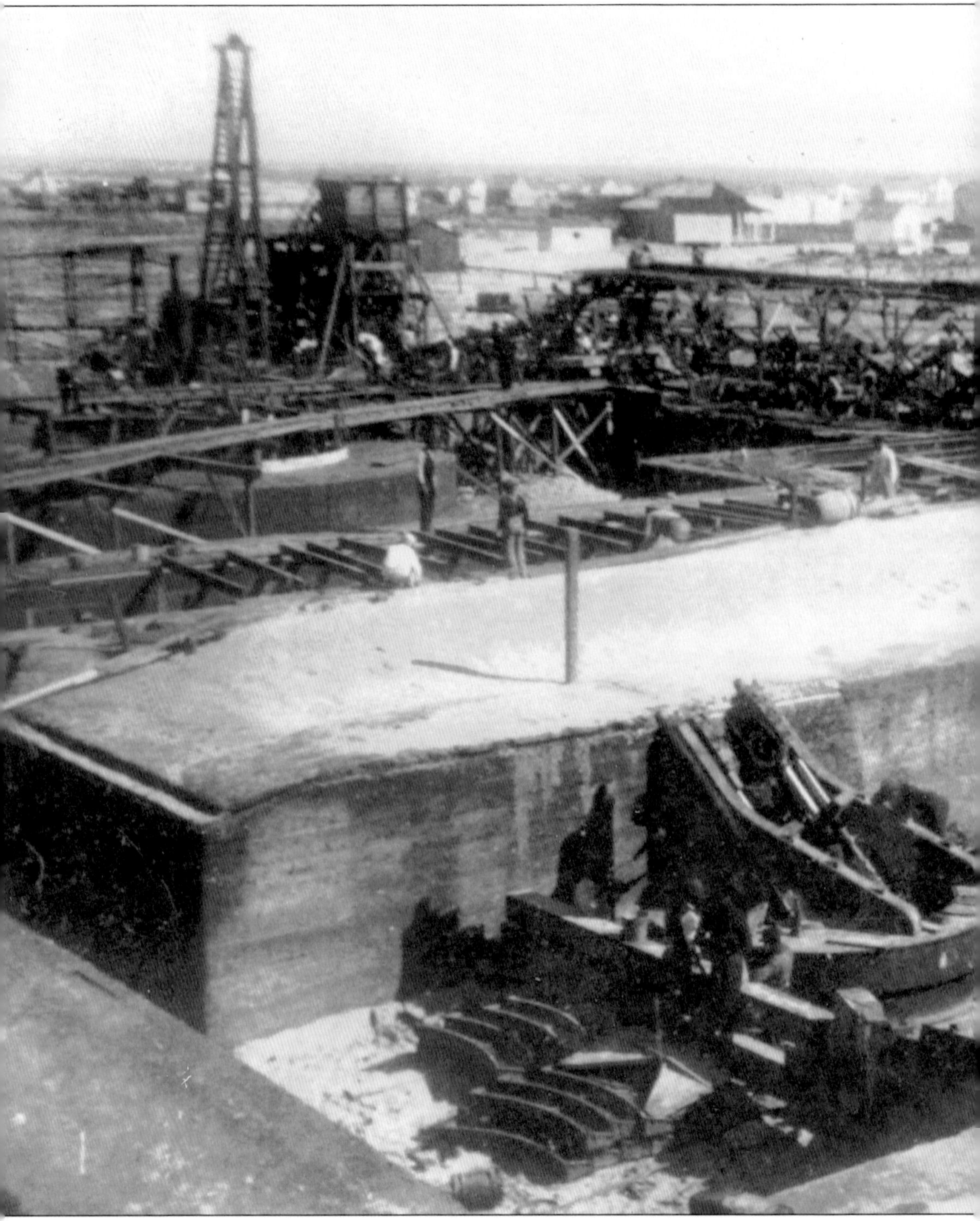

Battery Pierce Butler/Battery Capron, Northeast Corner of Middle Street and Station 20 1/2. This picture looks eastward toward the ocean. These batteries were constructed c. 1900 as mortar batteries for Fort Moultrie. Each of the batteries' four emplacements contained a cluster of four 12-inch mortars designed to propel a 700-pound projectile vertically.

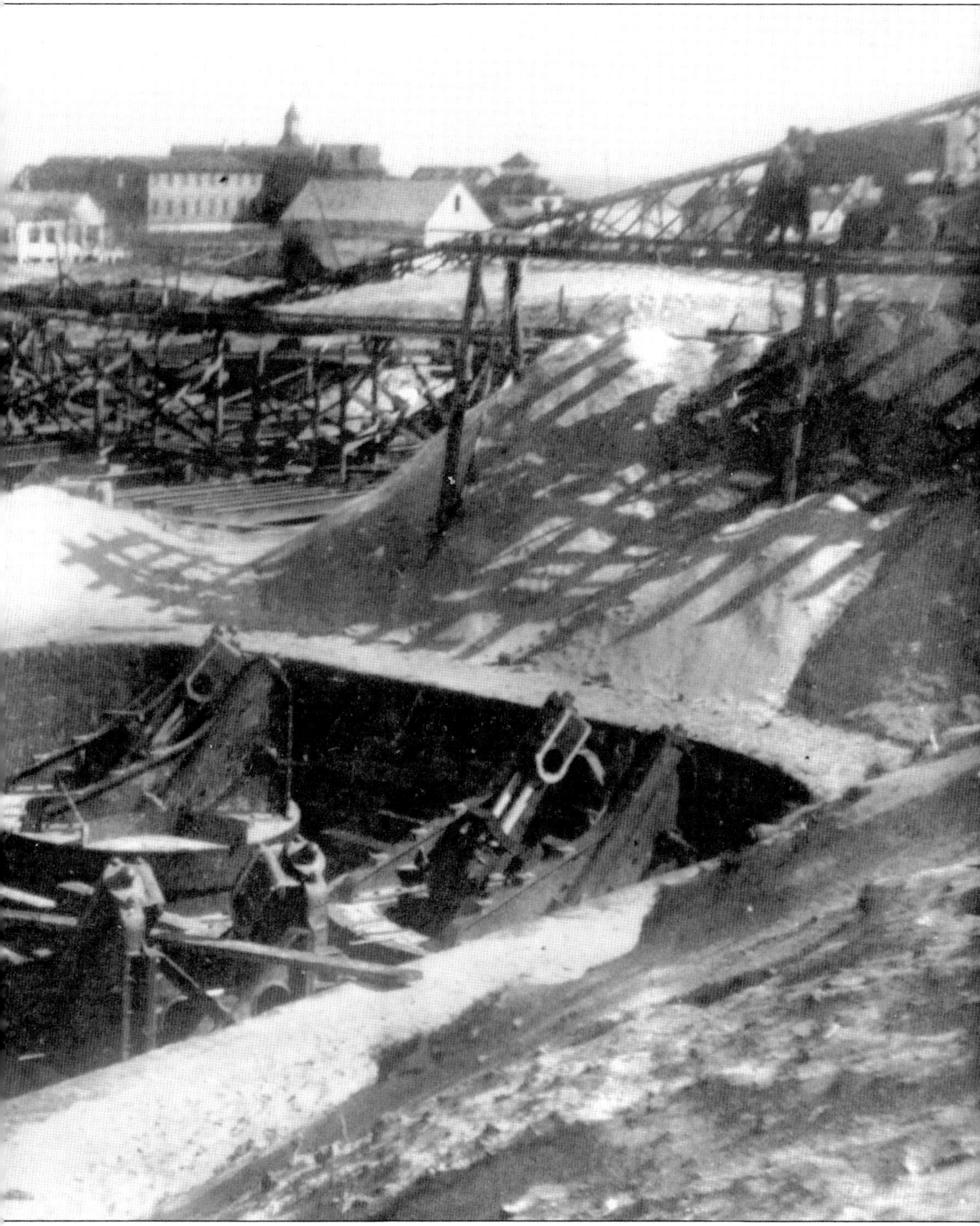

This picture, taken during construction, shows the Atlantic Beach Hotel near the center of the picture, J. Schroeder McInery's house on Middle Street behind the hotel, and the Conner House on I'on Avenue, with its cupola directly to the right of the hotel. [Part of a significant grouping of military structures.] (Courtesy of Marshall Stith.)

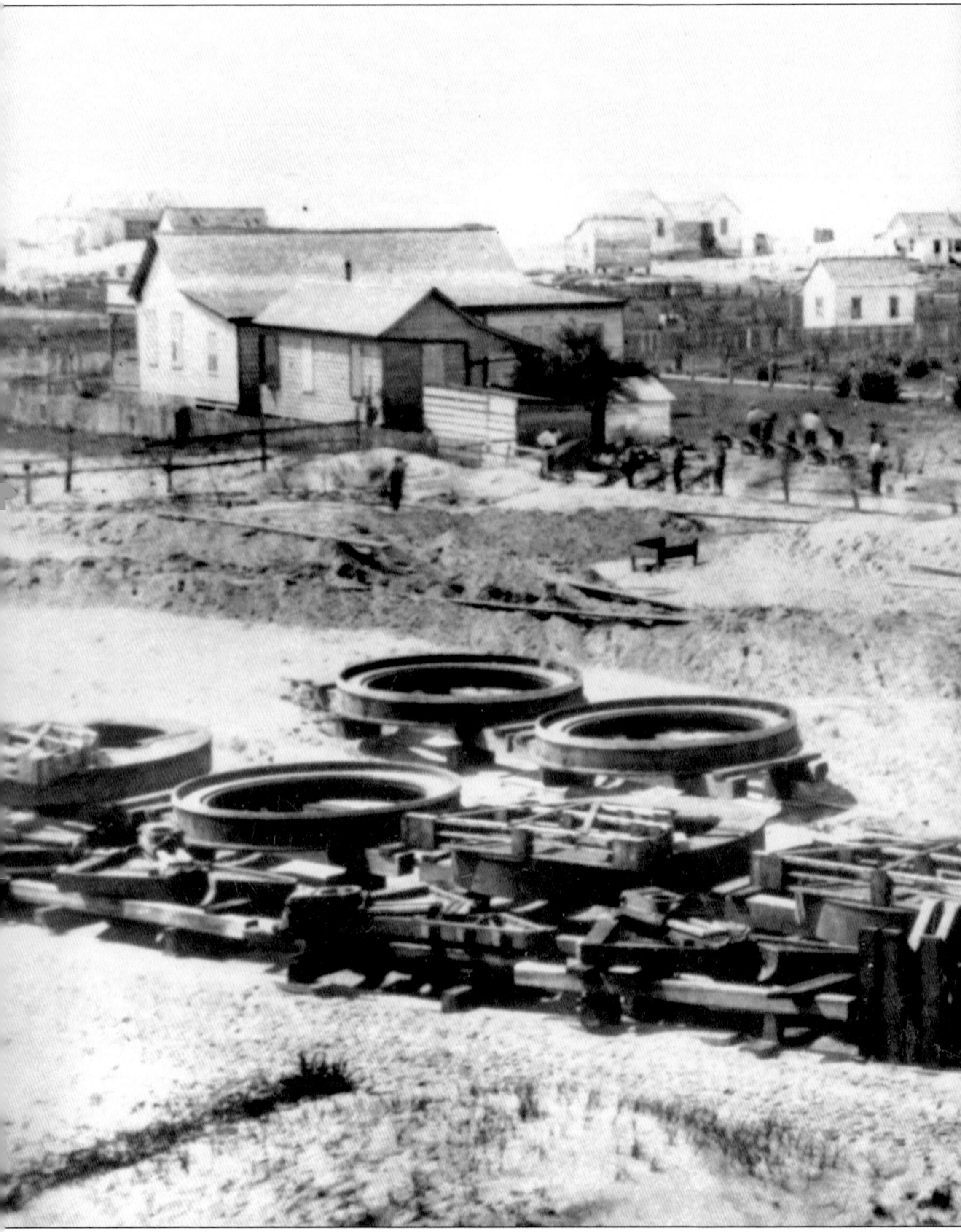

Westward view of Battery Pierce Butler/Battery Capron. This picture looks westward toward the inner harbor. Work on the Sullivan's Island installation did not commence until 1897, when tension between the U.S. and Spain resulted in the

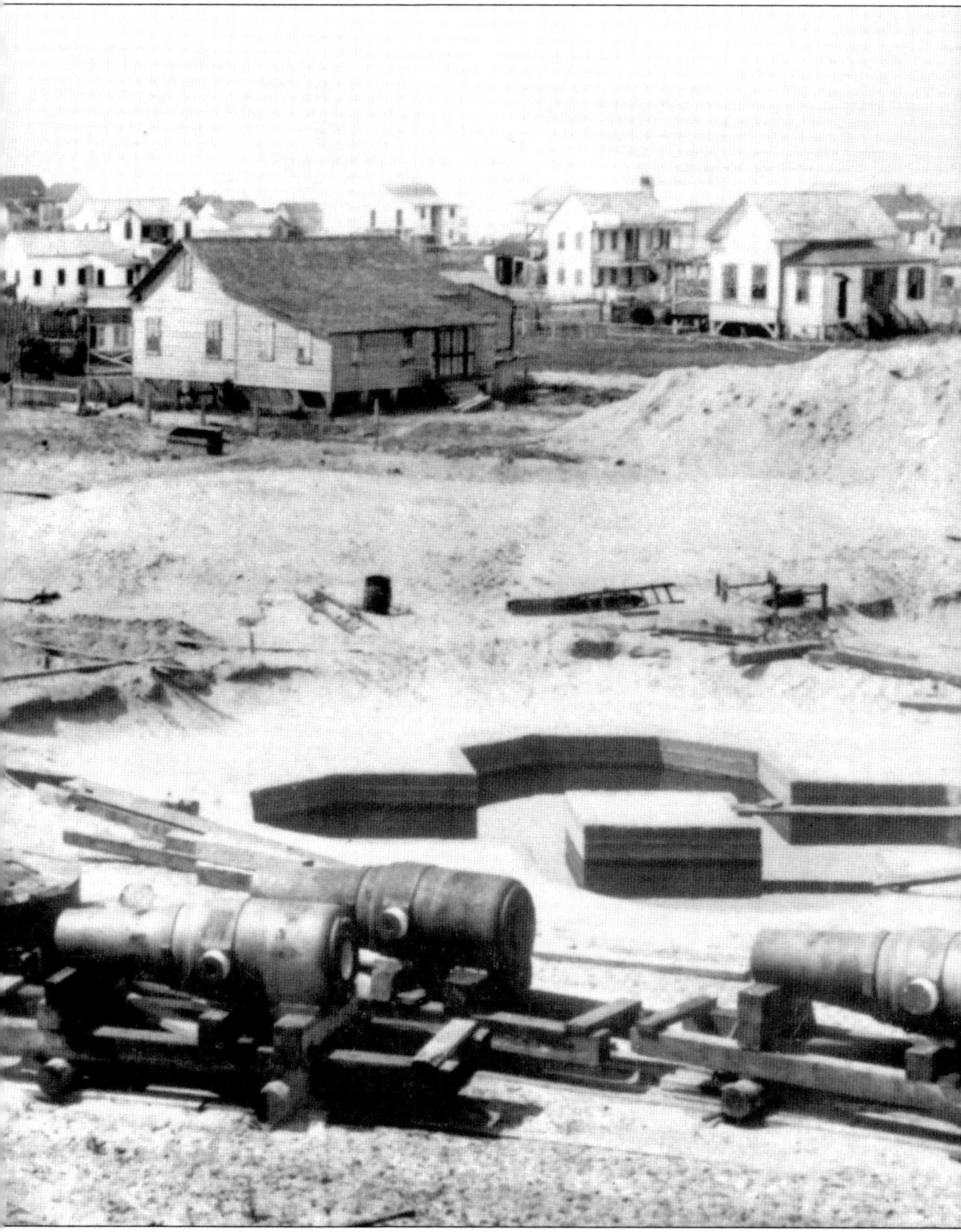

implementation of the Endicott Board's proposals. The installation was declared surplus after World War II and was acquired by the Town of Sullivan's Island. [Part of a significant grouping of military structures.] (Courtesy of Marshall Stith.)

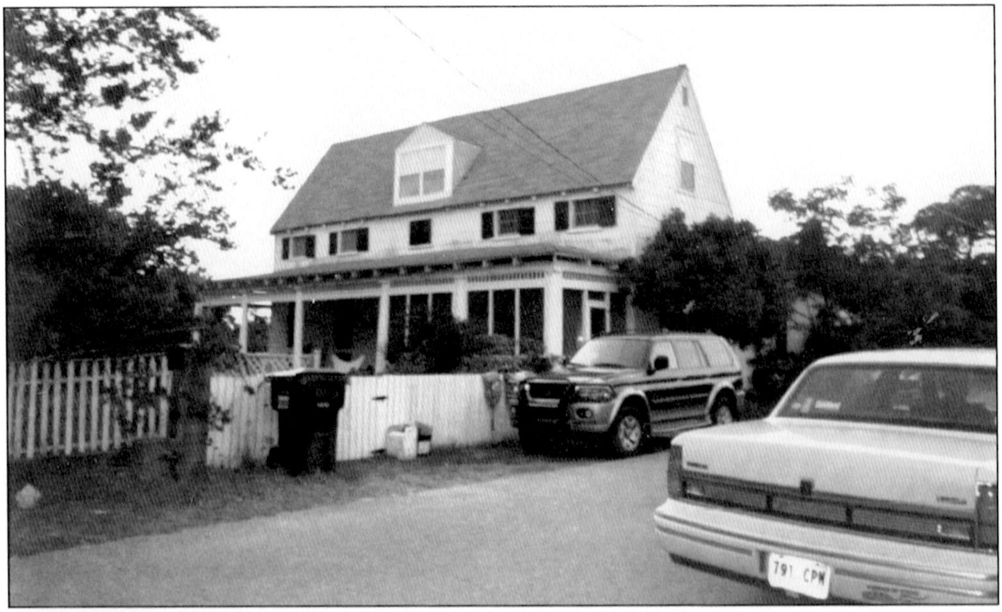

211 STATION 22, 1870. John E. Blanchard moved this house to its current location in 1902 when Fort Moultrie expanded. The Sullivan's Island School operated here from 1904 to 1925. Daniel F. Blanchard Sr. acquired the property in 1929, and the family took in sergeants from Fort Moultrie as boarders for a number of years. The front porch has exposed rafter ends and a decorative sawn screen at the porch level. [Good 19th-century example.] (Courtesy Marshall Stith.)

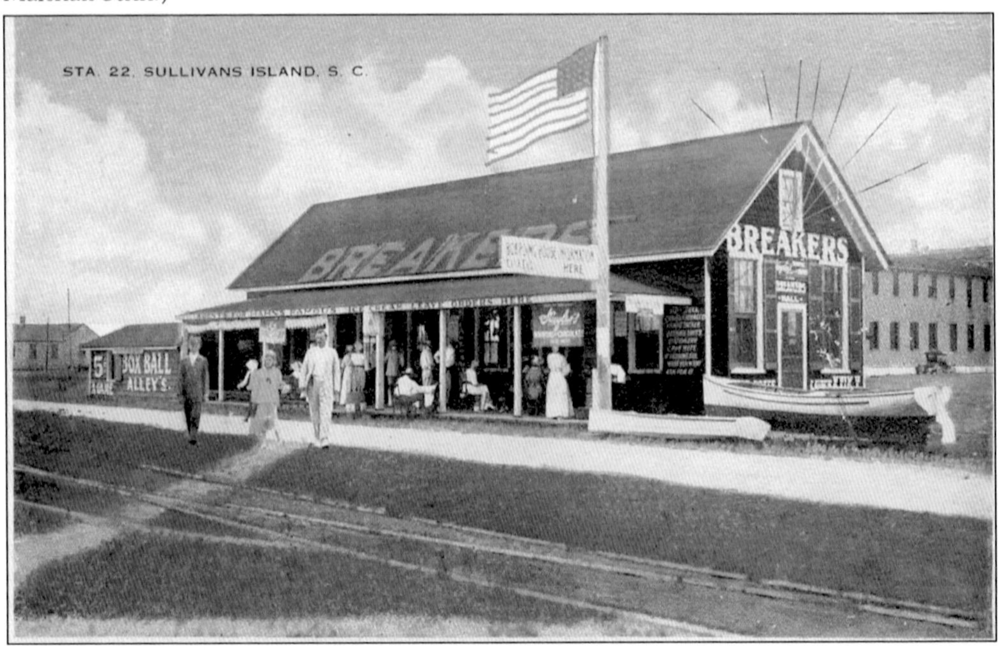

STATION 22, THE BREAKERS. This dance pavilion with a snack bar and bowling alley was located behind the Atlantic Beach Hotel. Weekly dances were held and attended by soldiers, summer people, and permanent residents. The first Breakers opened in the 1920s and was later torn down and replaced. Its replacement was torn down c. 1940. (Courtesy of Deborah Lofton.)

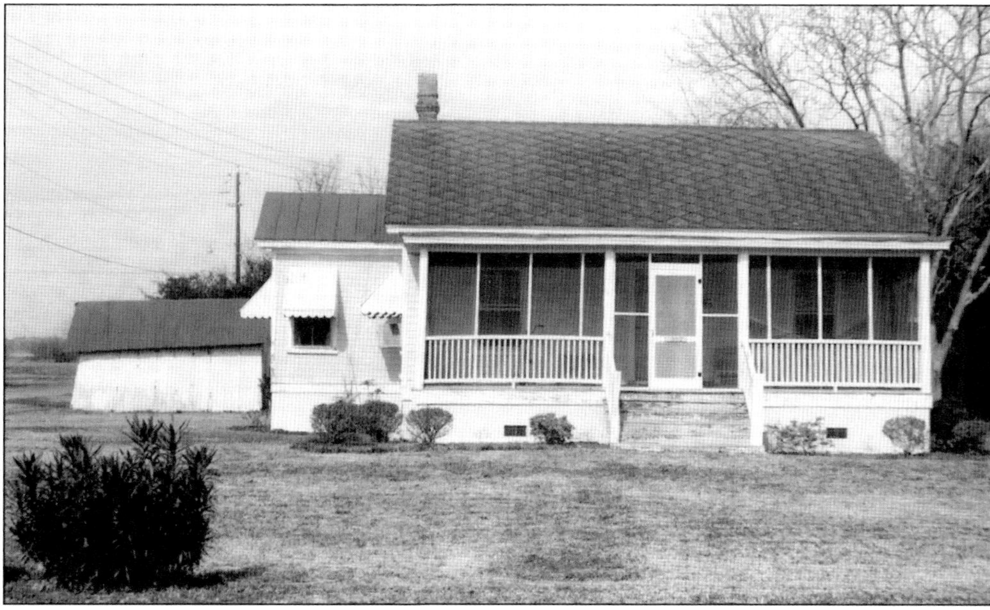

1802 Central Avenue c. 1890. The Max Kimbrell House was probably moved to this site as it is not shown on a 1917 plat or the 1924 Sanborn map and appears to be a much earlier structure. The west wing was added in the 1940s, and the rear porch enclosed in the 1950s. [Good late 19th-century example.] (Courtesy Marshall Stith.)

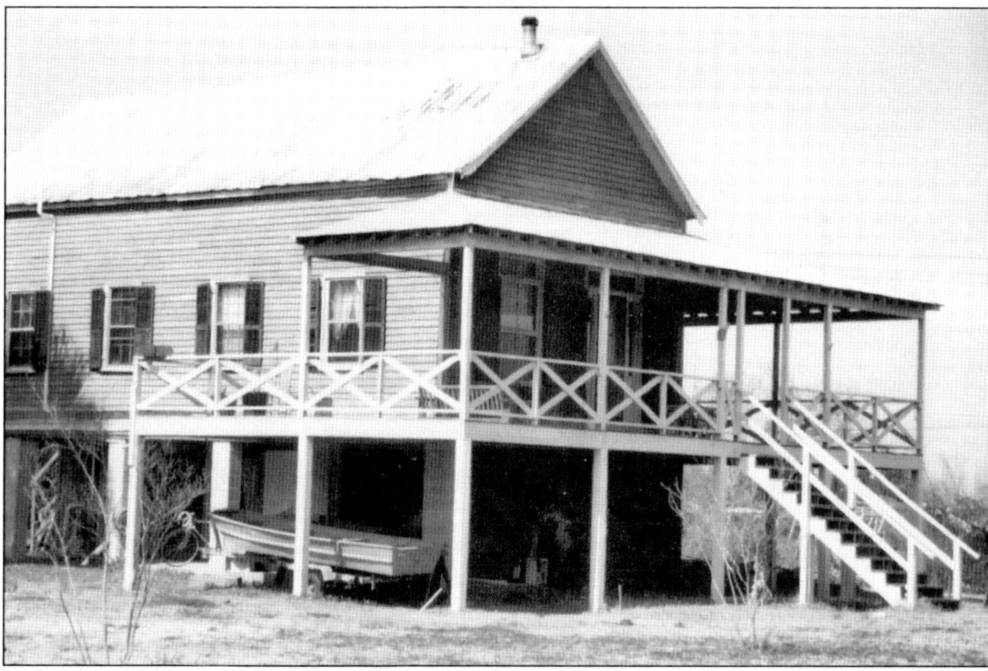

1820 Central Avenue c. 1905. Lumber merchant J.F. McInerny built a store (with an African-American carpenter named Percy), which was operated by his son Joseph P. McInerny. The building has been used as a residence, the Moultrieville Post Office, and a laundromat. It was moved from the front to the rear of the lot in 1983. [Although altered, the building is a good example of early 20th-century island commercial architecture.] (Courtesy Marshall Stith.)

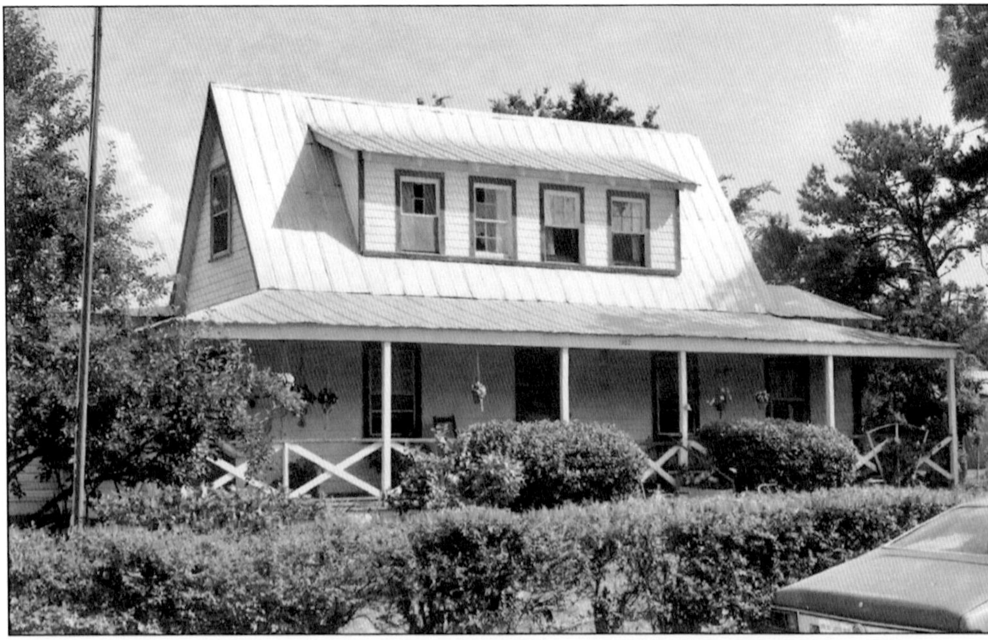

1902 Central Avenue c. 1905. This property was transferred in July 1926 to Vincent O. Coste, a member of the Life Saving Service (which in 1915 had become part of the U.S. Coast Guard). On May 6, 1895, license #35 was granted by the Town of Moultrieville to Henry L. Cade. It was shown as Lot M on H.S. Lamble's April 1902 plat of Moultrieville. This plat also shows Lots O and P as "Life Saving Station." [Representative of a modest early 20th-century island residence.] (Courtesy S.C. Department of Archives and History.)

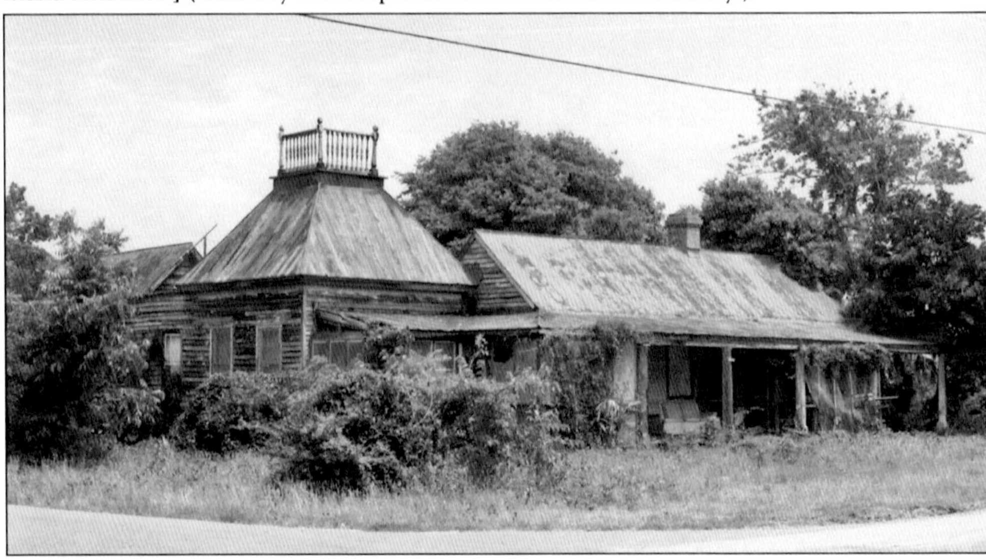

2002 Central Avenue c. 1885. The Blanchard House was the home of John E. Blanchard, a building contractor who worked with construction of the mounds and Marshall Reservation. He was involved with moving many of the houses that were relocated from Fort Moultrie c. 1902. Mr. Blanchard was the father of C.W. Blanchard Sr. who built a number of houses on Sullivan's Island in the 1930s. The house was later occupied by three Blanchard sisters. [Important 19th-century example.] (Courtesy S.C. Department of Archives and History.)

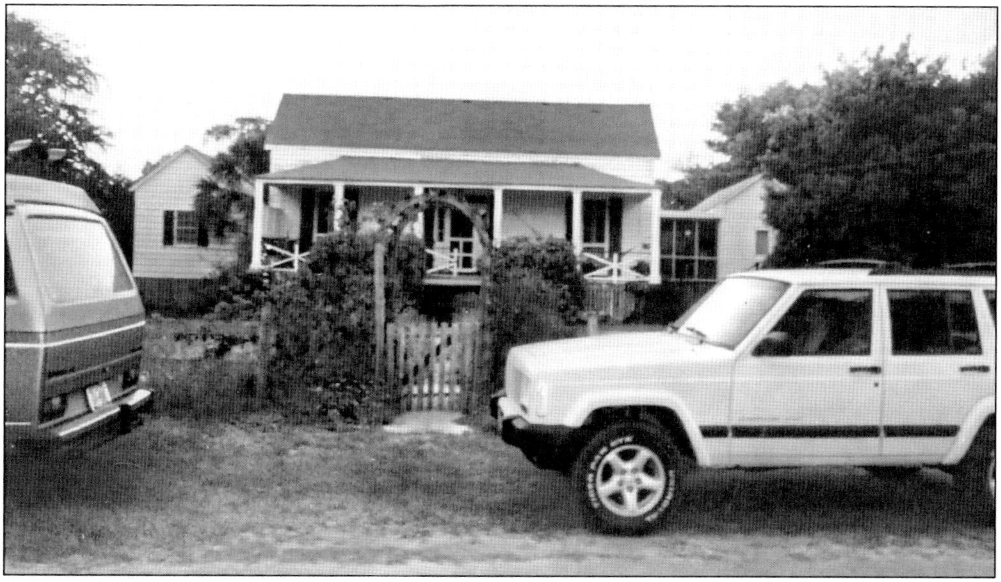

1808 I'ON AVENUE c. 1900. The house had previously belonged to Dr. John Seigling and was a summer residence before the Knopf family bought the property in the 1970s as a summer house. They moved there permanently after Hurricane Hugo. Wings on the east and the west are connected to the main house by screened-in breezeways. (Modest example of an early 20th-century island house.] (Courtesy Bonnie A. Williams.)

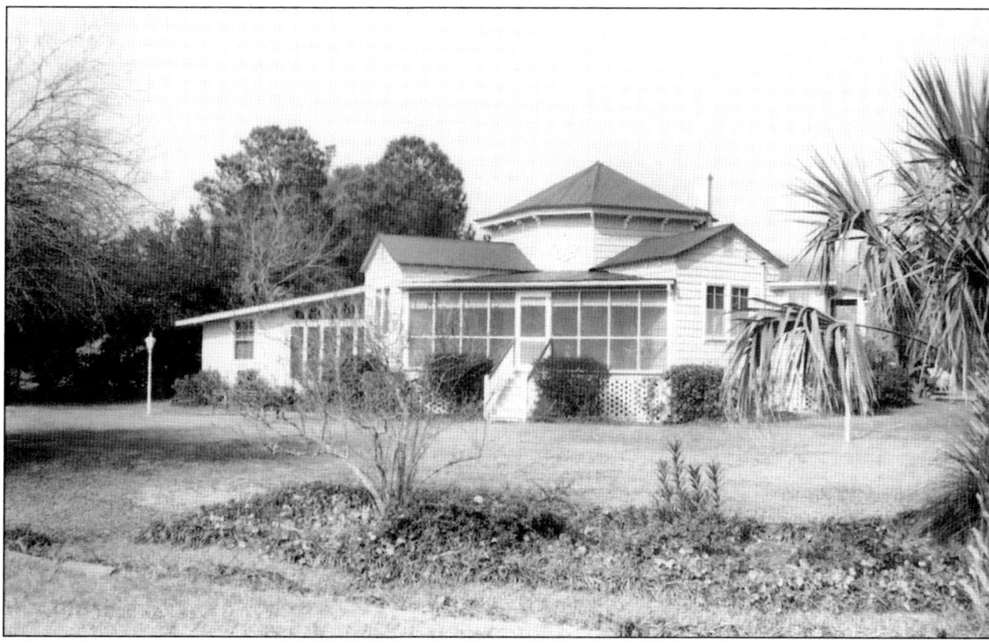

1820 I'ON AVENUE c. 1870. The Poker Cottage was built *c.* 1870 as an octagonal cottage (five rooms, four triangular porches) for Dr. J.B. Patrick, who lived at 1820 Middle Street. The house is said to have been built as a club house for Dr. Patrick's sons and was locally known as the Poker Cottage. Former owners include the Warley, Stoney, Hurley, Smith, Murrell, Them, and Hooker families. The current owner is Make Macmurphy. [Although altered, the building is an exceptional example of 19th-century island architecture.] (Courtesy Marshall Stith.)

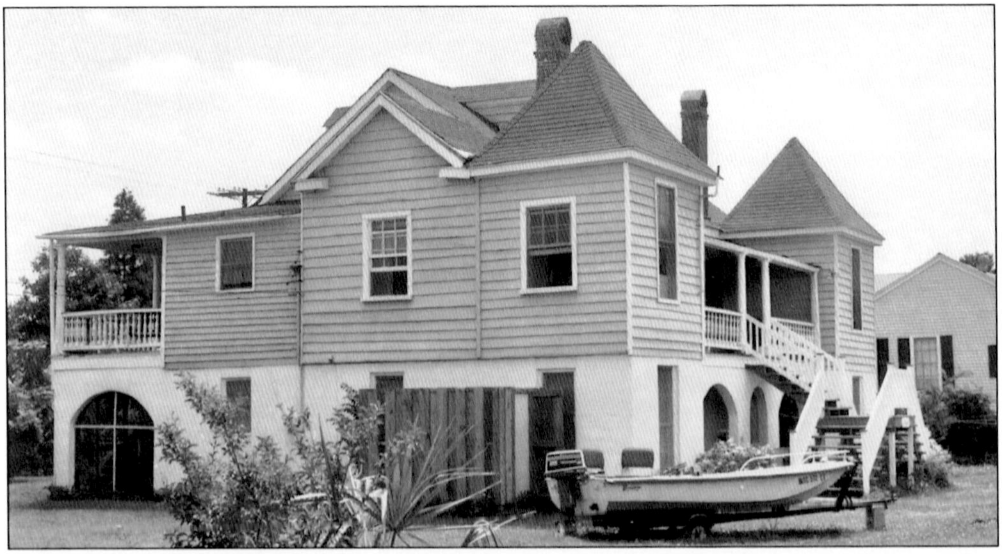

2114 I'ON AVENUE c. 1915. The main block of the house is rectangular with one-by-one bay wings to the east and west and pyramidal appendages to the northeast and northwest that flank the rear porch. The building is raised on a finished basement level. There are dormers with six/six windows on the north and south slopes of the main roof. The chimneys have arched rain hoods. The house was rehabilitated in 1987, and dormers and other features may have been added at that time. [A very good example of island architecture.] (Courtesy S.C. Department of Archives and History.)

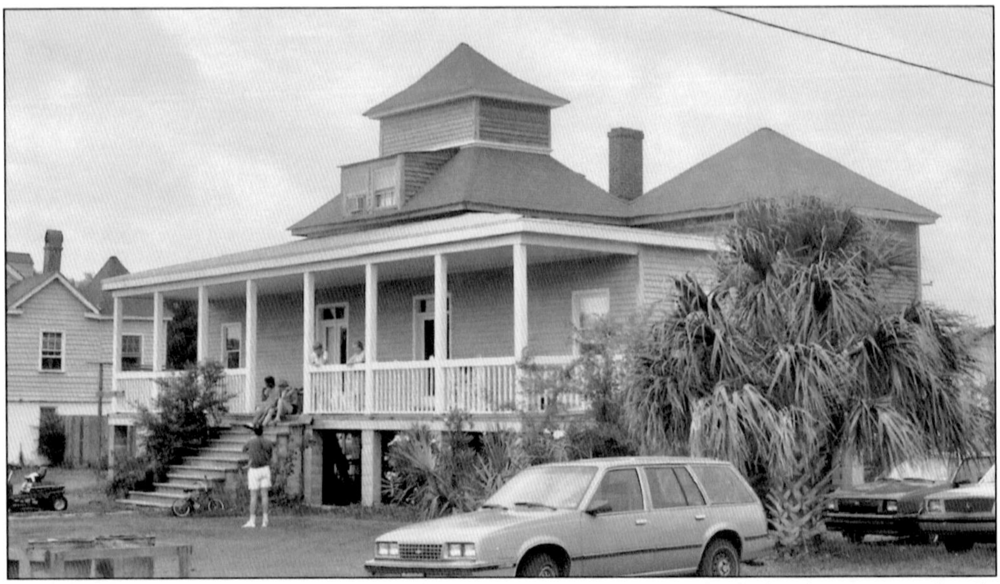

2118 I'ON AVENUE c. 1895. The John S. O'Conner House was built for the Conner family ("O" dropped), who still own it. The family tradition is that the house was used as a casino in conjunction with the Atlantic Beach Hotel, which was across the street. The house is rectangular with pyramidal wings to the northeast and northwest; the central section of the hip roof is raised. [A very good example of late 19th-century island residential architecture that has been compromised by unfortunate recent alterations.] (Courtesy S.C. Department of Archives and History.)

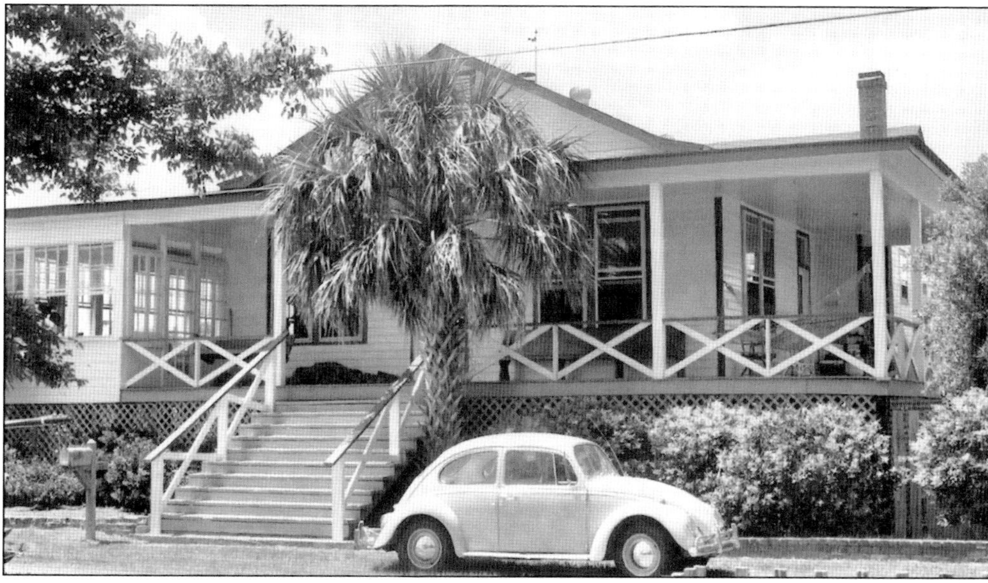

2202 I'ON AVENUE C. 1925. The Crossed Fish House was built on part of the site of the Atlantic Beach Hotel. The house has a T-shaped main block with a wrap-around porch at the front elevation on the west side. [Good example of early 20th-century island architecture.] (Courtesy S.C. Department of Archives and History.)

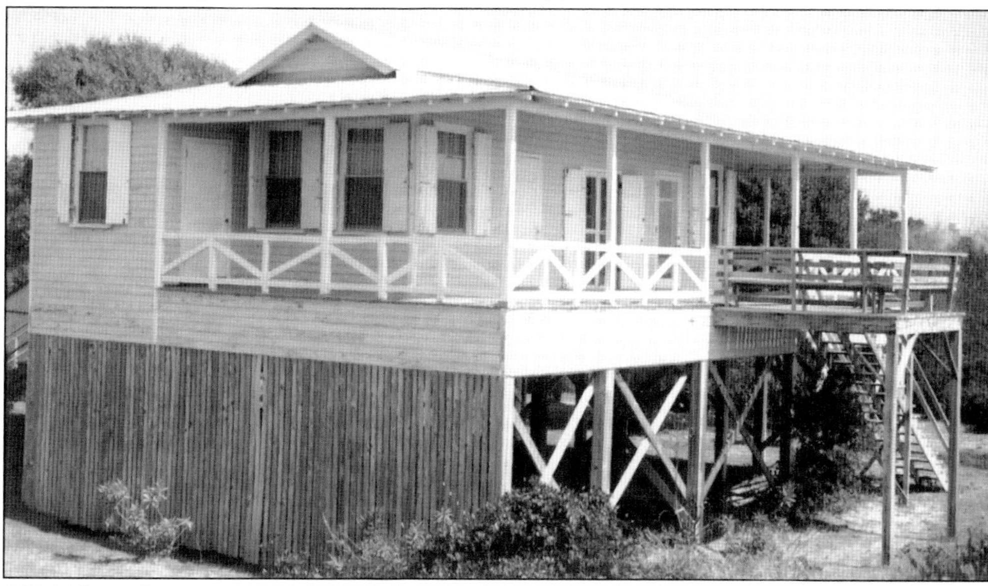

1901 THEE STREET C. 1926. Built by Claude W. Blanchard Sr. and John E. Blanchard for Arthur Gayer, this cottage is rectangular with porches around the south, east, and west and partially infilled on east and west. The house is similar to 1908 Thee Street, which was built c. 1926 for Arthur Bonnell Schirmer; 1902 Thee Street, built for Frank Schirmer; and 1856 Thee Street, also built at the same time for other members of the Schirmer family. The houses ranged in cost from $900 to $1,200 each. A Mr. Canady is said to have also built some of these houses, and the area became known as Schirmerville. [All the houses are representative of modest island houses built during the early 20th-century.] (Courtesy S.C. Department of Archives and History.)

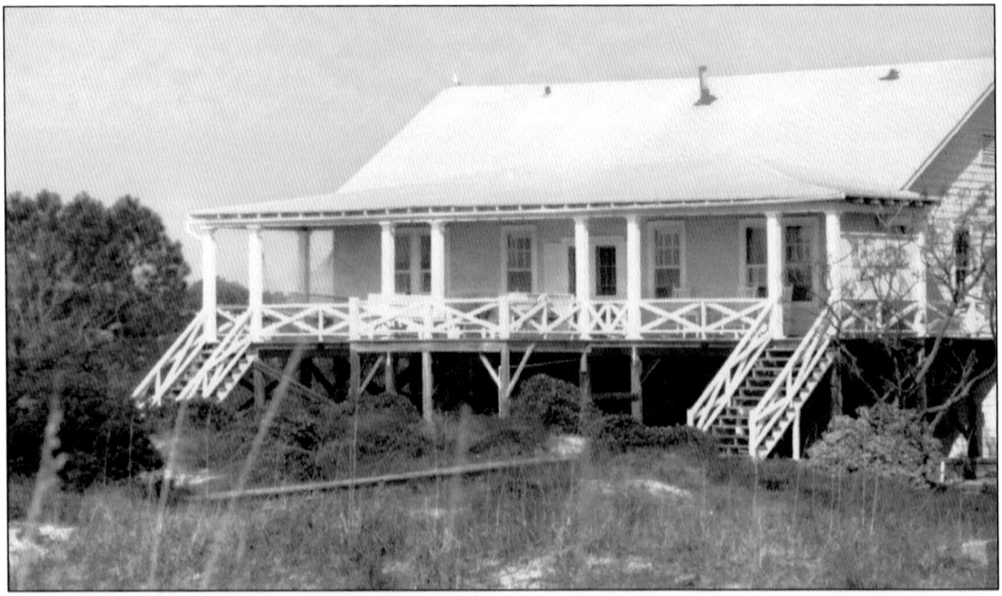

2061 Pettigrew Street c. 1930. This residence was built by Claude W. Blanchard Sr. for the O'Neill family of Charleston, who moved here from 2068 Pettigrew. Mr. O'Neill served as chairman of the Sullivan's Island Township Commission for many years and was a partner in the Heyward-O'Neill Insurance Agency in Charleston of which DuBose Heyward, the writer and poet, was a founding member. The house later belonged to Dr. R. Michael Williams. The square wood posts on the porch have molded bases and capitals. The house is built with projecting rooms on the northeast and southwest to capture prevailing breezes. [Representative of a large beachfront residence.] (Courtesy Marshall Stith.)

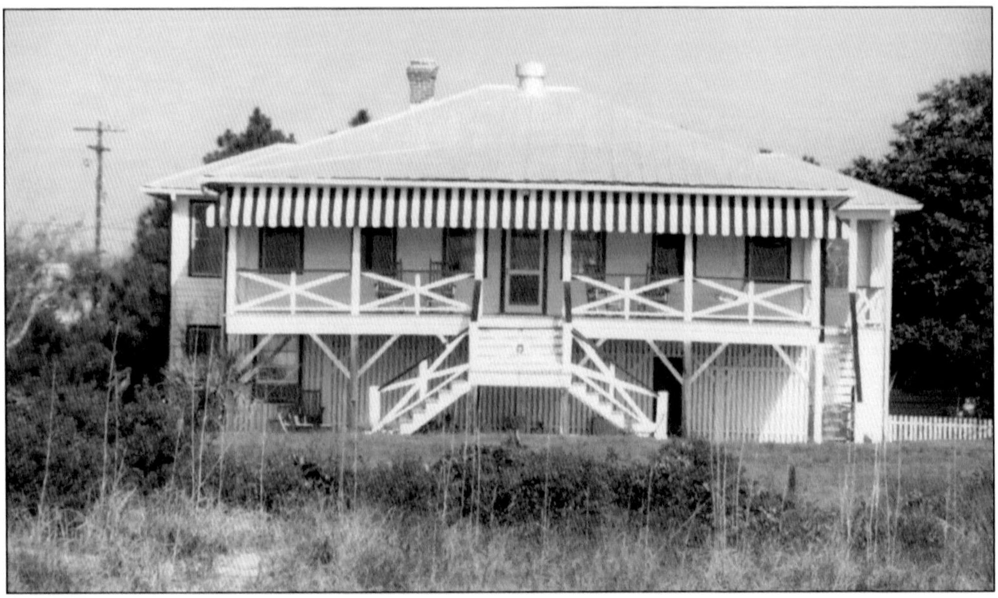

2101 Pettigrew Street c. 1935. This rectangular house has small wings to the northeast and northwest to take advantage of island breezes. It was built for the Frampton family of Charleston by Claude W. Blanchard Sr. [Representative of a large beachfront residence.] (Courtesy Marshall Stith.)

2105 Pettigrew c. 1935. This summer house was built for Dr. Robert M. Hope and his family, who lived at 12 Meeting Street in Charleston. Lumber for this house, as well as 2103, 2109, 2115, and 2119 Pettigrew, was provided by an uncle of Robert Pringle. [Representative of the type of large beachfront residences that were constructed in the 1930s.] (Courtesy of Marshall Stith.)

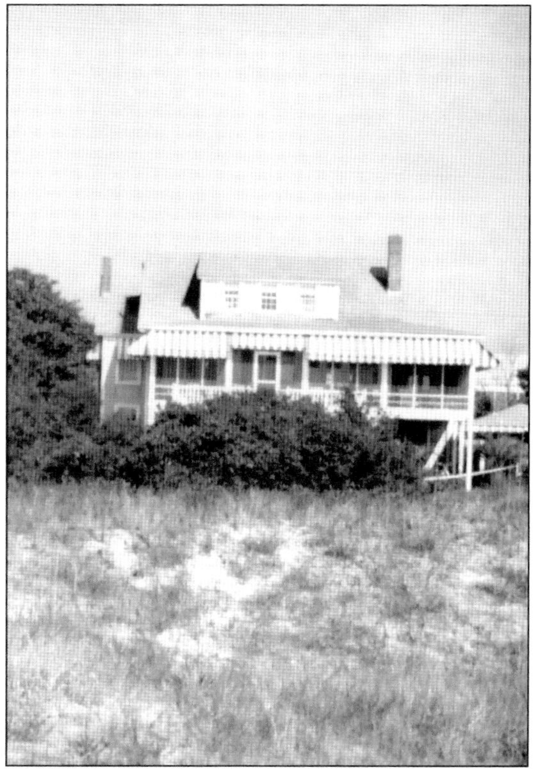

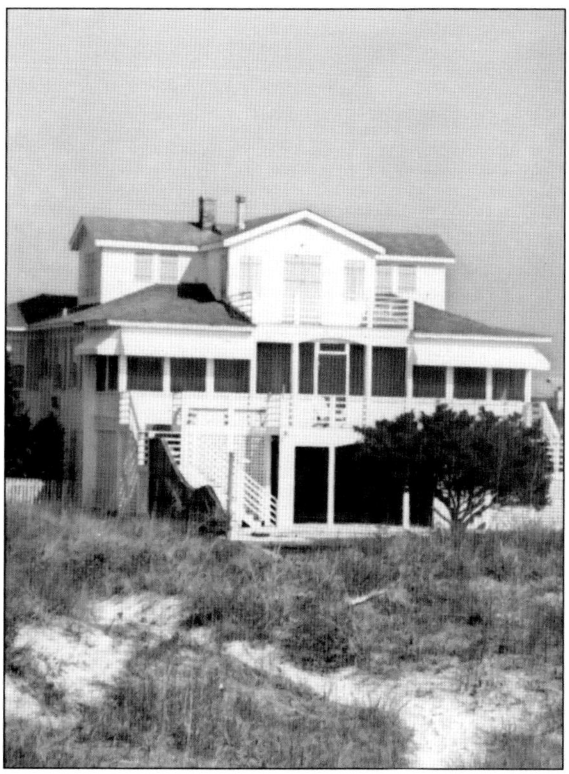

2109 Pettigrew Street c. 1935. This residence was built for the Prettyman family of Charleston by Claude W. Blanchard Sr. The cross gable, second-level addition and the front porch were glassed in c. 1987. Lumber for this house was also provided by an uncle of Robert Pringle who lived at 2102 Pettigrew. [Representative of a large beachfront residence.] (Courtesy Marshall Stith.)

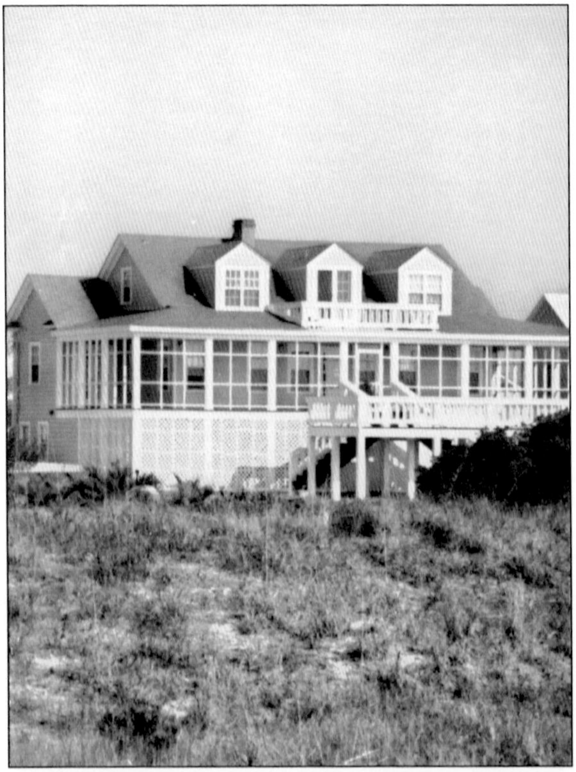

2115 Pettigrew Street, 1937. This residence was built by Claude W. Blanchard Sr., with the lumber coming from an uncle of Robert Pringle. The original porch was one story, front facing, with a wrap-around to the west elevation; it was removed as part of the 1987 remodeling, and a new porch and a deck were added. [Although altered, the structure is representative of the type of large beachfront structure built in the 1930s.] (Courtesy Marshall Stith.)

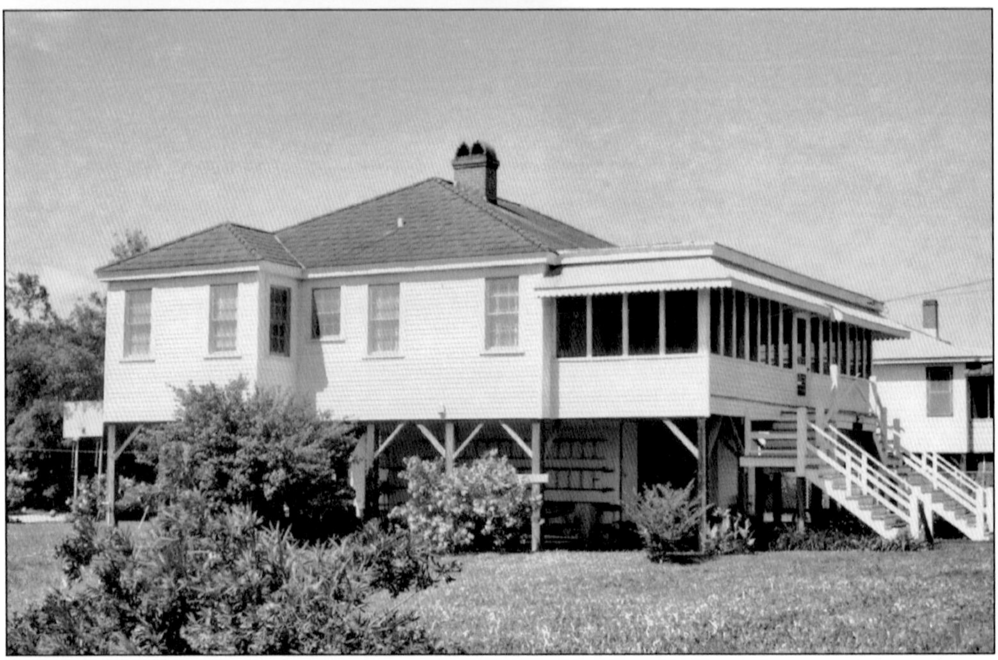

2216 Atlantic Avenue c. 1937. The Simmons House was built on the site of the Atlantic Beach Hotel as a summer residence for the Jack Simmons family; their Charleston home was on Church Street. [Representative example of early 20th-century island architecture.] (Courtesy S.C. Department of Archives and History.)

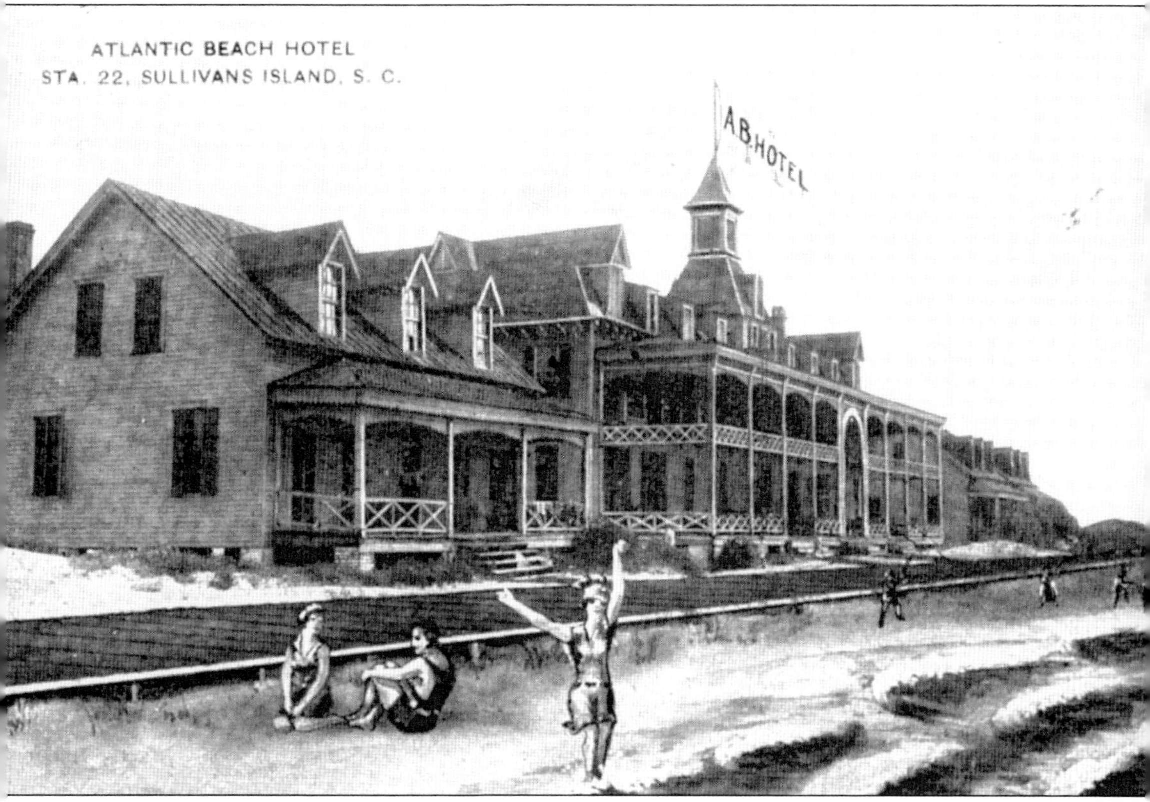

STATION 22, ATLANTIC BEACH HOTEL. This hotel was originally named the New Brighton Hotel when it opened in 1884 on land donated by the Town of Moultrieville to Robert Chisolm. It was built on the front beach and stood over nine feet above the high water level and faced the sea. The owner, J.F. Burnham, was a "Northern gentleman of means." The three-story hotel provided 112 rooms, music entertainment, semi-detached cottages fitted out with speaking tubes and electric bells, and separate bathing houses for ladies and gentlemen. A wooden plank way took bathers directly to the surf and enabled them to reach their dressing rooms without wading through the sand. The original plans and estimates contemplated a building that would cost about $25,000, but Mr. Burnham, who was in constant supervision of the work, made changes in the original plans for the so-called "storm-proof" structure, which would eventually cost him $80,000. Seven lumber mills were involved in furnishing materials for the complex, and there was an average work force of 100 men. The main building of the hotel with its veranda was 120 by 40 feet, the dining room was 90 by 40 feet, and the casino was 120 by 40 feet. The complex also included a separate kitchen and servant quarter building, cottages, a water tower and water works, and bathing houses. The French windows on the second floor opened upon small balconies, one to each room. Under the dining room, and extending about half its length, was a 65,000-gallon cistern; adjoining the cistern was a cellar 40 by 45 feet, built of solid brick and Portland cement and used for the storage of provisions and wines. Several years later the McCullough family from Columbia, South Carolina, acquired the New Brighton Hotel and reopened it as the Atlantic Beach Hotel in 1896. The hotel burned on January 9, 1925, after a dance. According to local legend, a bootlegger looking for his stash in the myrtles next to the hotel set the bushes on fire, which spread to the structure. It may have been storm-proof but it was not fire-proof. (Courtesy of Deborah Lofton.)

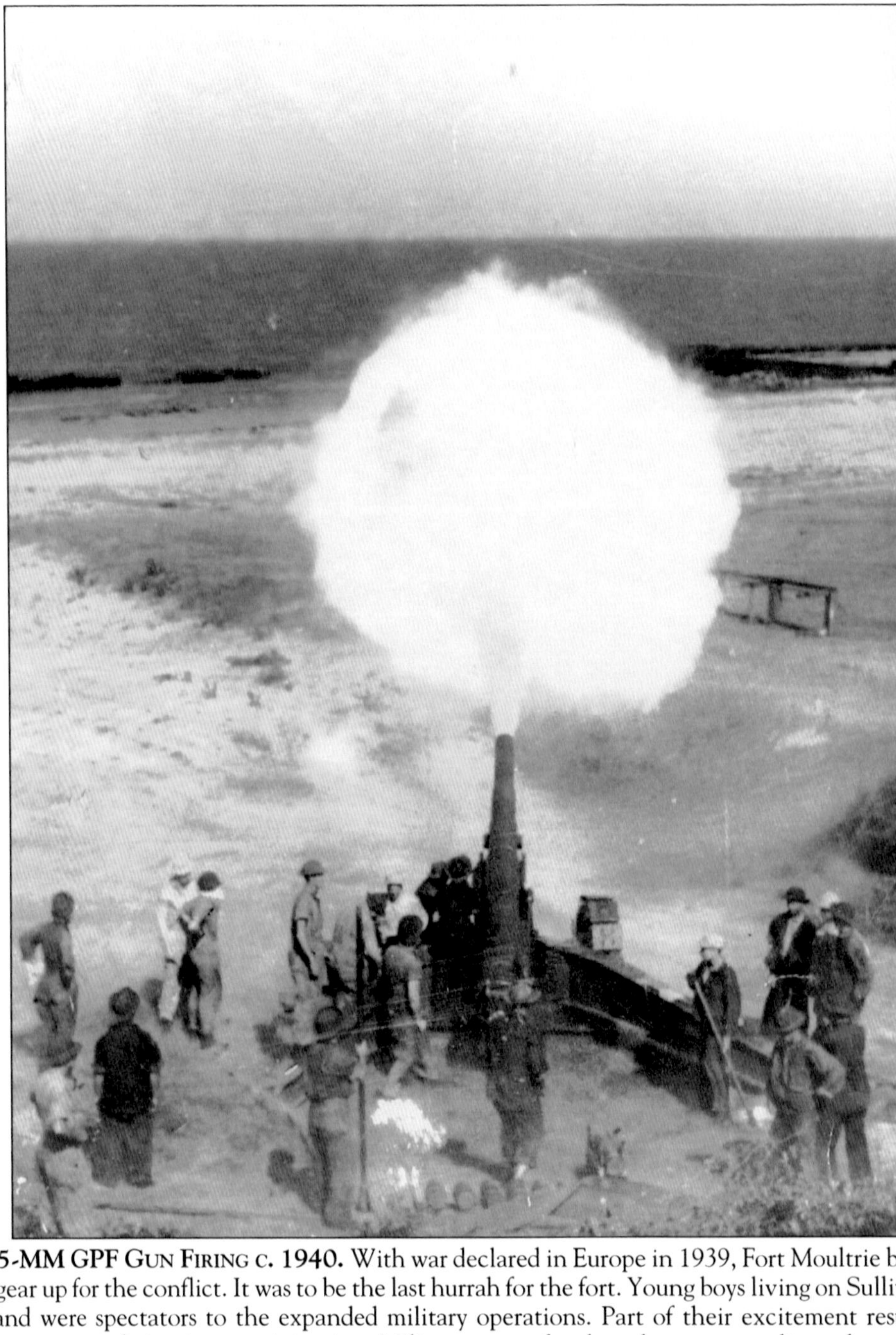

155-MM GPF GUN FIRING C. 1940. With war declared in Europe in 1939, Fort Moultrie began to gear up for the conflict. It was to be the last hurrah for the fort. Young boys living on Sullivan's Island were spectators to the expanded military operations. Part of their excitement resulted from a sense of vicarious participation. Military games for them became a reality unknown to youngsters from non-military places. Adding to the sense of war games was the ability to find an abandoned canteen, spent shell, or empty cigarette pack left behind by the soldiers. These souvenirs could be found at sites such as this one after the gun was fired. In earlier years the firing of the guns did not give the same excitement to parents as it did to children, since plaster oftentimes cracked or fell. Many island homes had to replace plaster with beaded wall board and ceilings. (Photo courtesy of Marshall Stith.)

Four

ATLANTICVILLE
Stations 22–28

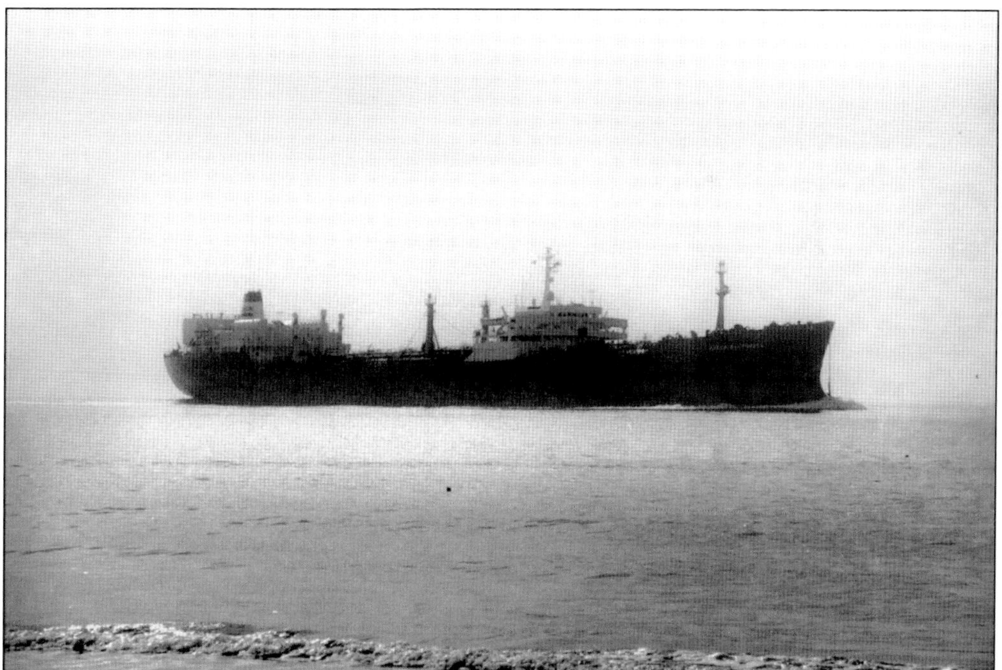

MERCHANT SHIP. Because of the bend in the island, Atlanticville does not face the inner harbor but eastward to the Atlantic Ocean. The origins of the name Atlanticville may have been suggested by its location on the easternmost of part of the island. (Courtesy of Marshall Stith.)

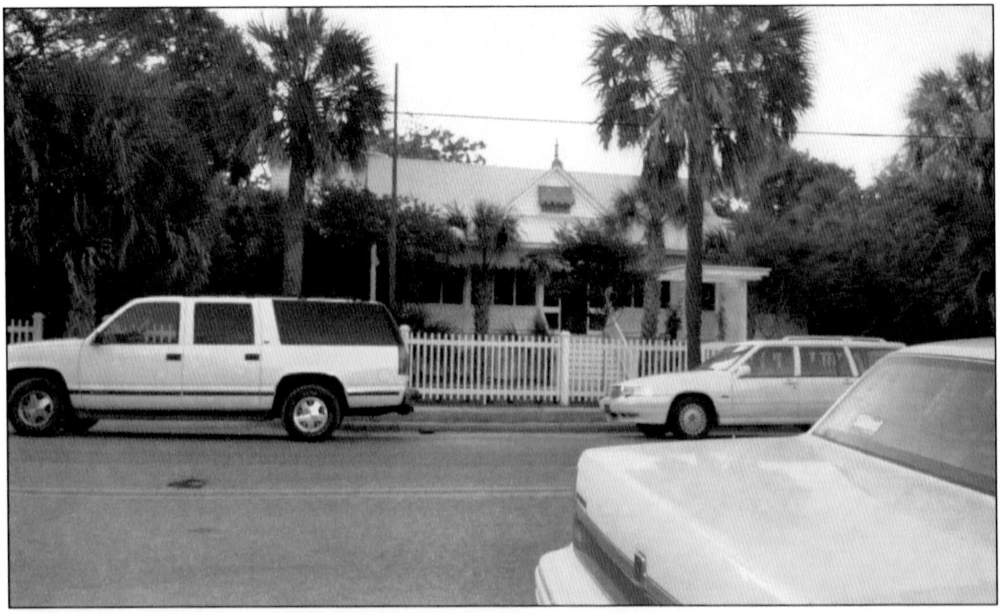

2262 MIDDLE STREET C. 1898. This house (Melrose) was formerly owned by a military officer. The house has an extended hall plan. The north end of the hall is finely detailed with ceiling molding and a wooden mantel piece. The dwelling has four-paneled doors and molded window and door surrounds, and the porch has a decorative sawn balustrade. In the front yard is a World War II–era flag pole. [Very good late 19th-century example.] (Courtesy Bonnie A. Williams.)

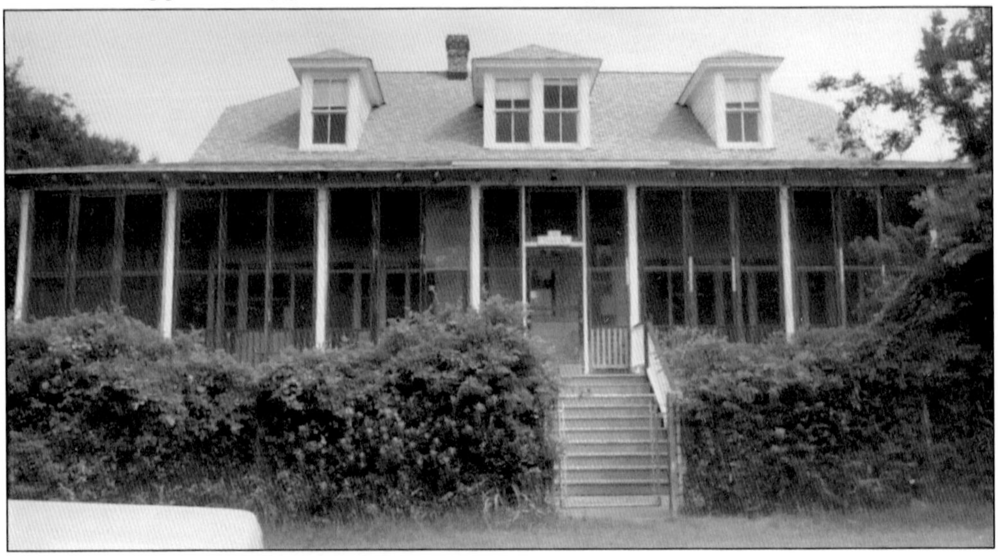

229 STATION 23 C. 1910. This property was bought by the Wulbern family of Charleston late in 1909, and the house (Summer Salt) was started for them. One or two dated boards remain marked "1910." Legend has it that in the August 1911 storm the house was known to be well built (each fall the family replaced louvered shutters with made-to-fit winter storm windows) and provided refuge for at least 20 people while water washed under the house. The house has a gable roof with jerkin heads and a large central hipped dormer with paired two/two windows flanked by smaller hipped dormers with single two/two windows. [Good early 20th-century example.] (Courtesy Bonnie A. Williams.)

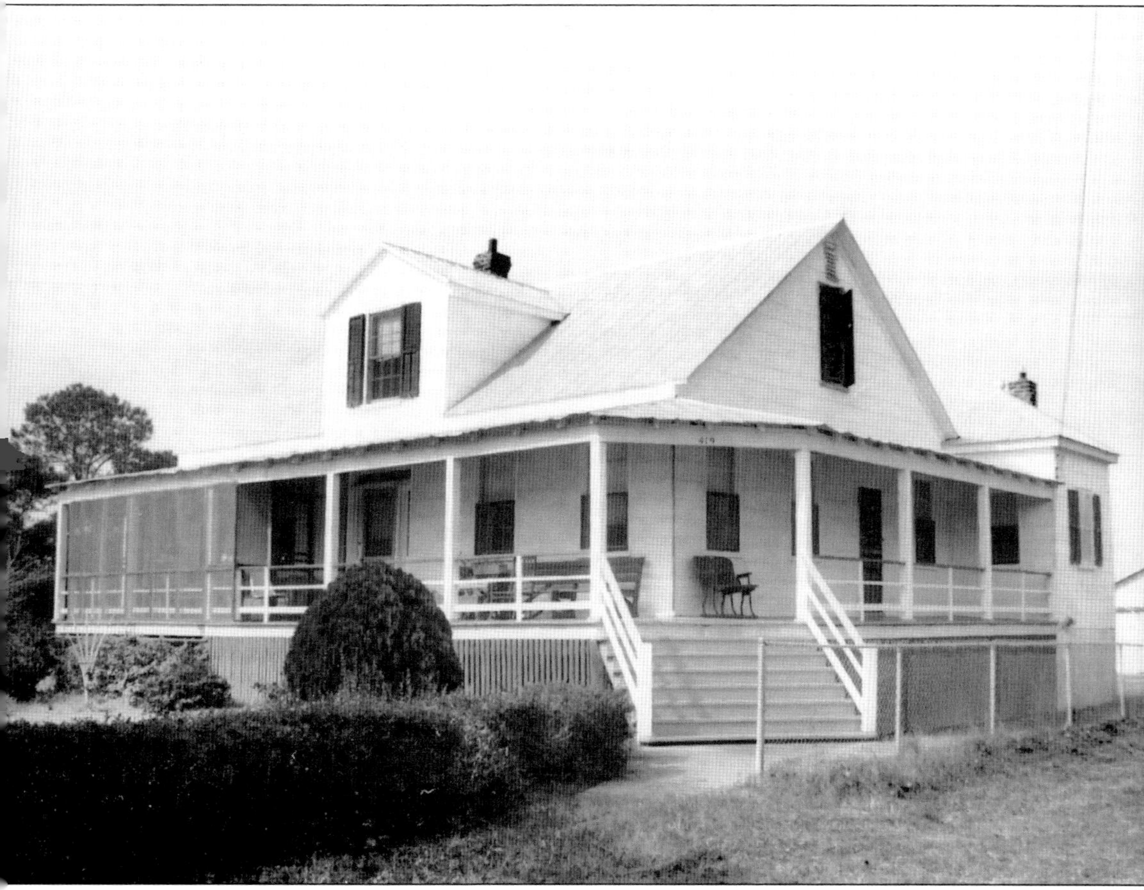

419 Station 23 c. 1902. This house was built by Allen P. Jones. The front facing gable dormer is a recent addition. The gable end windows of the main house have paneled shutters with diamond-shaped cutouts. The principal entrance has a transom and sidelights with a four-paneled door, while the side entrance has French doors. The house also has one-by-one bay projections on the northeast and northwest wings. Mr. Jones, an African American, and other male family members of the family have been highly respected carpenters and craftsman on Sullivan's Island for generations. They have been sought by island house owners to maintain and build many of the historic properties because of their knowledge and expertise. The Jones family owns this house; they are year-round residents. [Very good late 19th- to early 20th-century example.] (Courtesy Marshall Stith.)

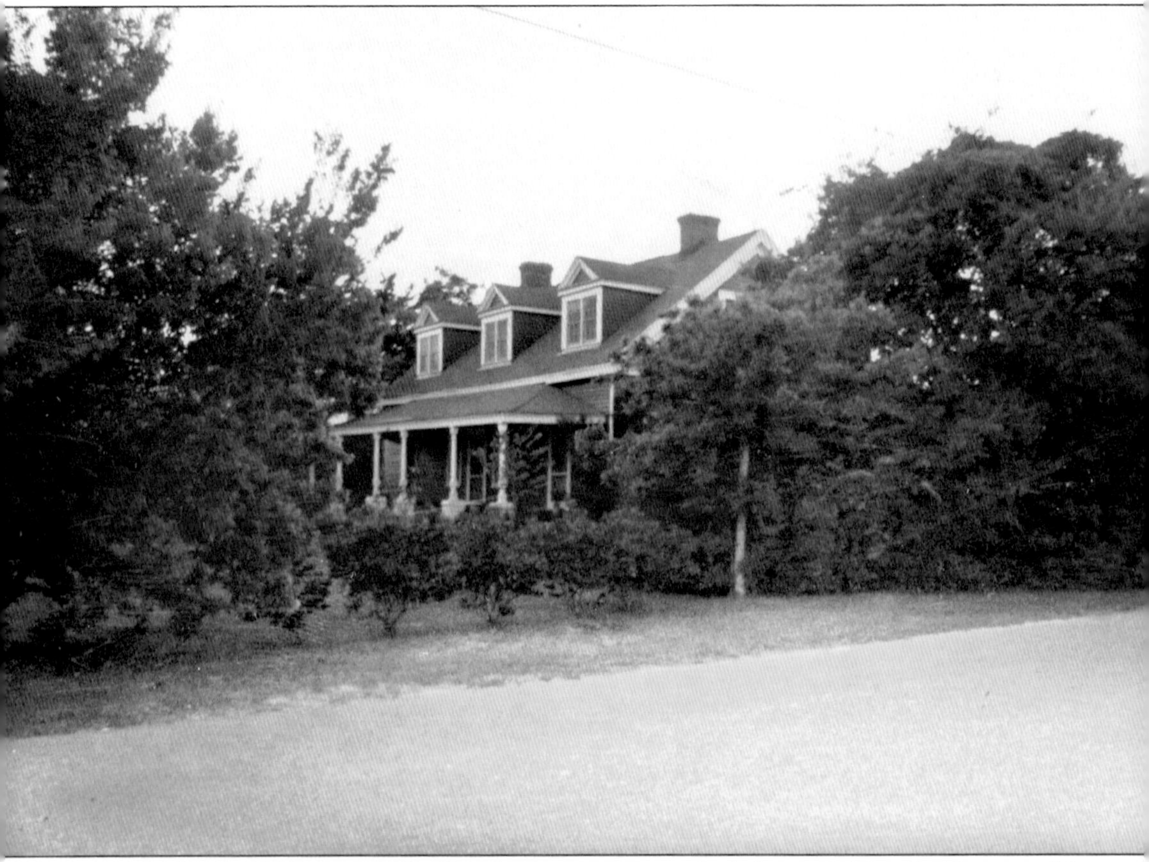

2320 MIDDLE STREET C. 1900. This large structure was built by a Mr. Von Dohlen, possibly Conrad Albert Von Dohlen, the father of James Albert Von Dohlen, for whom a house was built at a similar date at 2502 Middle Street, and later owned by George Lauriat, who is said to have been a captain of the *Sprig Carroll*. The Avinger family lived in the house for about 30 years and used the small building at the rear as a cobbler's shop. The house is basically a rectangular block with a smaller detached structure to the northwest, which is now linked by infill. There are corbelled caps on the chimneys and boxed cornices with returns at the gable ends. A continuous shed addition runs along the north elevation. The addition to the west provides kitchen and bathroom space, and a wooden stair has been added to the east elevation. The porch has a beaded board ceiling. The house is said to be haunted by a young woman in a flowing dress. The property includes an interesting collection of bottles along the walk way, made in Ireland and dug up on site by a former owner. [Very good early 20th-century example.] (Courtesy Bonnie A. Williams.)

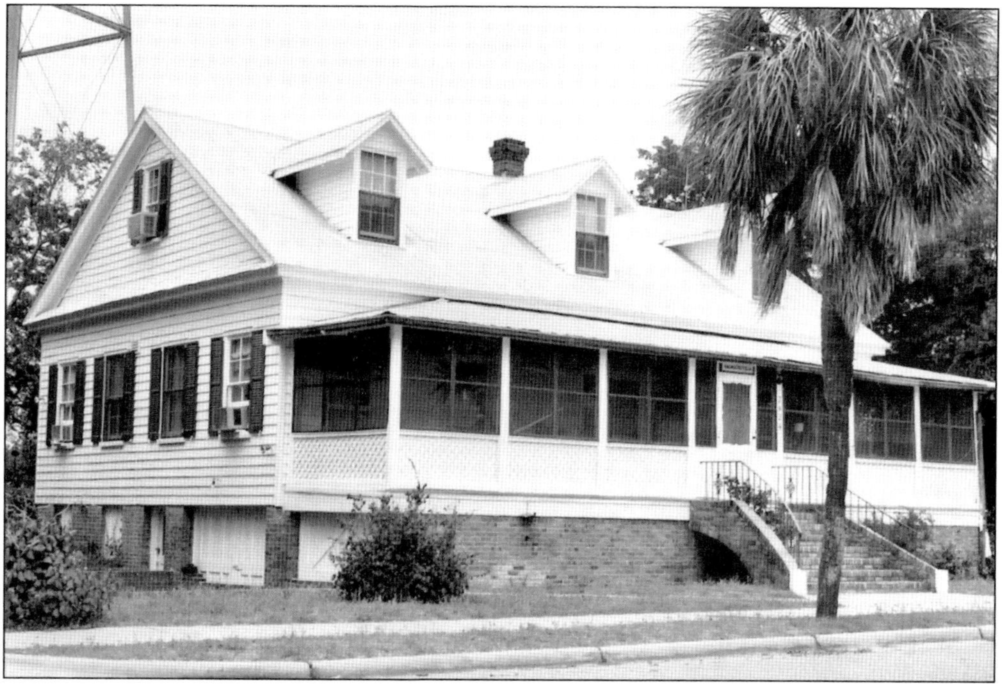

2424 MIDDLE STREET c. 1915. The Minot/Blanchard House (Vagabond Villa) was purchased c. 1937 from William Minot by Theodore S. Blanchard, superintendent of construction at Fort Moultrie. Author Dorothea Benton Frank, a granddaughter of Theodore Blanchard, grew up here at the family home. [Good example of early 20th-century architecture.] (Courtesy S.C. Department of Archives and History.)

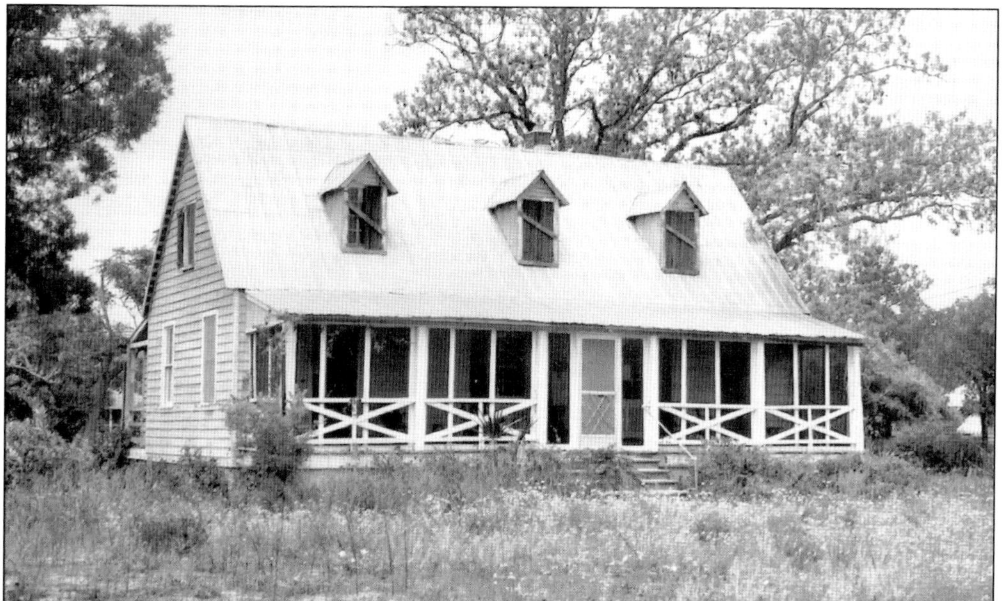

2430 MIDDLE STREET c. 1900. The Bischoff House has three gable dormers with six/six windows and board and batten shutters. [Good example of early 20th-century building.] (Courtesy S.C. Department of Archives and History.)

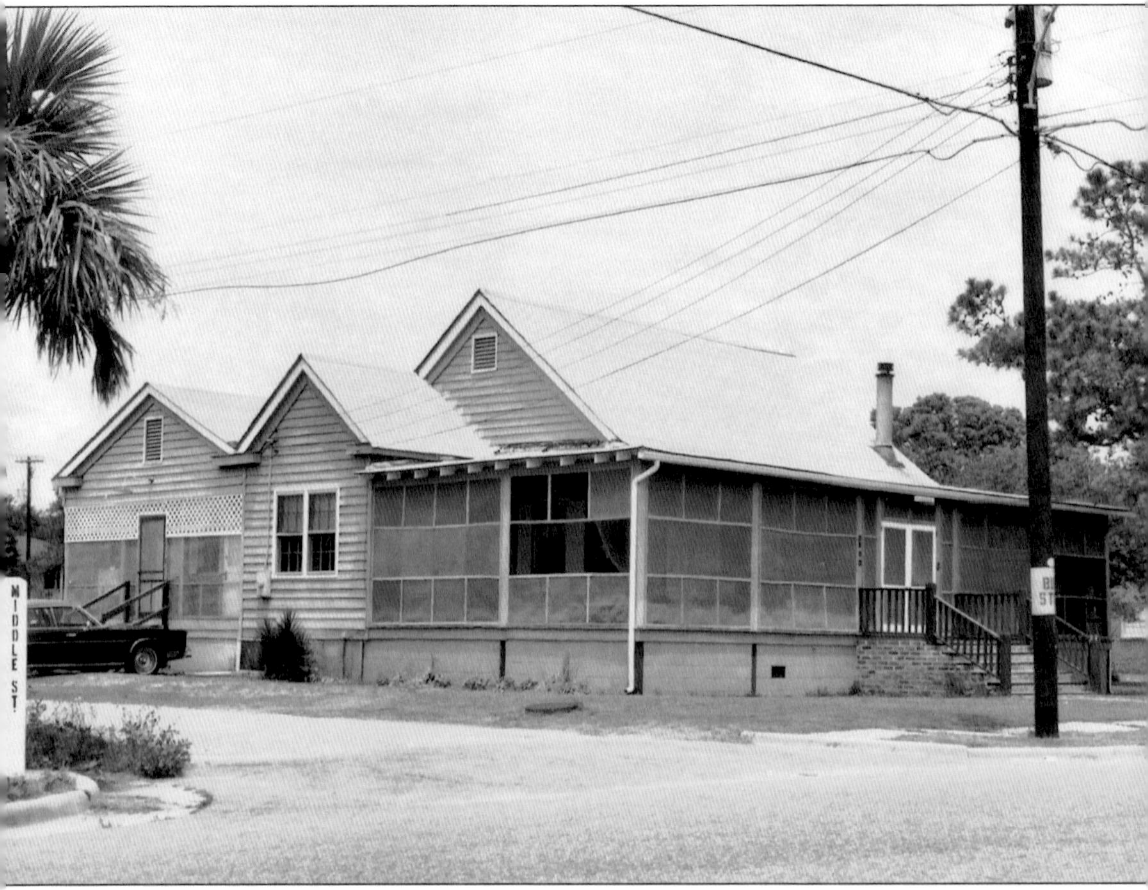

2502 Middle Street, 1899. The Von Dohlen/Mehrtens house was built for James Albert Von Dohlen, president of the J.A. Von Dohlen Steamship Co. of Charleston. Mr. Von Dohlen's daughter married Jennings Cauthen, a longtime reporter for the *News and Courier* and Charleston County coroner. The Cauthen family lived in Charleston on Broad Street and spent their summers at 2502 Middle Street. The house was lost to Hugo, but the Mehrtens rebuilt at the same location. The wings and rear addition dated from *c.* 1942. [Modest example of 19th-century building; Gone.] (Courtesy S.C. Department of Archives and History.)

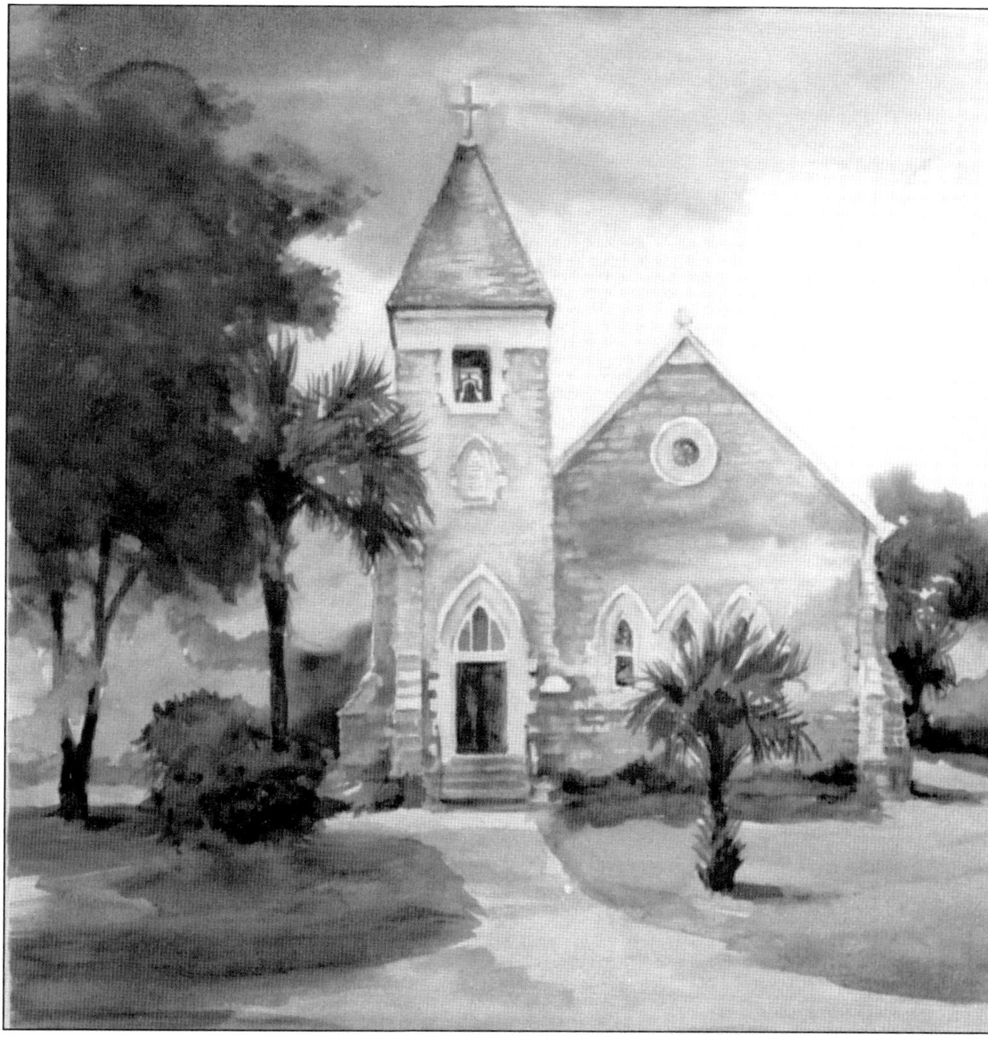

2520 Middle Street. The Church of the Holy Cross (Episcopal) was built in 1907 after the earlier church at 1401 Middle Street was condemned by the federal government as part of its expansion of Fort Moultrie. The Church then acquired this property between 1905 and 1907 and built the present sanctuary in the Gothic Revival style; this building opened in June 1908. The church was built after the style of its predecessor and the memorial windows, bells, and chancel were moved and incorporated within the building. The hurricane of August 27, 1911, badly damaged the chapel, and services were discontinued for the remainder of the year. With the beginning of World War II, the church was turned over to be used as a first aid center for the duration of the war. While the church was being repaired, the services were held in the chapel at Fort Moultrie. The church was fully repaired by 1947. In 1962 the church was accorded parish status for the first time. It was renovated in 1966, and stained-glass memorial windows were installed in 1972. The Rev. John B. Burwell is rector of Holy Cross and the Rev. Chris S. Warner is associate rector. [Exceptional structure; significant as an example of early vernacular 20th-century church architecture and for its historical associations.] (Courtesy Jim Darlington.)

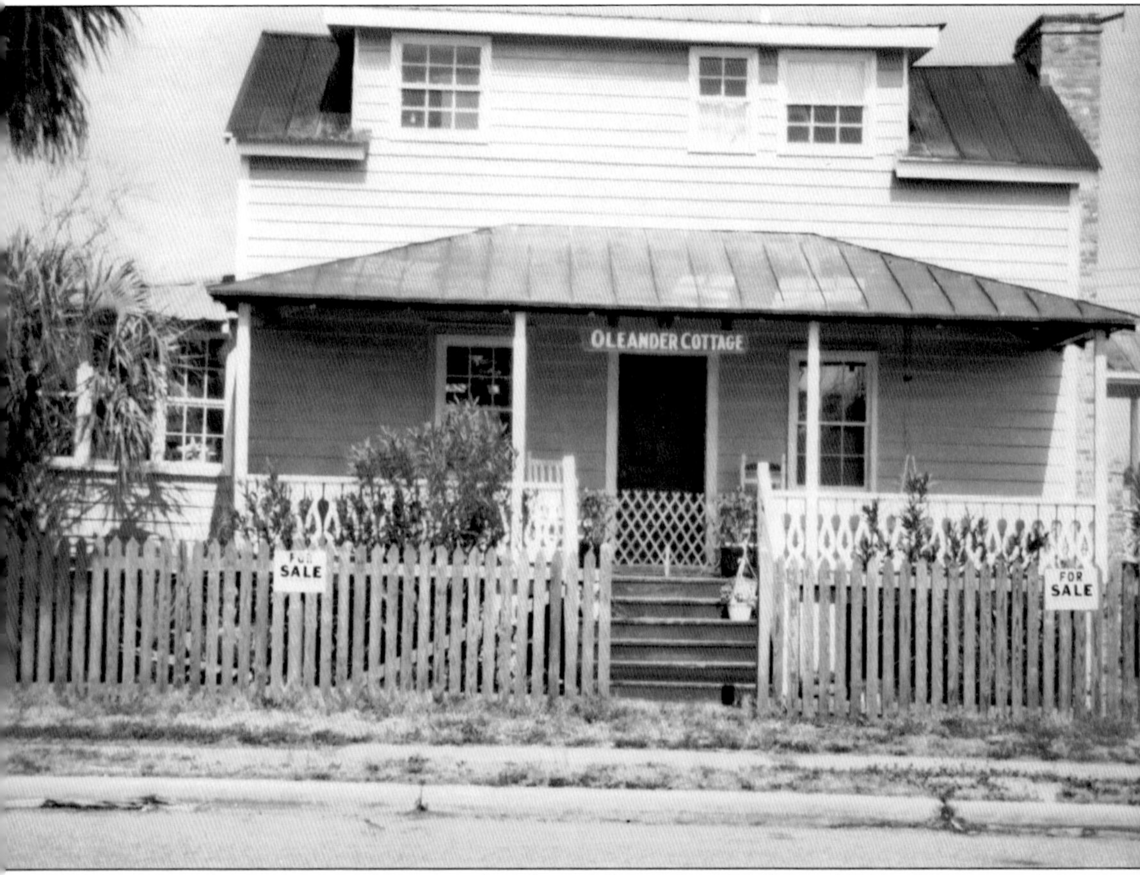

2630 Middle Street c. 1880. Local tradition claims that this house (Oleander Cottage) was built in 1901–1902 as part of the South Carolina and West Indian Exposition, which was held in what is now the Hampton Park area in Charleston. After the exposition the house was dismantled and floated over to Sullivan's Island. The porch at the west elevation is enclosed. The front porch features a decorative sawn balustrade. The dormers were added at a later date. The Neyle family is the current owner. [Additional research is necessary to determine possible historical association with the South Carolina and West Indian Exposition. Good example of late 19th-century building.] (Courtesy Marshall Stith.)

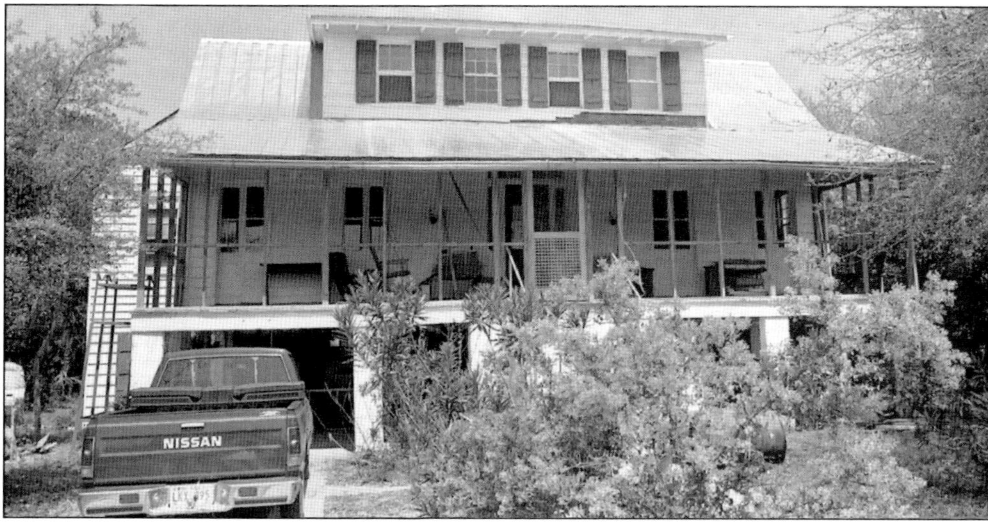

2814 MIDDLE STREET, 1909. The dormer on this house (the Wren's Nest) was added *c.* 1950. During the 1940s Mr. and Mrs. Hugh Fraser of Charleston summered there with family members, including their granddaughter Angelica Roystone. In the next block was a prisoner of war camp where it is said Italian prisoners were kept. Angelica would walk up to the fence to stare at the Italians and they at her. The Obadiah Dugans, who founded the Star Gospel Mission of Charleston, summered next door at Faith Cottage, 2820 Middle Street [gone]. They used Faith Cottage as a summer retreat for underprivileged children. [Representative of the modest island residences built during the early 20th century.] (Courtesy S.C. Department of Archives and History.)

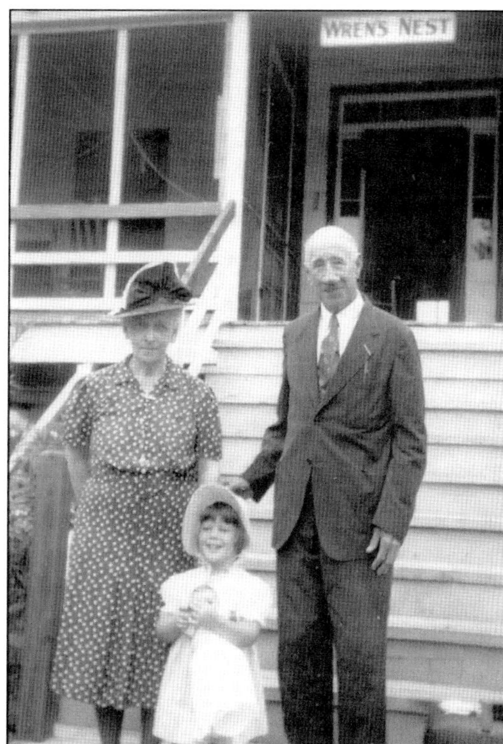

2814 MIDDLE STREET, THE FAMILY. Mr. and Mrs. Hugh Fraser are with their granddaughter Angelica at the front steps of their summer home in August 1942. (Mrs. Angelica R. Sudduth.)

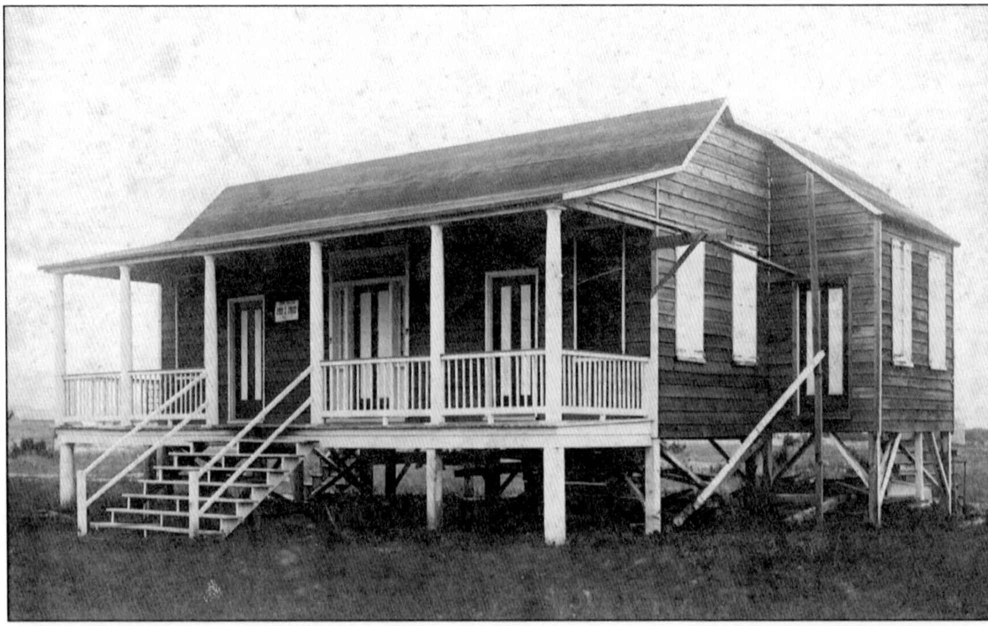

2830 Middle Street (Front) c. 1900. The Paturzo House, prior to the 1911 hurricane, was further forward on the lot and lower to the ground. The house has historic nine/nine windows. [This dwelling is a variation of the "island house" form as constructed on the island from prior to the Civil War through the mid-20th century.] (Courtesy Marshall Stith.)

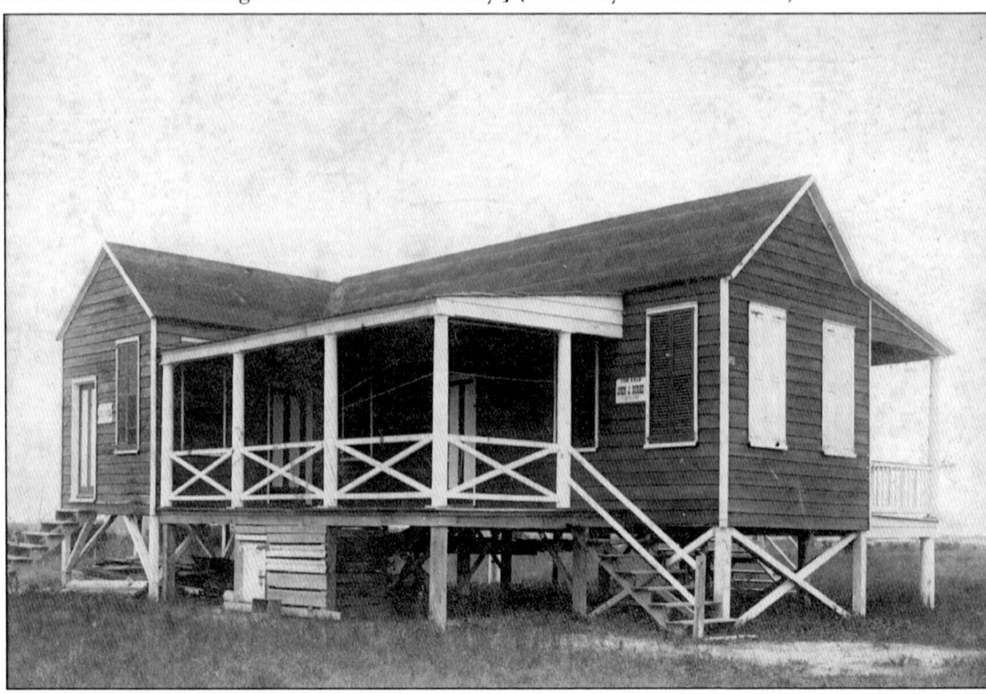

2830 Middle Street (Back). The back of the house has a porch infill to create additional space. Historic wooden siding has been covered with asbestos shingles. The Paturzo family purchased the property c. 1915. Note the "for sale" sign by John J. Burke to the left of the louvered shutters. (Courtesy Marshall Stith.)

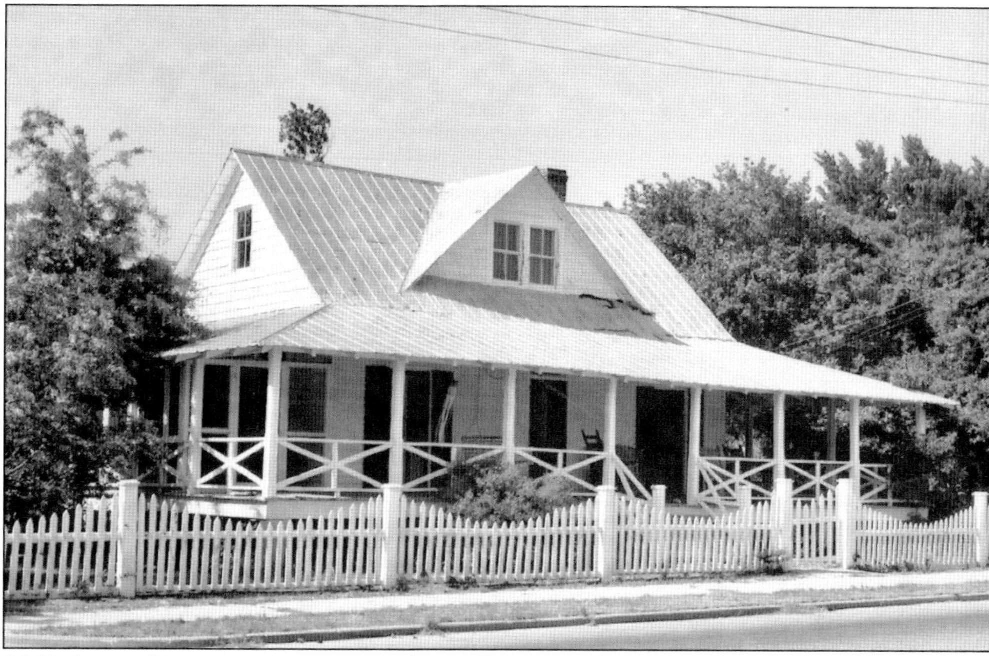

2262 Jasper Boulevard c. 1890. The Miller House has decorative shingling at the front facing gable. The entrance has French doors with transom. The house has four-paneled doors, molded surrounds, original light fixtures, beaded board, and a central hall plan. Dr. Jerrold M. Buckaloo and family are the current owners. [Exception example of late 19th-century architecture.] (Courtesy S.C. Department of Archives and History.)

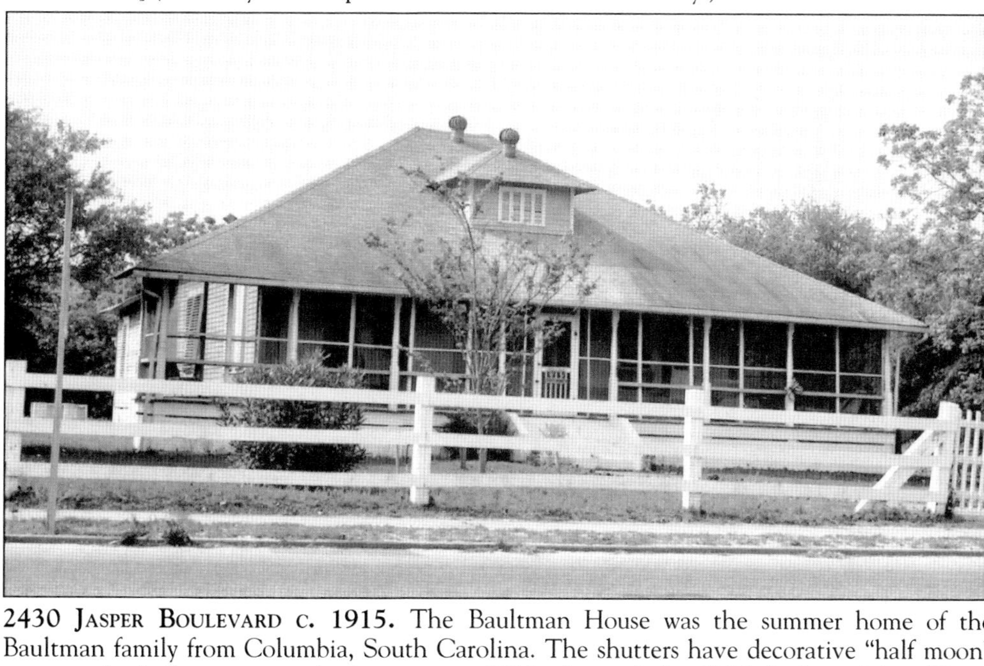

2430 Jasper Boulevard c. 1915. The Baultman House was the summer home of the Baultman family from Columbia, South Carolina. The shutters have decorative "half moon" cutouts. A similar structure is shown on a 1917 plat and the 1924 Sanborn Map. [Good example of early 20th-century island architecture.] (Courtesy S.C. Department of Archives and History.)

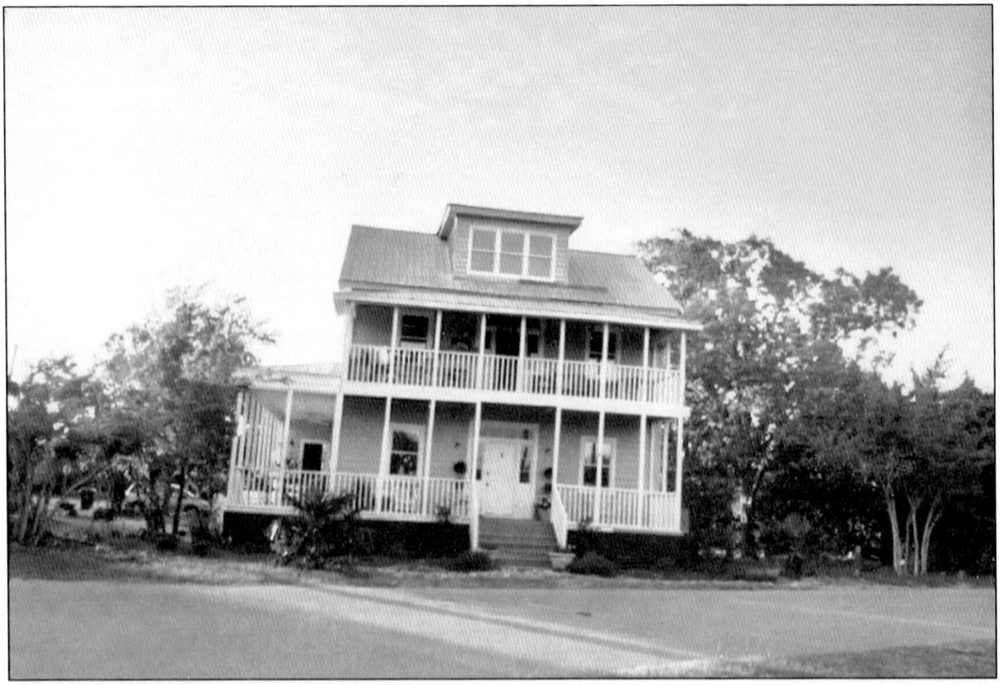

2402 QUARTER STREET c. 1900. The Alexander Scharlock House has a paneled entrance with a transom and sidelights. Kitchen and laundry additions were made in the 1930s. Judge Louis Stith was born here. [Good early 20th-century example.] (Courtesy Bonnie A. Williams.)

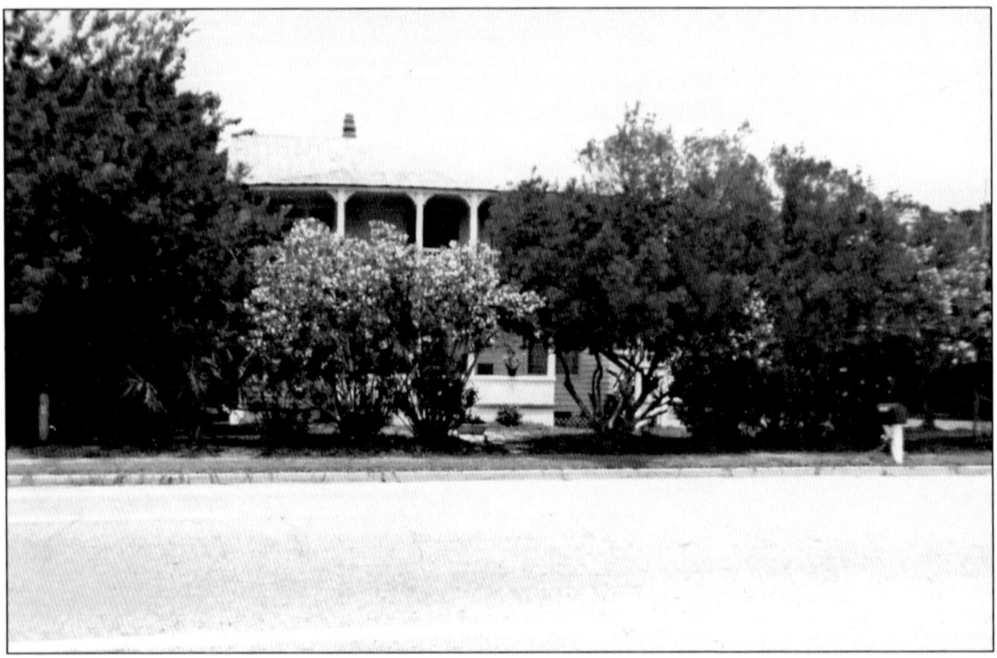

2520 JASPER BOULEVARD c. 1895. The Schirmer/Werner house appears on a 1917 plat and 1924 Sanborn Map. The porch has been altered and an exterior stair added c. 1965. There are decorative sawn brackets at the porch. [Good example of late 19th-century architecture compromised by alterations.] (Courtesy Ruth A. Hood.)

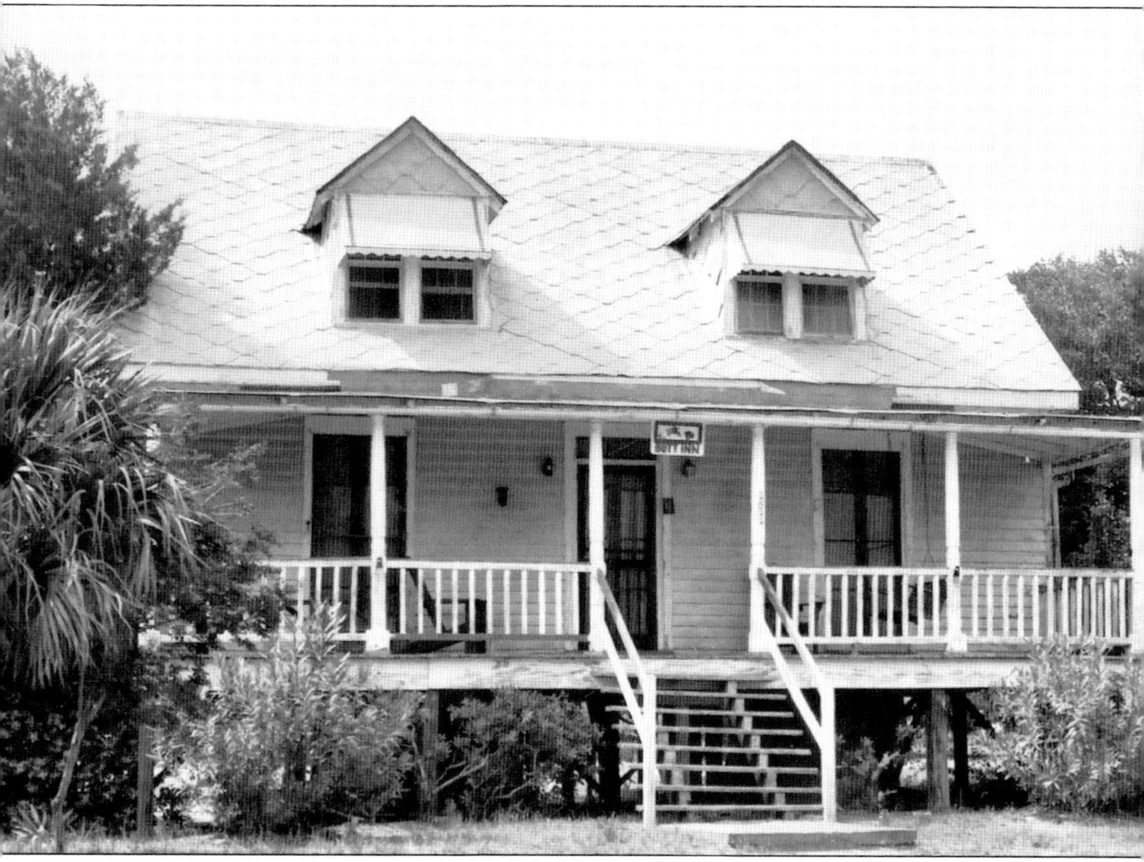

2622 Jasper Boulevard c. 1885. This was the summer home (The Butt Inn) of the Butt family of Charleston from 1935 to 1986. The building stands on high ground and was used as a refuge during summer hurricanes by families living or staying on the front beach. The Norris family is the current owner. [Very good example of late 19th-century island residential architecture.] (Courtesy S.C. Department of Archives and History.)

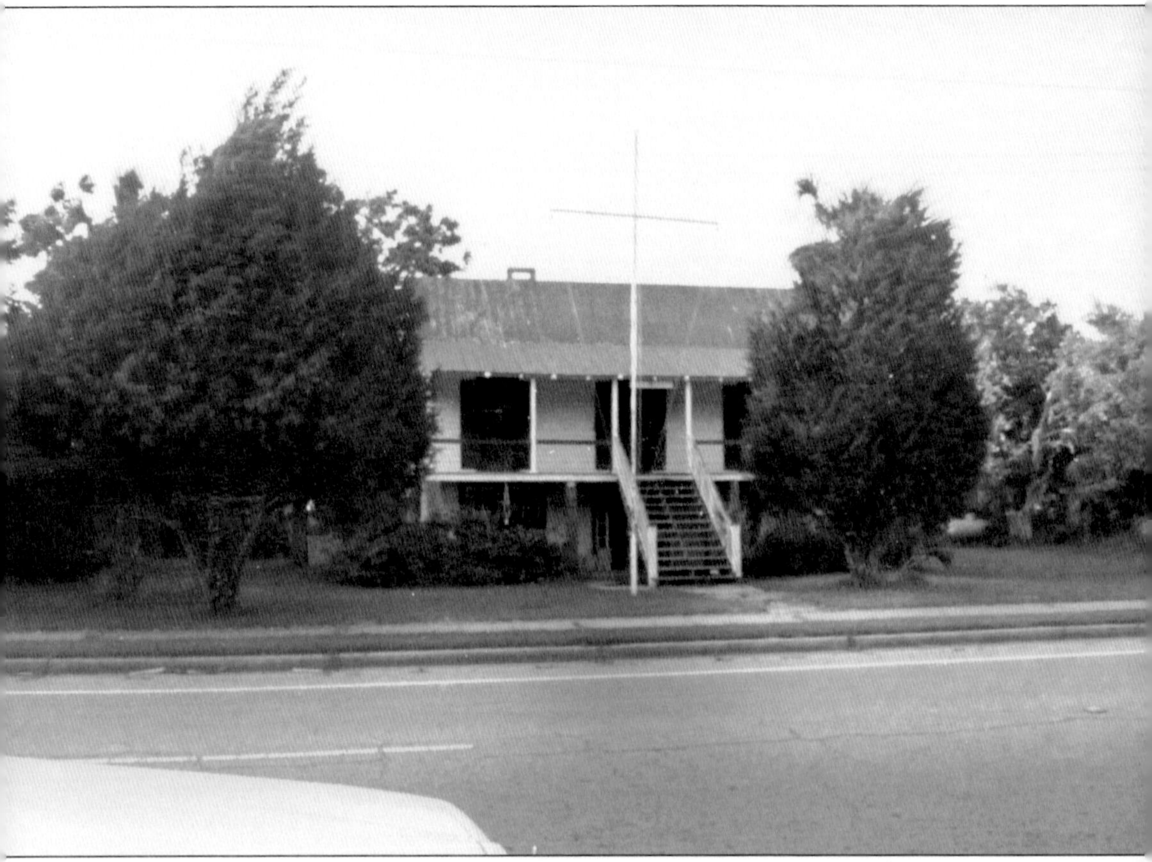

2662 Jasper Boulevard. This lot (Dixievilla) was bought in 1907 for $33 by William S. Pregnall, and the house which he began building was nearly completed in 1911 when a hurricane removed the porch roof. The house was completed by 1913 by Mr. Pregnall's sons after his death. Heavy timbers for framing were reclaimed from the ferry *Commodore Perry*, formerly used as a CSA blockade runner. The downstairs was finished in 1938, and the door is said to have been put together using two windows from the ferry. *Commodore Perry* had been bought and dismantled by Pregnall Shipyard, located on the Cooper River waterfront in Charleston. The Richardsons now own the property. [Simple variation of island house form; structure is typical of many constructed on the island from before the Civil War through the mid-20th century.] (Courtesy Bonnie A. Williams.)

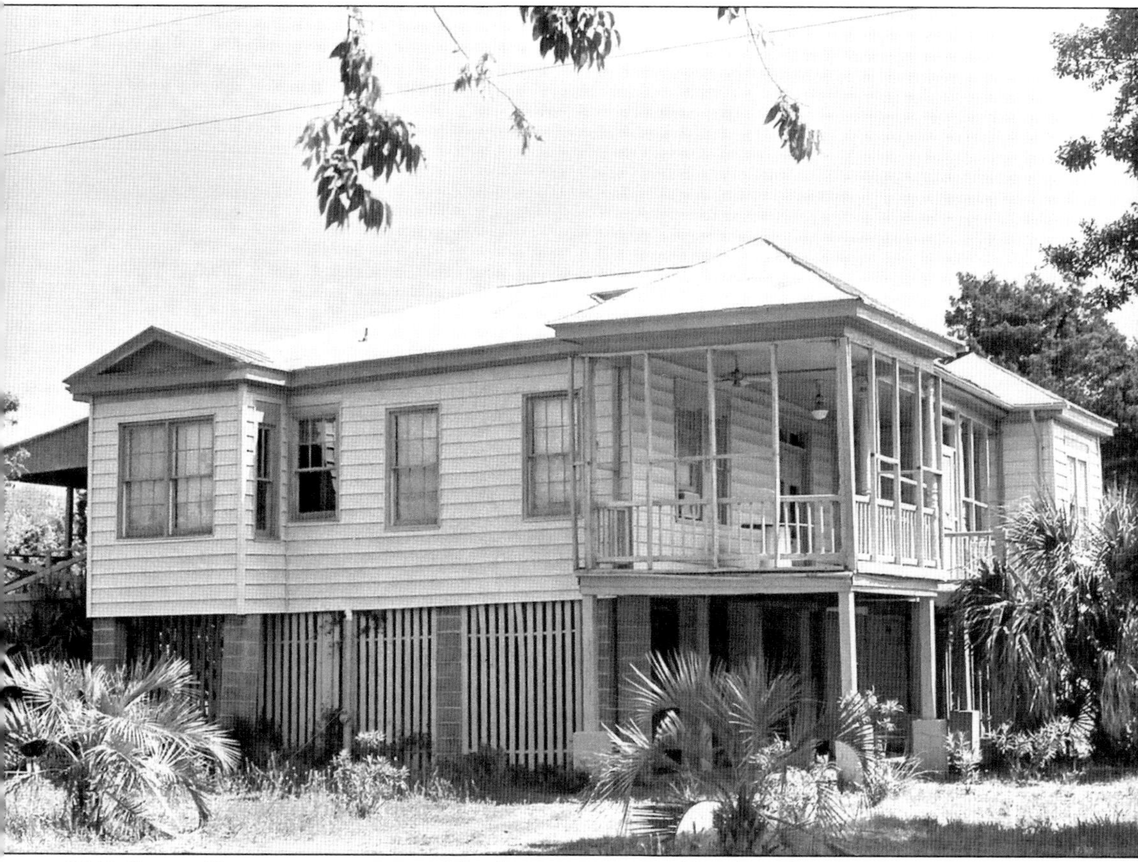

2702 JASPER BOULEVARD c. 1900. This house was owned by the Edward K. Pritchard family and was their summer house from 1934 to c. 1955. They lived on Tradd Street in Charleston. In 1934 there was a bath/shower in the enclosed ground floor area, but that year remodeling placed the baths upstairs into existing spaces. The rear kitchen addition and ground floor enclosures were added c. 1940. The porch has two flanking pavilions with two pyramidal roofs. A rear intersecting gable was added with pedimented gables. The hipped dormer has three two light windows. [Elaborate early 20th-century beach residence with distinctive architectural features.] (Courtesy S.C. Department of Archives and History.)

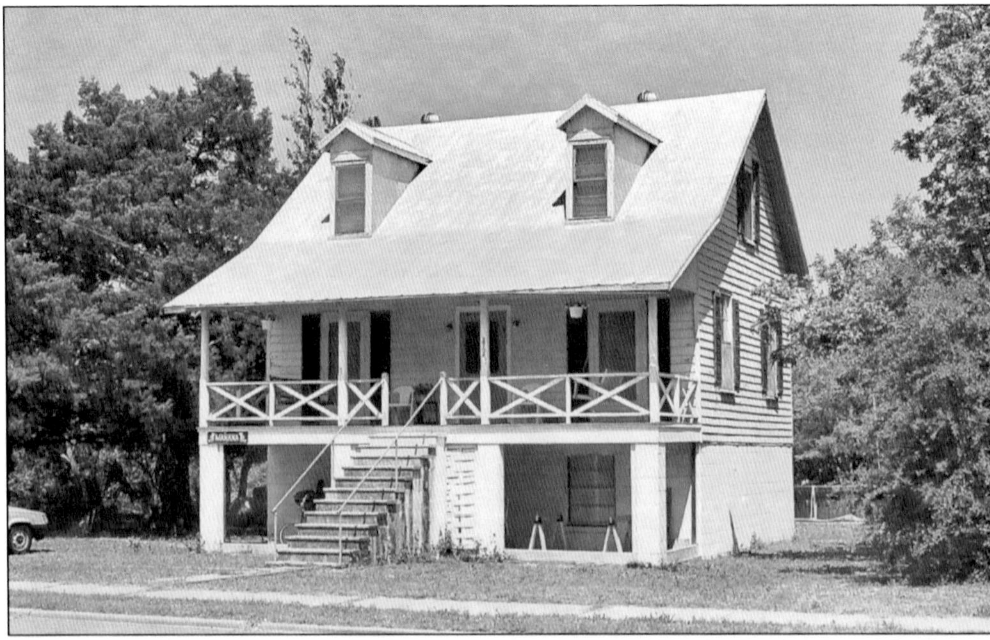

2708 Jasper Boulevard, 1905. The principal entrance of this house (Manana) leads into a central hall, flanked by two entries into parlors/chambers. The flanking doors on the porch could indicate the front parlors/chambers were rented to summer boarders. The original tabby pilings were replaced c. 1965; the remnants remain on the site. [Representative of the modest summer dwellings built in the early 20th century, Gone.] (Courtesy S.C. Department of Archives and History.)

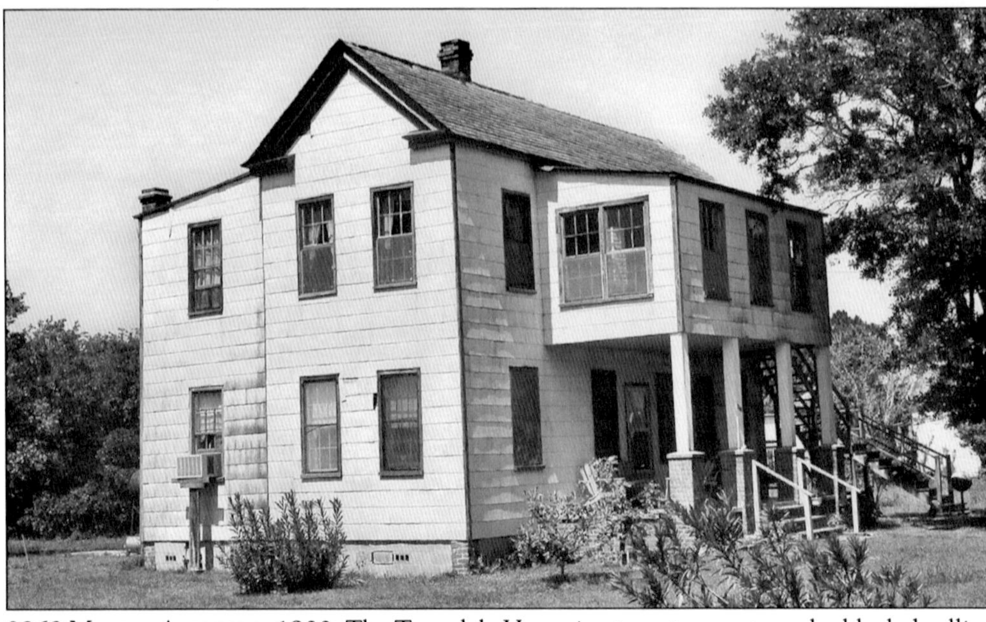

2262 Myrtle Avenue c. 1900. The Truesdale House is a two-story rectangular block dwelling that has a two-story rear wing with a one-story addition. The building is shown on a 1917 plat without the rear additions. [Good example of late 19th- to early 20th-century island residence.] (Courtesy S.C. Department of Archives and History.)

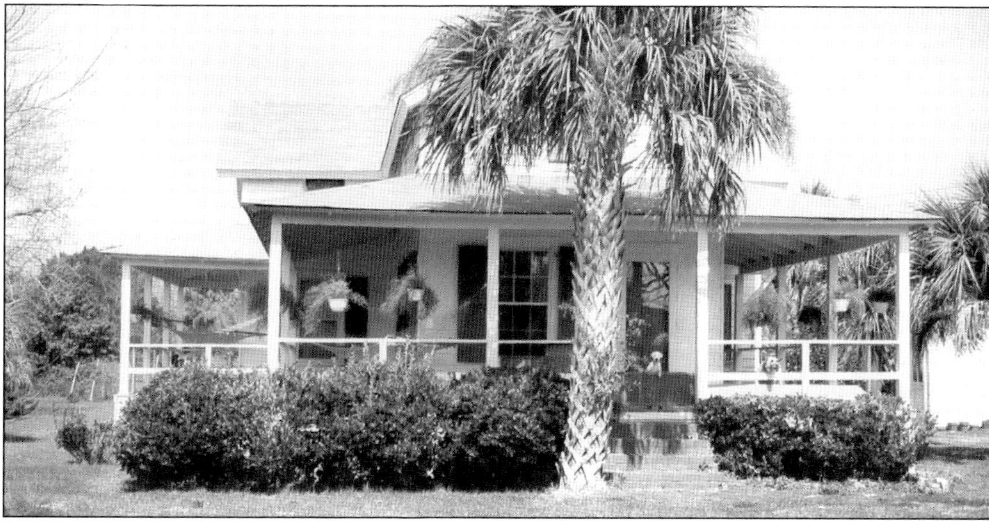

2408 Myrtle Avenue c. 1890. The date of construction of this house is uncertain. It is said to have been built *c.* 1890, but letters found in the house date it to *c.* 1903. It is laid out in the historic T-shape design with a cross gable roof. The wrap-around porch has square wood posts. The house was formerly occupied by a retired soldier from Fort Moultrie. [Good example of late 19th- to early 20th-century island architecture compromised by alterations.] (Courtesy Marshall Stith.)

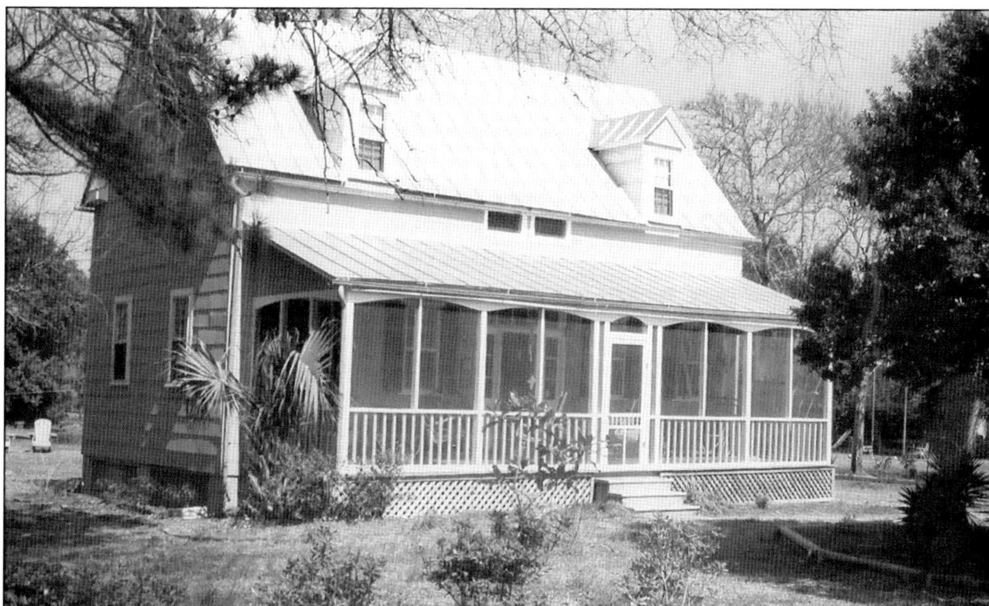

2508 Myrtle Avenue, 1893. The McGuire/Pozaro House was conveyed by the Town of Moultrieville to John McGuire in December 1905. The house was probably built by him before he sold the license to Maggie Pozaro in September 1906. Maggie Pozaro sold the property to Abbie L. Burn and Emily Dixon on May 16, 1913. Burn and Dixon, in turn, sold to Gladys Tatum Burn on June 8, 1948. Burn sold to Ann and Mack Fleming on April 23, 1979, and the Flemings sold to Mitch and Phyllis Feller on May 11, 1982. [Good example of early 20th-century island architecture compromised by alterations.] (Courtesy Marshall Stith.)

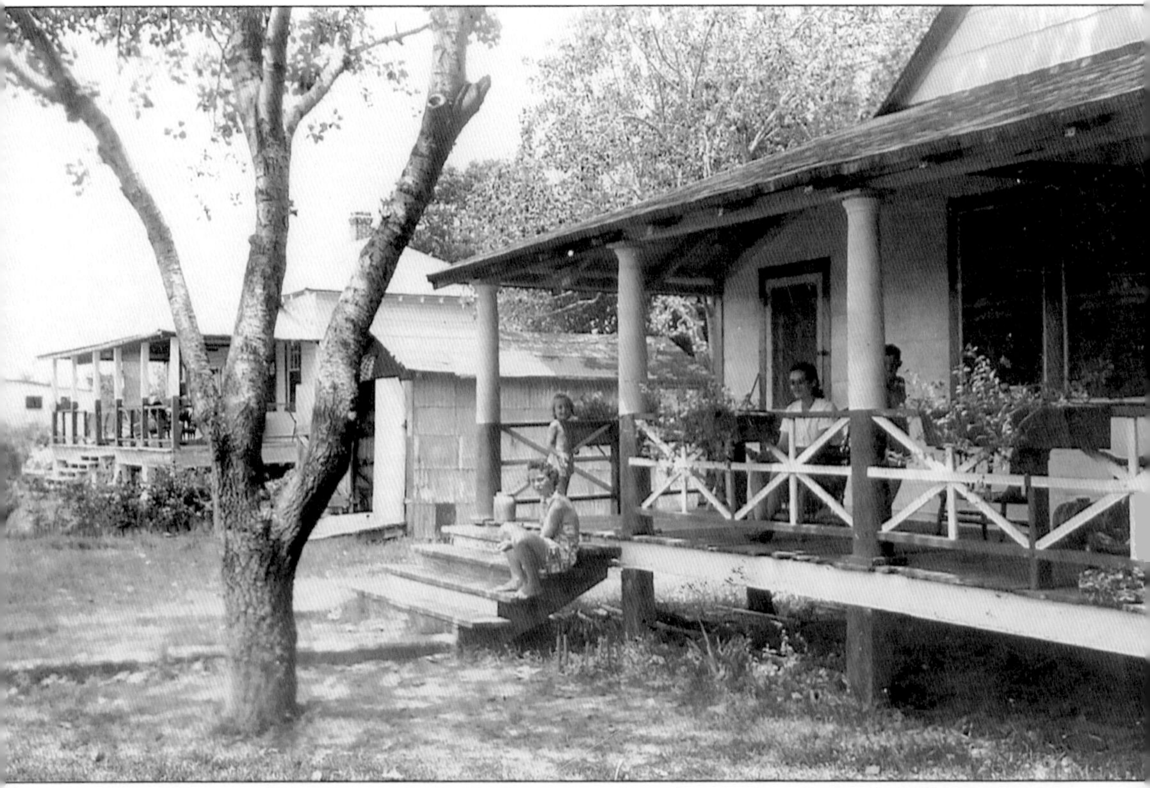

2620 Myrtle Avenue c. 1910. Probate records indicate that Anna J. Dohring Leppert, the mother and guardian of Ernest O. Dohring, paid all his debts after he died in June 1916. She also collected all assets, and "there came into her hands, as administrator, the lease hold interest in lot 88 and the buildings, home, etc . . . in Atlanticville." The house may have been built as early as 1910 by Edward Wulbern, who got the license originally. Later Oscar Leppert and his family would live in the house. The Leppert house is gone but to the left of the picture is the Jacob Meitzler House c. 1910, at 2614 Myrtle Avenue. Charlotte Dixon Hartnett purchased the house from Mrs. Meitzler, whose husband was in the army. Jacob Meitzler had added the front section to a much smaller house. The house features a central hall plan and a beaded board porch ceiling. [Good example of early 20th-century island architecture.] (Courtesy Oscar Leppert Jr.)

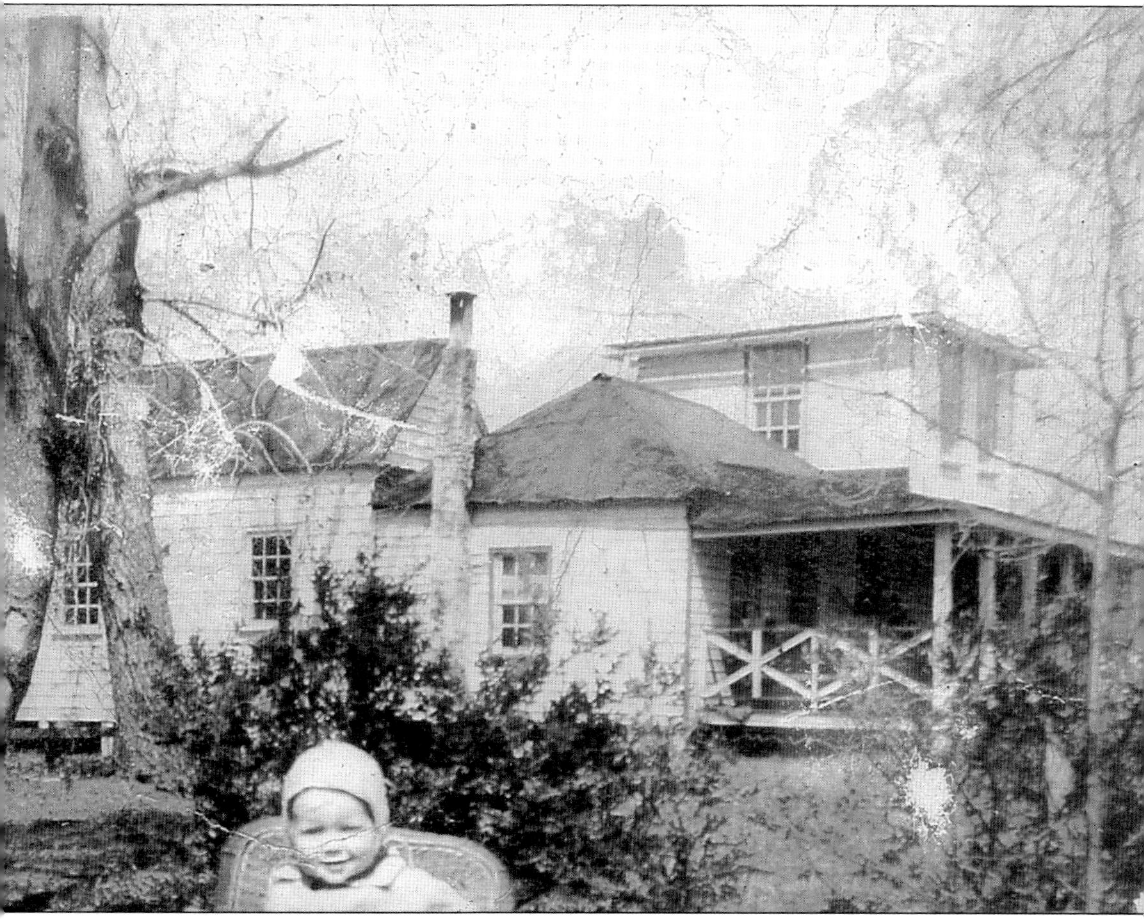

2624 Myrtle Avenue. Frederick Harrison Legare, shortly after his marriage to Henrietta Ethel Moore, bought Lot 89 and "buildings" on July 9, 1923, from Margaret Pozaro for $5 and other consideration. The only alteration the Legare family made was to add a second-story addition in the 1930s. The kitchen wing may have been attached to the property before the Legare ownership. Fred Legare carried on the family freight business his father had started with his brothers Dan and Rupert. They carried goods from the government wharf on Sullivan's Island to Adger's Wharf in Charleston and back. "Miss Etta" dabbled in real estate. At one time she owned the property where the Sea Island Shopping Center in Mount Pleasant is now located. Before Highway 703 was built, the property was described as being in "in the middle of nowhere." Like many island residents during the Depression, the Legares had a garden, chickens, and a cow. [Good early 20th-century example.] (Courtesy Linda Dayhoff Smith.)

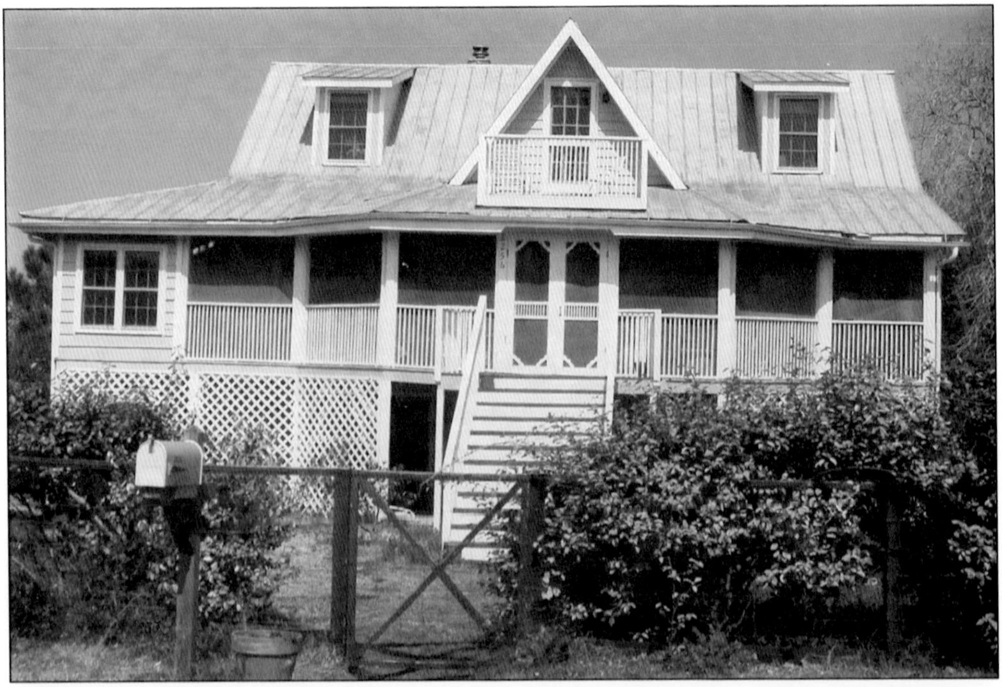

2256 I'ON AVENUE C. 1895. This house was moved to this site in 1978 from Station 28 and extensively remodeled. It was formerly the property of the Fischbein family. Dormers appear to be recent additions. An entrance and dock were added at the front-facing gable, and the porch was enclosed at the west end. Nona Hastie is the current owner. [Good example of late 19th-century island architecture compromised by alterations and relocation.] (Courtesy Marshall Stith.)

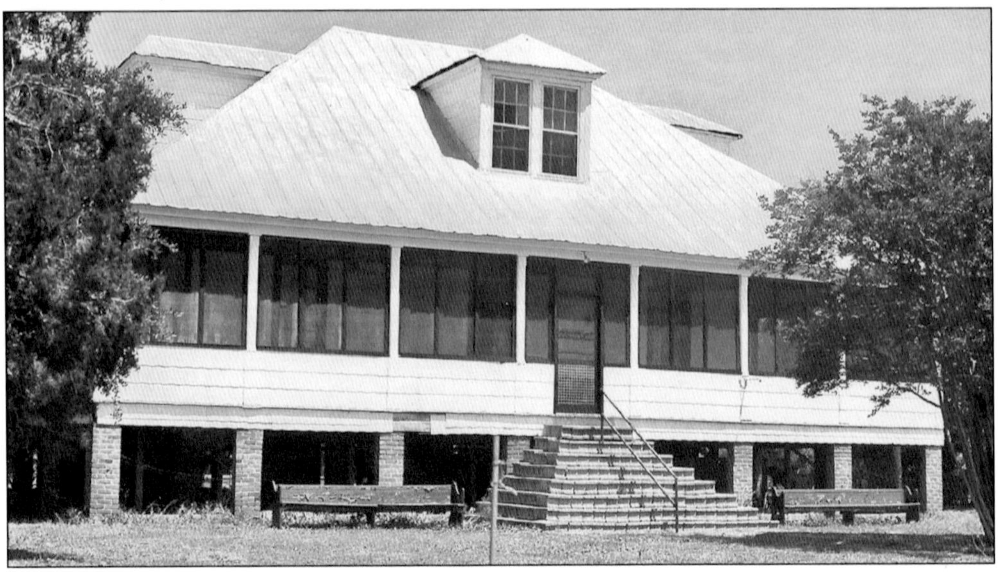

2263 I'ON AVENUE (2262 ATLANTIC AVENUE) C. 1900. This building was formerly a boarding house run by Mrs. Myma Brown. It is now used by the Charleston Club as a clubhouse. [Good example of early 20th-century island architecture.] (Courtesy S.C. Department of Archives and History.)

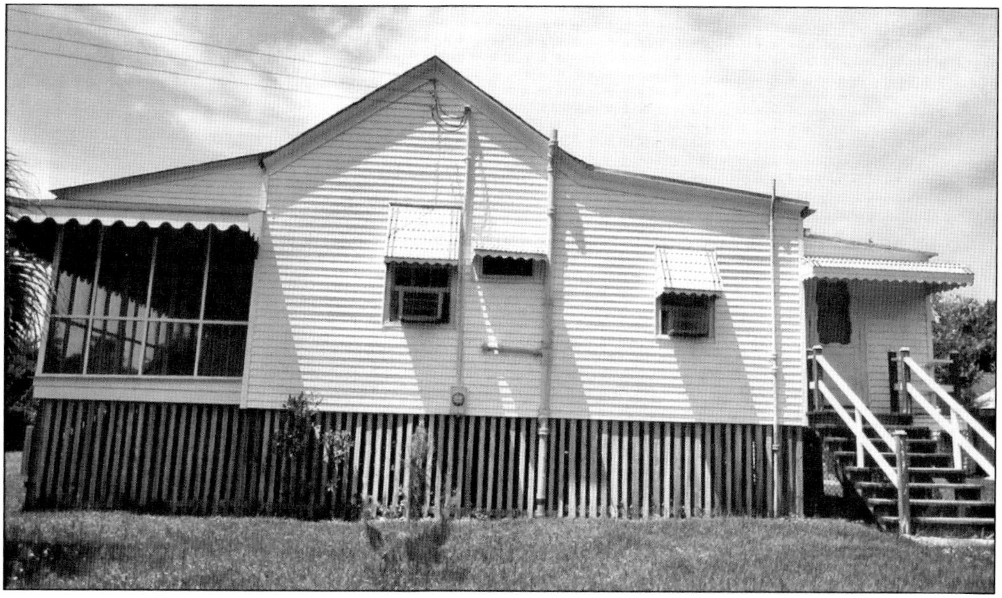

2269 I'ON AVENUE C. 1910. The John M. Rivers house was the summer cottage of radio and television executive John M. Rivers Sr. and his family. Rivers owned and operated WCSC-TV, Charleston's pioneer television station. [Variation of the "island house" form as constructed on the island from prior to the Civil War through the mid-20th century; Gone.] (Courtesy S.C. Department of Archives and History.)

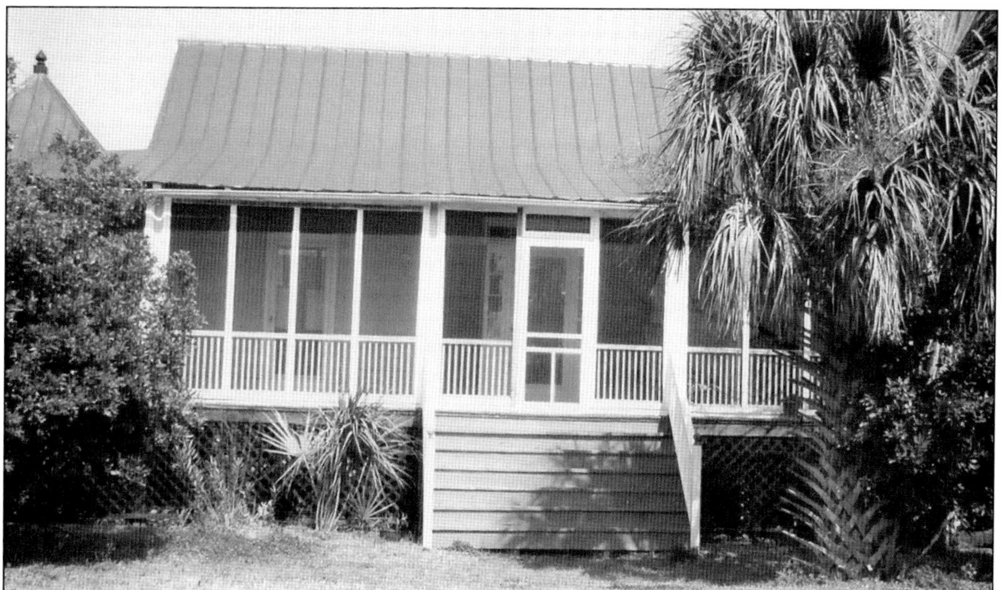

2408 I'ON AVENUE C. 1900. The LaCoste House is a rectangular block with a pyramidal appendage to the west and an attached kitchen house to the north. Decorative elements include sawn barge boards and sawn rafter ends on the porch. The principal entrance has a transom and sidelight. It is shown on the 1912 Sanborn Map and on a 1917 plat. The residence was regularly rented as a summer home by the Ehrhardt family. [Greatly altered.] (Courtesy Marshall Stith.)

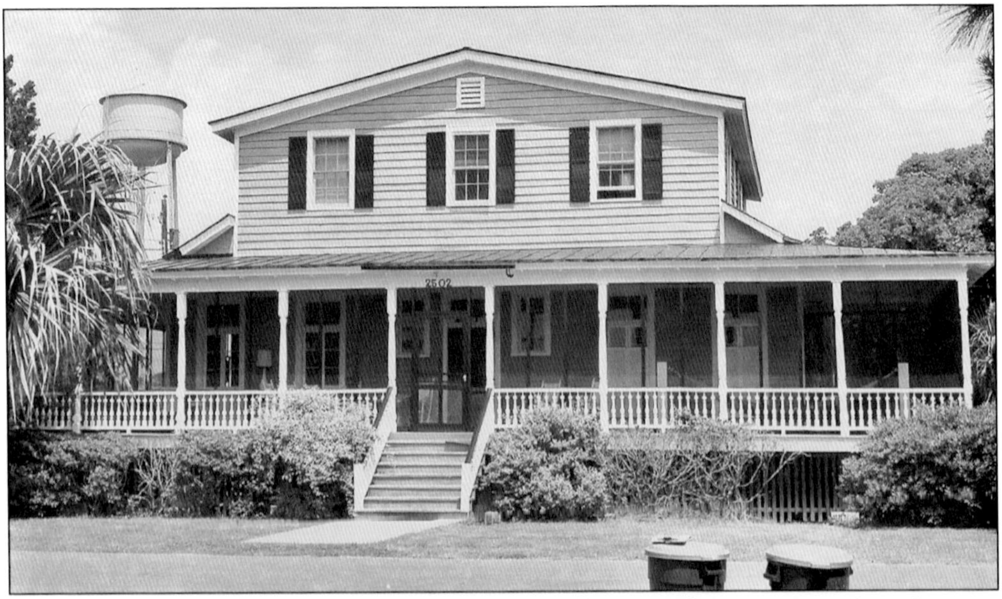

2502 I'ON AVENUE (FRONT) C. 1885. The Barton Muller House has wrap-around porches on a basic rectangular frame. There are louvered shutters and windows with wooden pediments. The porch has turned columns and a balustrade with bracketed eaves. The entrances have transoms, and there is lattice infill at the foundation. The second story is a later addition. The current owner is Sonny Meavers. [Good example of late 19th-century island architecture.] (Courtesy S.C. Department of Archives and History.)

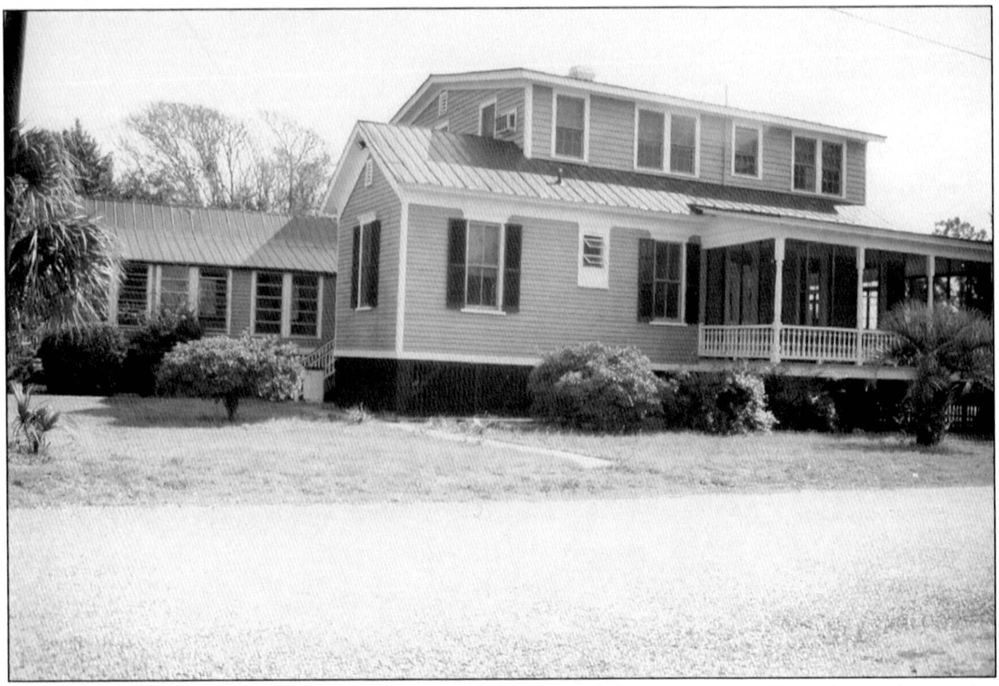

2502 I'ON AVENUE (SIDE) C. 1885. The side view of the Barton Muller House shows the wrap-around porch on the western elevation and an addition at the rear of the main house. The stables have been converted to a garage. (Courtesy Marshall Stith.)

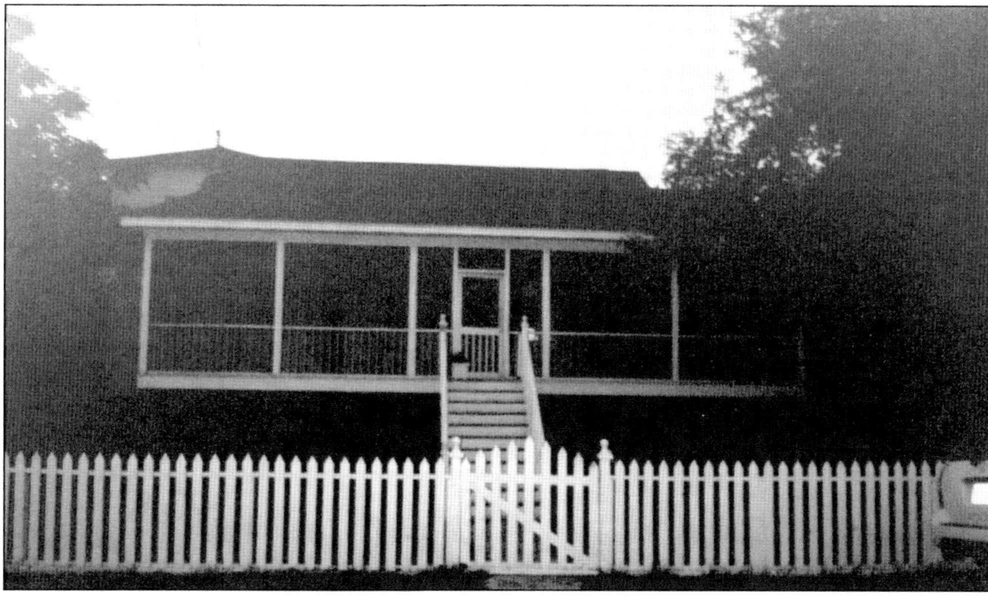

2508 I'on Avenue c. 1895. The vacation home (Summer Yard) was the beach house of Dr. Archibald Baker Sr. In 1912 he, along with Dr. Lawrence Craig of Dillon, founded Baker Hospital at 55 Ashley Avenue in Charleston. It was the first modern, private hospital specializing in surgical and obstetrical patients. The house has porches on the south and north elevations, and the gable ends have boxed cornices with returns. Later owners include the Maybank family. The current owner is the T.W. Bouch family. [Good late 19th-century example.) (Courtesy Bonnie A. Williams.)

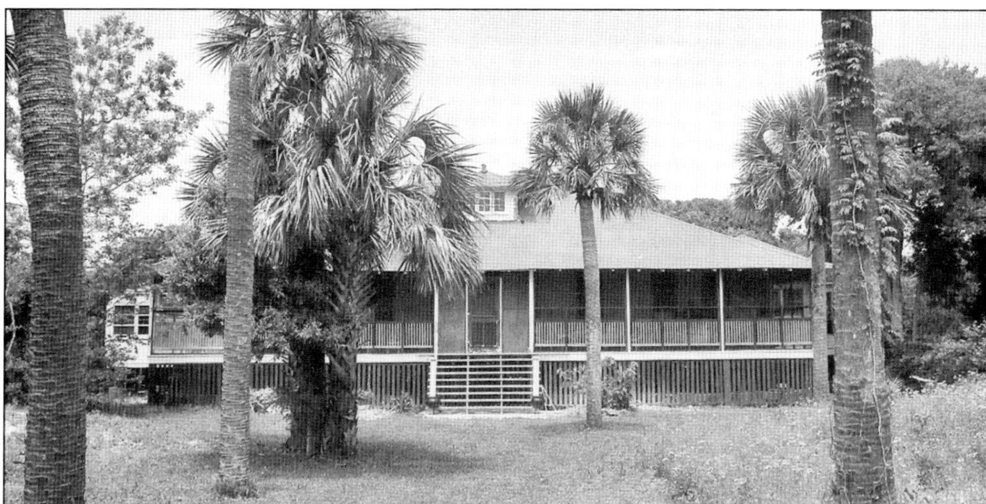

2513 I'on Avenue c. 1900. The Johnson House (Song of the Surf) is said to have been built by James Johnson, who operated a coal and ice business in Charleston. The house is built in the West Indian style with interior Victorian elements and an oddly shaped game room with its original servant's bell. The detached kitchen was joined to the main house in the 1940s. The garage sits on the site of the former stables. Alvira Zirkle owned the house from 1945 to 1970, when it was sold to Roy Williams III and Dr. R. Michael Williams. [Good example of late 19th-century island architecture.] (Courtesy S.C. Department of Archives and History.)

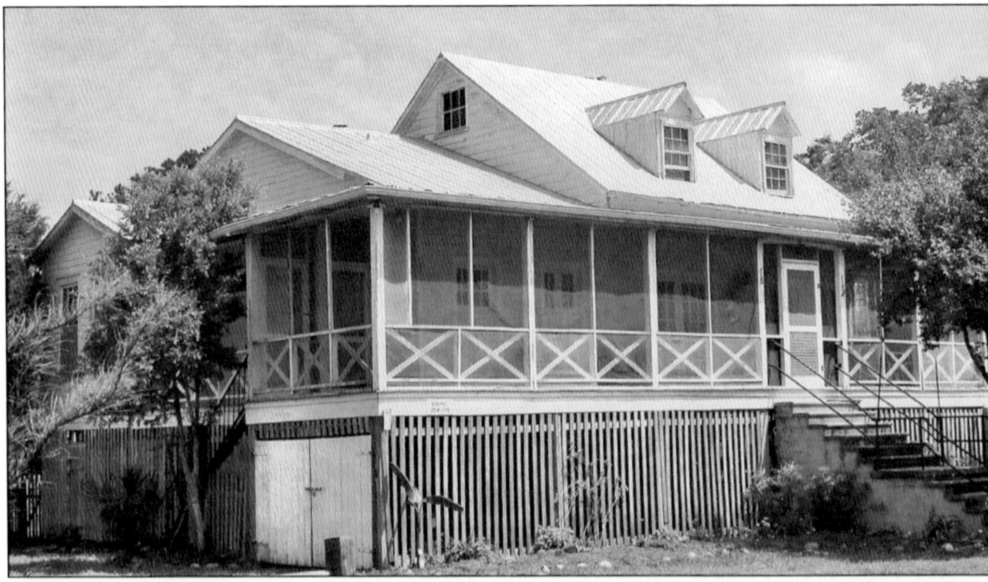

2514 I'ON AVENUE c. 1910. The S.C. Brown House is a rectangular structure with porches on the south, west, and north elevations. The kitchen house was attached to the main residence, and a bedroom addition was built *c.* 1930 on the west elevation by S.C. Brown. Mr. Brown came into ownership of the property through his marriage to Hannah Mendelsohn. Her father, I.M. Mendelsohn, had previously purchased the house from the Mazyck sisters. The interior of the house has beaded board ceilings and walls and heart-of-pine floors. The current owner is Blaine Ewing. [Good example of early 20th-century architecture.] (Courtesy S.C. Department of Archives and History.)

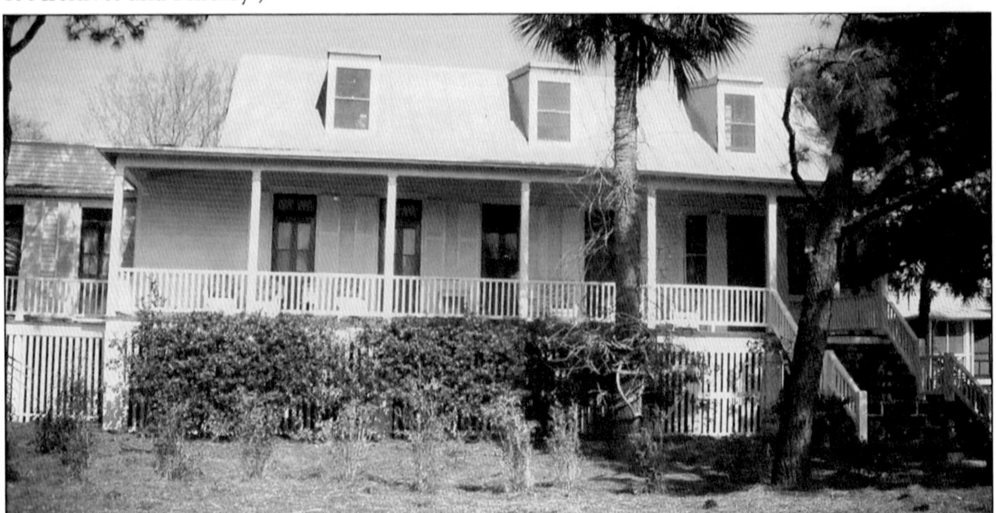

2520 I'ON AVENUE c. 1895. The Lesemann House's main block has one-story wings to the north and northwest with three shed dormers with six/six windows. The gable ends have boxed cornices with returns and plan board friezes. The porch roof has decorative sawn rafter ends with chamfered posts and molded capitals; the porch ceiling is beaded board. The Lesemann House is shown on the 1912 Sanborn Map. The house later belonged to the Carroll family and now belongs to Janyce McMenamin. [An important example of late 19th-century architecture; altered.] (Courtesy Marshall Stith.)

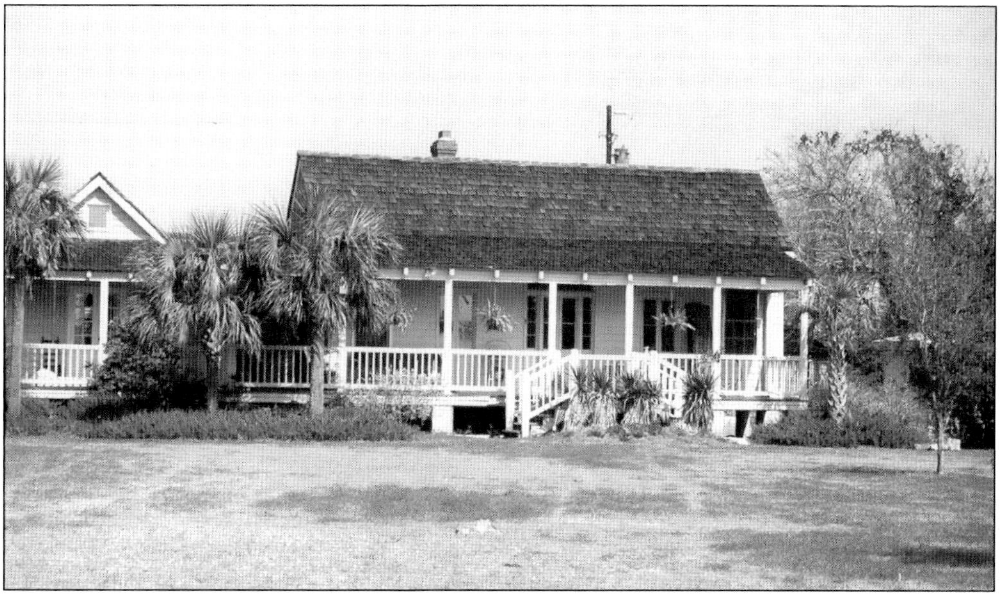

2523 I'ON AVENUE C. 1895. The Heyward Harvey House's rectangular main block has additions to the north. The principal entry has transoms and sidelights, and the porch has exposed rafter ends and a simple balustrade. The house appears on the 1912 Sanborn Map. Former owner Joel Wolfe sold the house to the current owner Dr. Barry Silverman, a cardiologist from Atlanta. [Good example of 19th-century island architecture; altered.] (Courtesy Marshall Stith.)

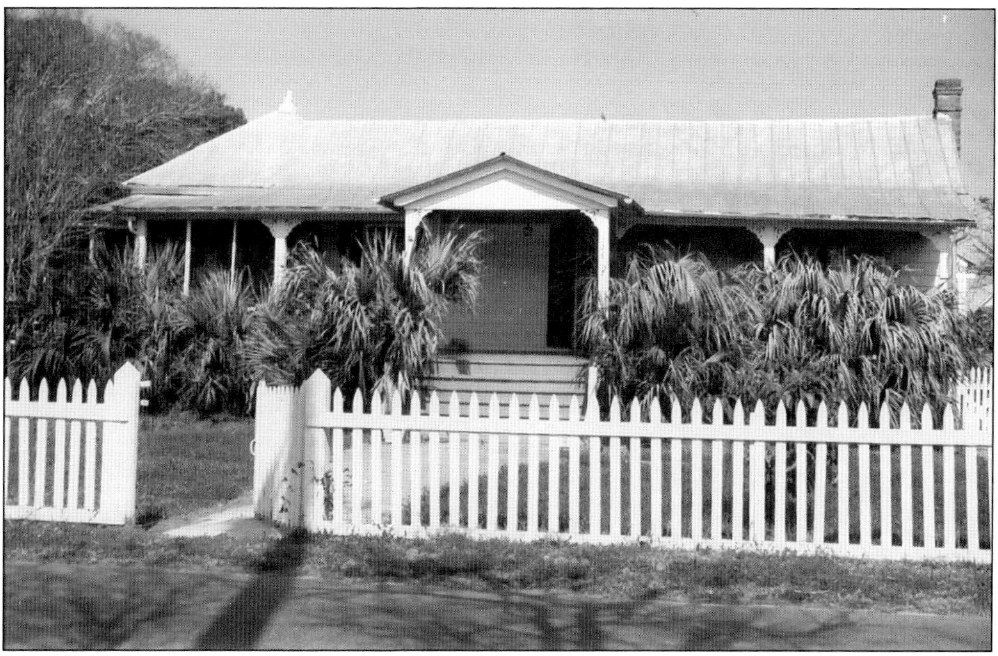

2608 I'ON AVENUE C. 1900. The Legerton House has a rectangular main block with a square flanker with a pyramidal roof to the northwest, additions to the rear, and a projecting gable over the entry bay. The house is shown on the 1912 Sanborn Map and a 1917 plat. [Good example of the modest island residences built during the late 19th-century.] (Courtesy Marshall Stith.)

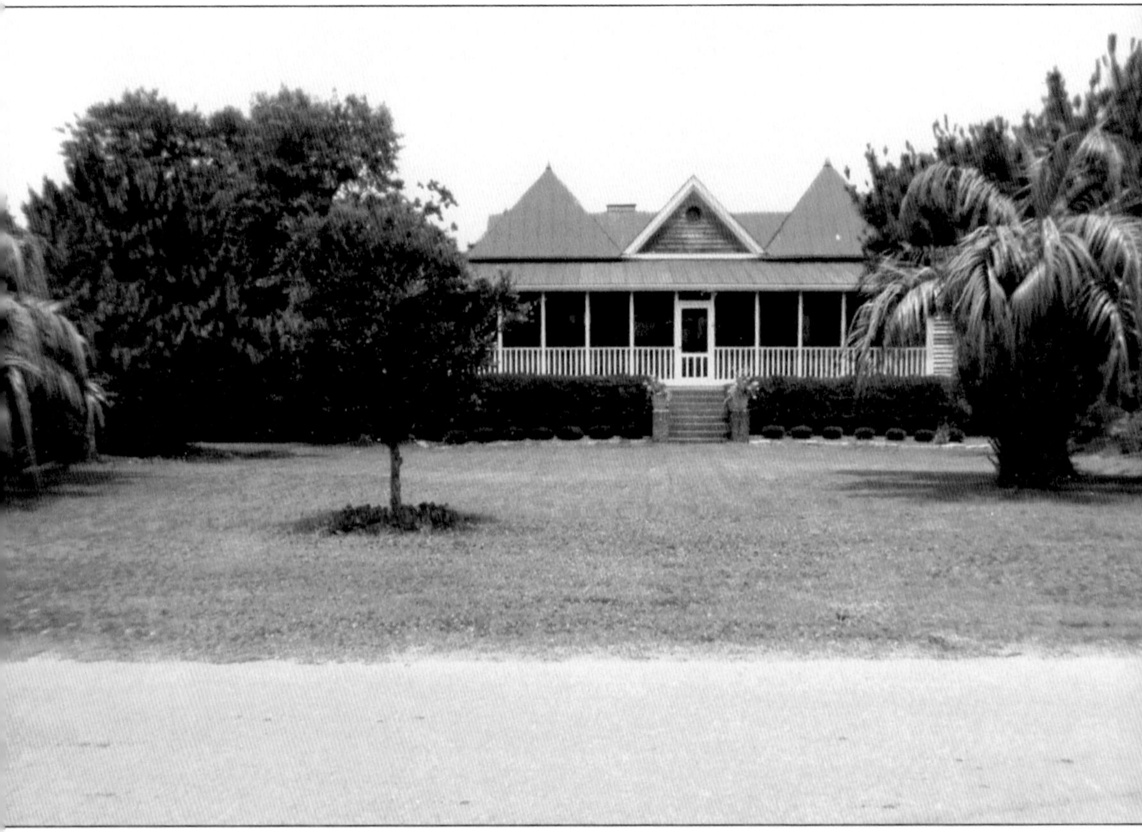

2629 I'ON AVENUE C. 1900. The T-shaped main block of this house has square flankers at each corner with pyramidal roofs. There is infill between the two rear flankers. The rear of the house now serves as the principal entrance to the house. There is an attached kitchen house with a recent dormer. The house has round attic vents at the gable ends, a rear wrap-around porch, and French doors. It appears on a 1917 plat and the 1924 Sanborn Map. The Pearlstine family owned the house for years. [Important example of early 20th-century island architecture.] (Courtesy Ruth A. Hood.)

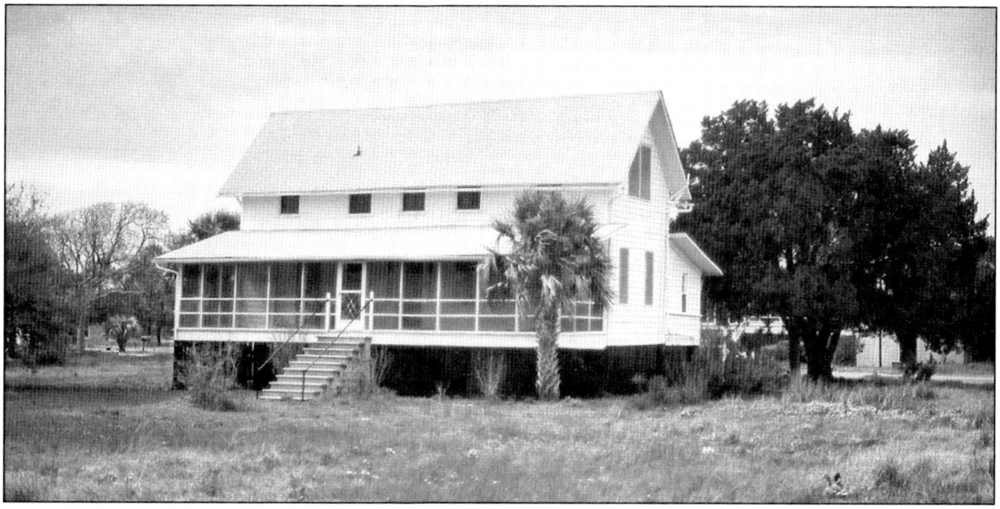

2707 I'ON AVENUE c. 1905. The Dr. William H. Speissegger House (Cabbage Patch) showed the craftsman architectural style influence. It was built for Swinton Anderson within the neighborhood once commonly referred to as Andersonville, so named because of the several houses built in close proximity for family members, including Maxwell, Pickens, and Titus Anderson. The lots were laid out by Maxwell Anderson with lumber for the houses from the Anderson Lumber Mill. This house had low profile six-light windows at the second level of the façade, bracketed eaves, and exposed rafter ends at the roof. [Excellent example of an early 20th-century beach house; Gone.] (Courtesy S.C. Department of Archives and History.)

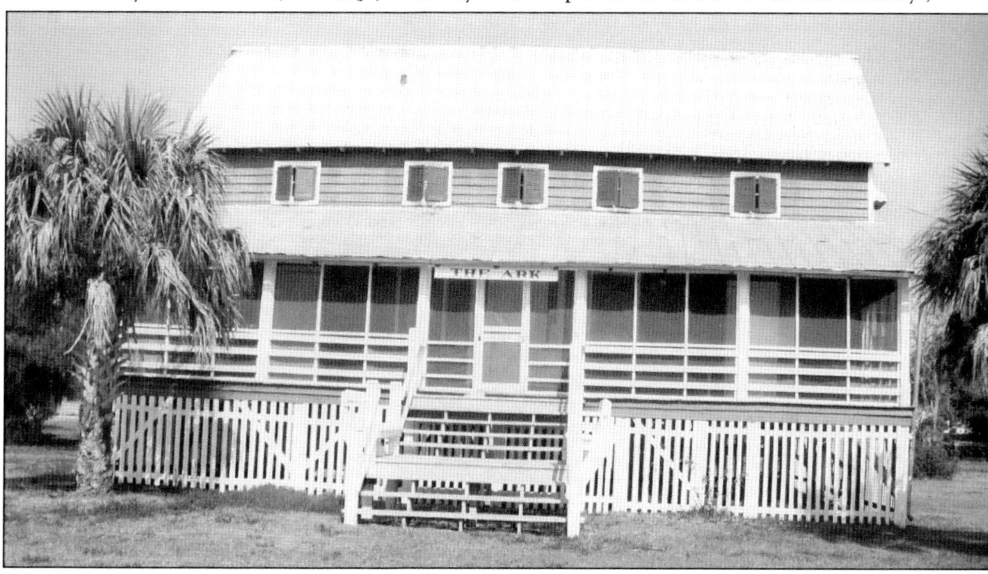

2714 I'ON AVENUE c. 1908. The Anderson family also built this house (The Ark) with materials barged to Sullivan's Island from the Anderson Lumber Yard at the foot of Broad Street in Charleston. One interior door retains the delivery notation. The structure appears on a 1917 plat and the 1924 Sanborn Map. During the 1911 hurricane, family members gathered here for safety, and from that time forward it was referred to as "The Ark." [Excellent example of an early 20th-century beach house, which contributes to the overall character of the eastern end of Sullivan's Island as it developed partly as a result of the trolley line in the late 19th and early 20th centuries.] (Courtesy S.C. Department of Archives and History.)

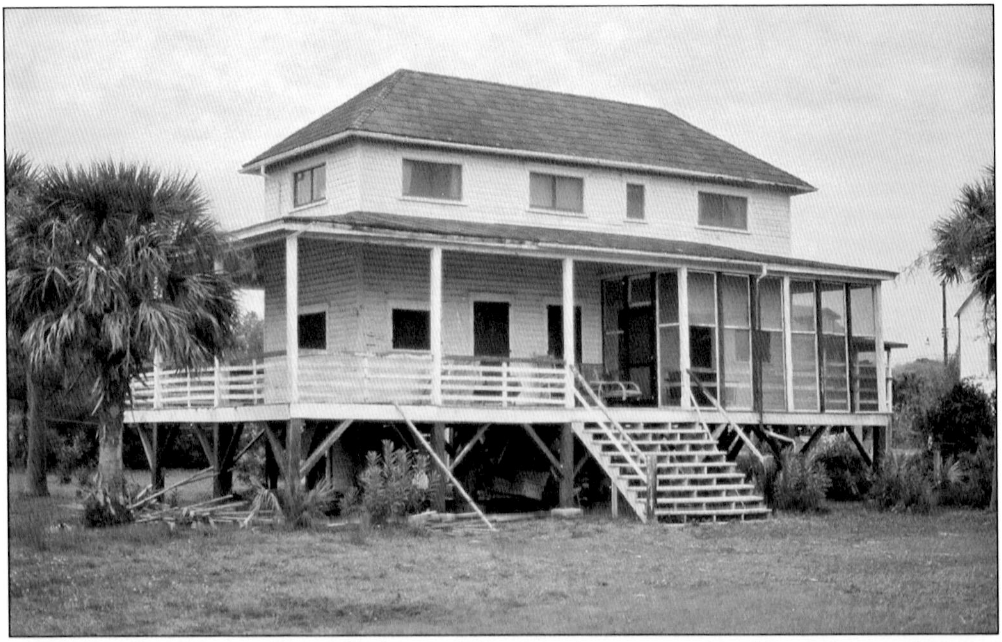

2723 I'ON AVENUE c. 1915. The house (Chez Lena) is accented with wooden window and door surrounds and includes a one-story gable addition off the rear "ell" with a gable raised, seam metal roof. [Excellent example of an early 20th-century beach house.] (Courtesy S.C. Department of Archives and History.)

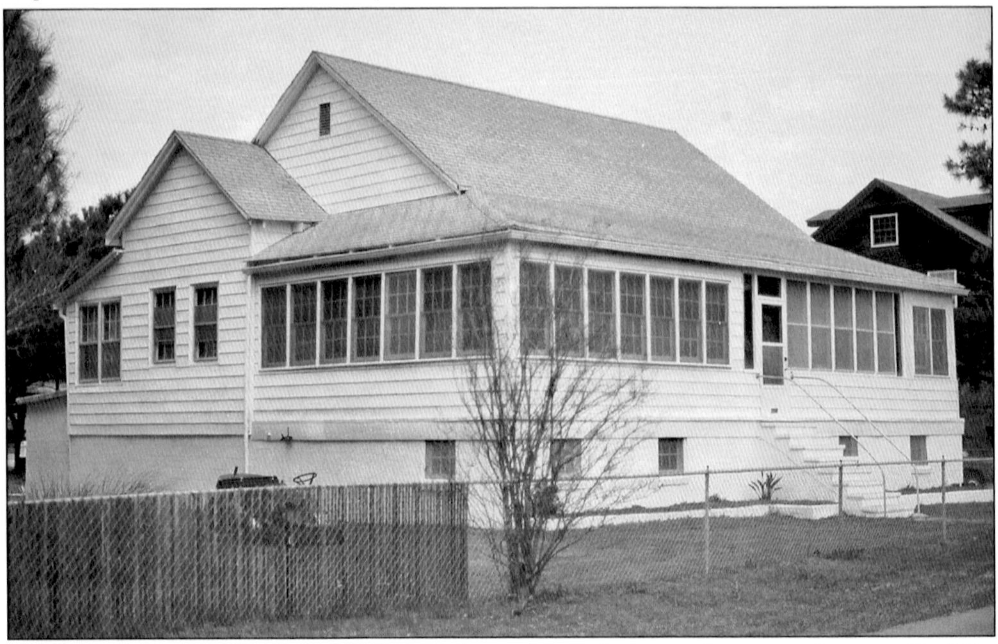

2730 I'ON AVENUE c. 1915. The house shows the craftsman influence architecturally. The craftsman influence incorporated large windows with diamond panes and wide dormers projecting from gable roofs. A second story was built after the 1987 survey by Preservation Consultants, Inc., when this photograph was taken. [Although altered, indicative of a rather substantial early beach house.] (Courtesy S.C. Department of Archives and History.)

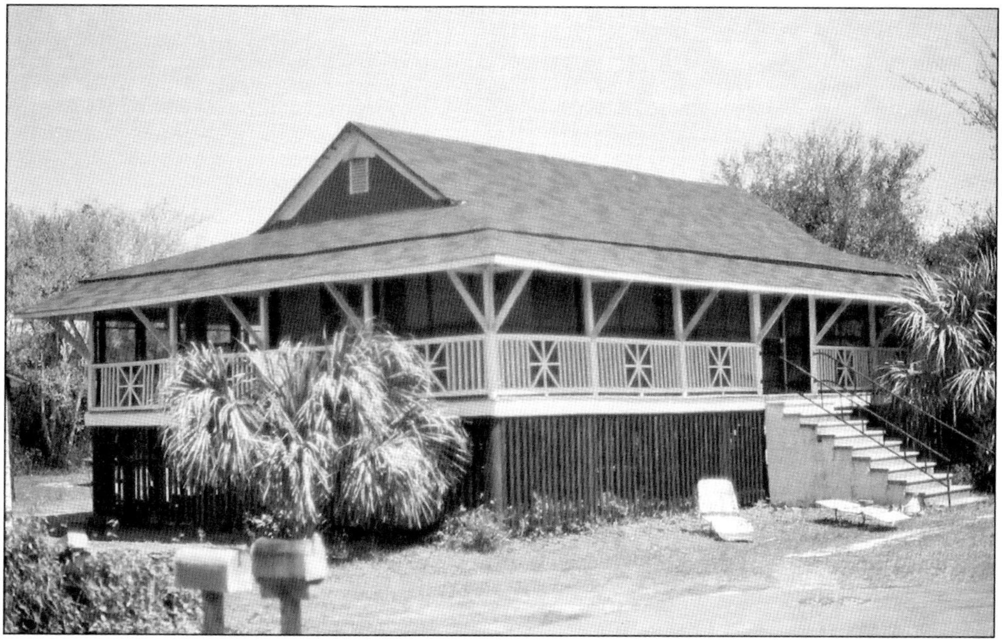

2808 I'on Avenue c. 1925. This house, built as a summer residence, has several small additions that have been constructed at the rear. Louvered attic vents in the gable ends and French doors at the porch are among the dwelling's local features. [Example of a typical modest early 20th-century beach dwelling.] (Courtesy S.C. Department of Archives and History.)

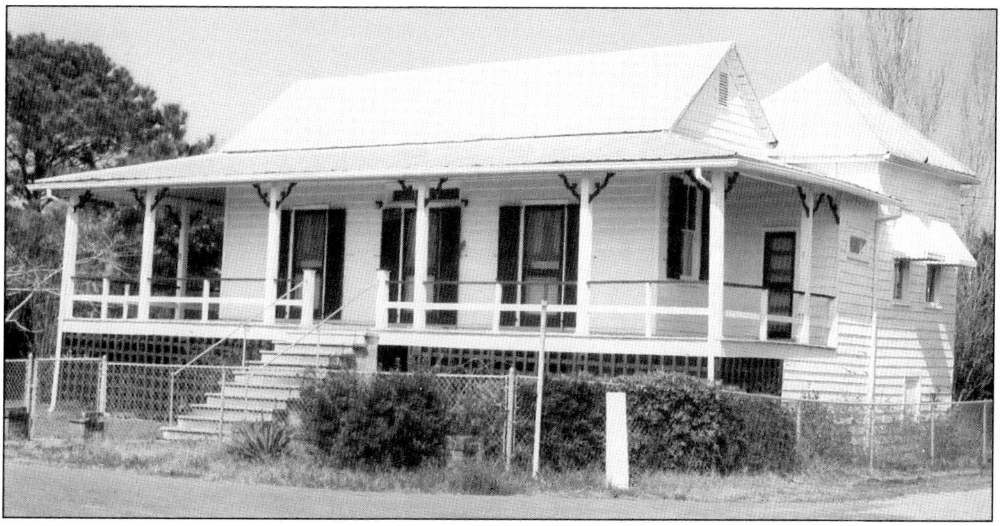

2830 I'on Avenue c. 1895. This cottage has a wrap-around porch with square posts and sawn brackets. The transom at the main entrance has louvered shutters at the principal doors and windows. Wood awnings are on the rear windows. The front of the house has lattice at the ground floor level that wraps around the sides. The rear porch has been enclosed between the pyramidal wings connected by a shed roof. The house is similar to 2824 I'on Avenue, although that home lacks the decorative features and has an apron wall at the porch. [Excellent example of a small late 19th-century beach house as it contributes to the overall character of the eastern section of Sullivan's Island that developed partly as a result of the trolley line in the late 19th and early 20th centuries.] (Courtesy Marshall Stith.)

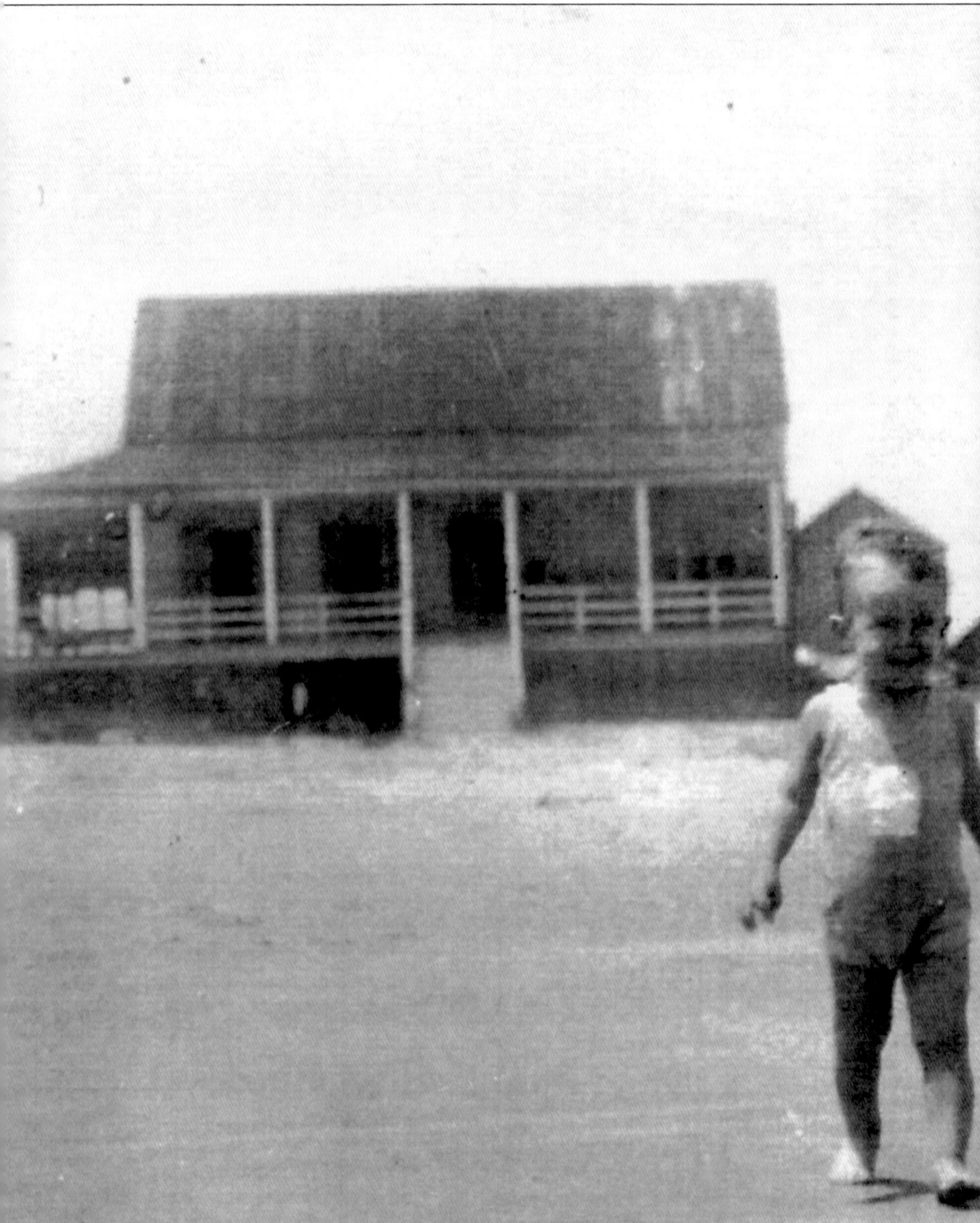

Station 22 1/2—Front Beach. The photo shows the youngster standing on the beach when the tides practically reached to the front steps of 2251 Atlantic (Kottage Kill Kare) and 2257

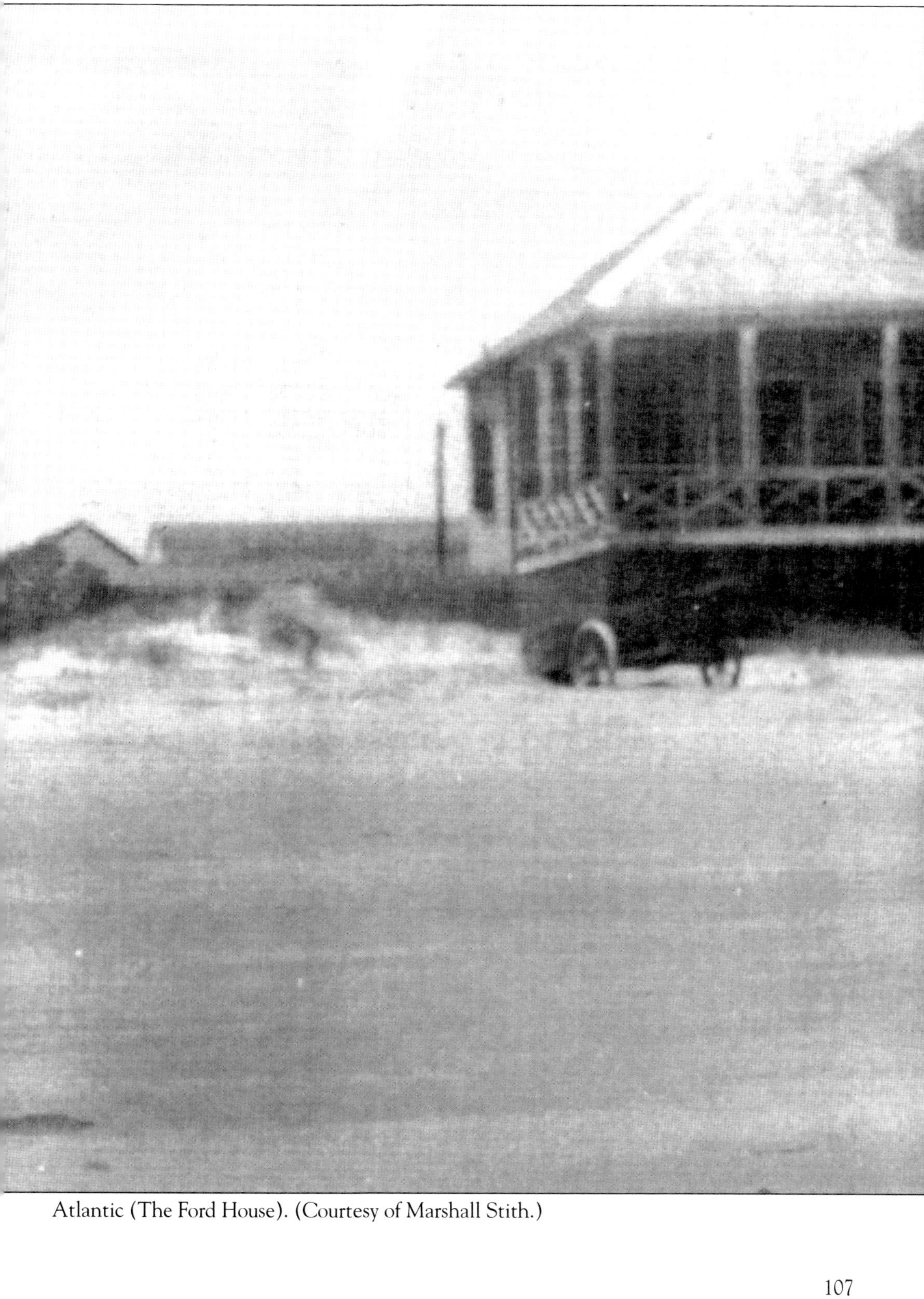

Atlantic (The Ford House). (Courtesy of Marshall Stith.)

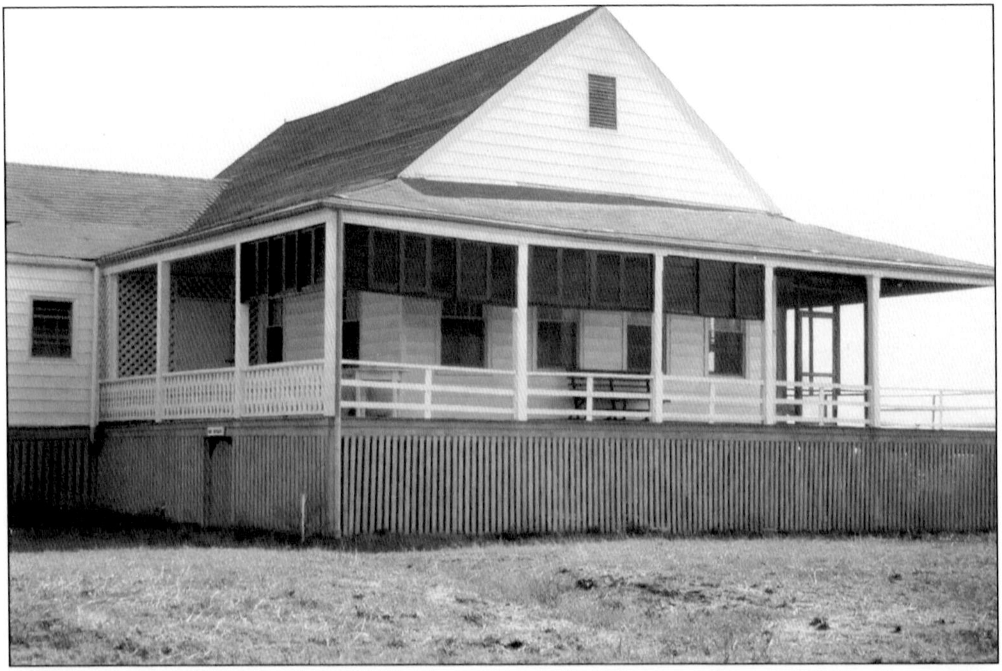

2251 Atlantic Avenue c. 1895. The homes at 2251 Atlantic (Kottage Kill Kare) and 2263 Atlantic were moved 15–20 yards toward the rear of their lots to escape high tides, only to be destroyed later by Hurricane Hugo. Pictured here is 2251 Atlantic. [Good example of late 19th-century island architecture; Gone.] (Courtesy of Marshall Stith.)

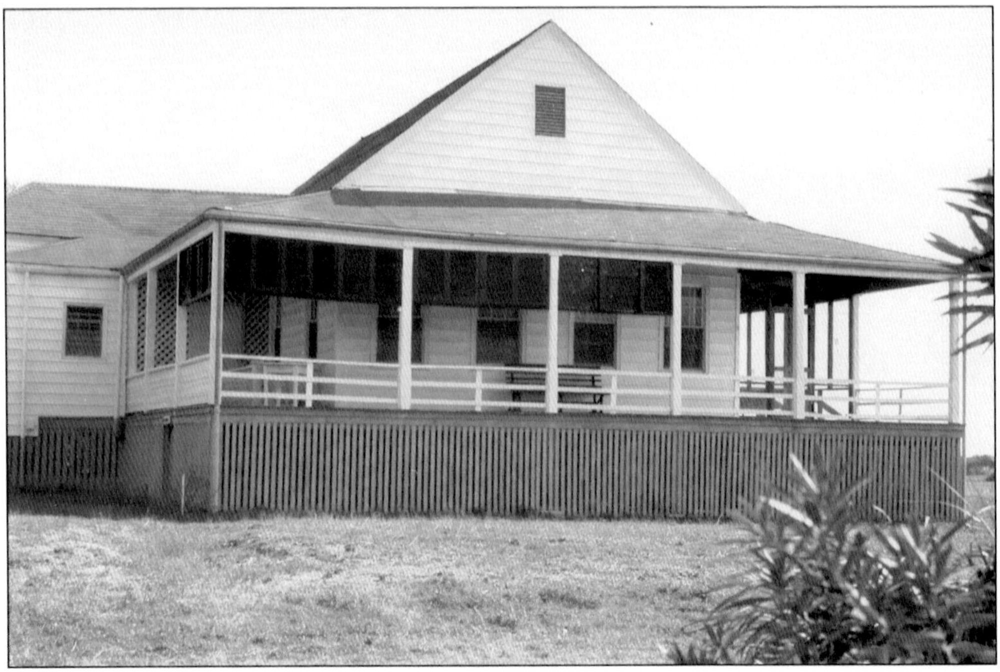

2251 Atlantic Avenue. The family who summered at this house kept voluminous scrapbooks of their halcyon days at the beach. All of the books were lost when Hurricane Hugo came ashore in 1987. (Courtesy of Marshall Stith.)

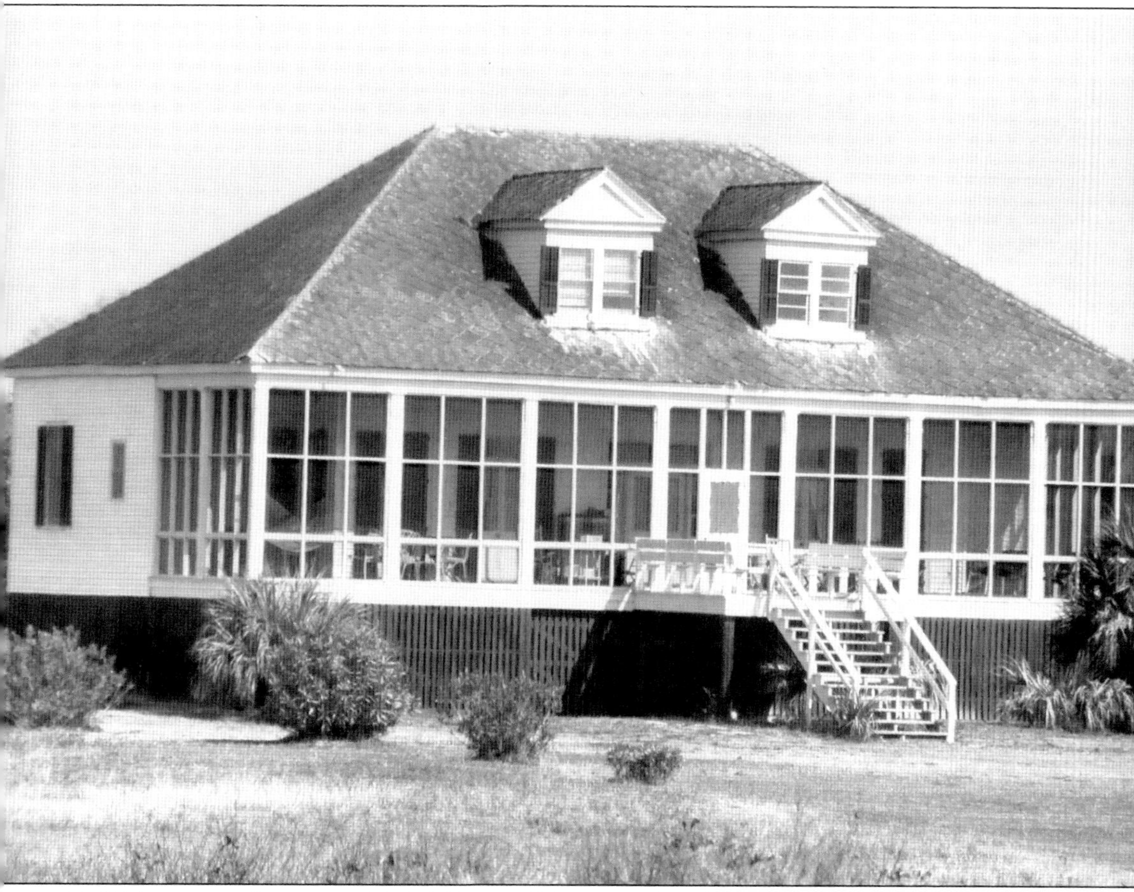

2257 Atlantic Avenue c. 1910. The Ford House was bought from Wilbur Thornhill in 1935. The high tides formerly came up to the immediate front of the house. The house has iron rods that anchor side walls to horizontal beams 15 feet underground. The dwelling is rectangular in shape with an integral porch to the south and a hipped porch to the northeast. The building has a hipped roof with two front-facing, pedimented gable dormers that have been altered. The principal entrance has a transom with a sidelight flanked by French doors. W.H. Ford is the current owner. [Good example of early 20th-century island architecture.] (Courtesy Marshall Stith.)

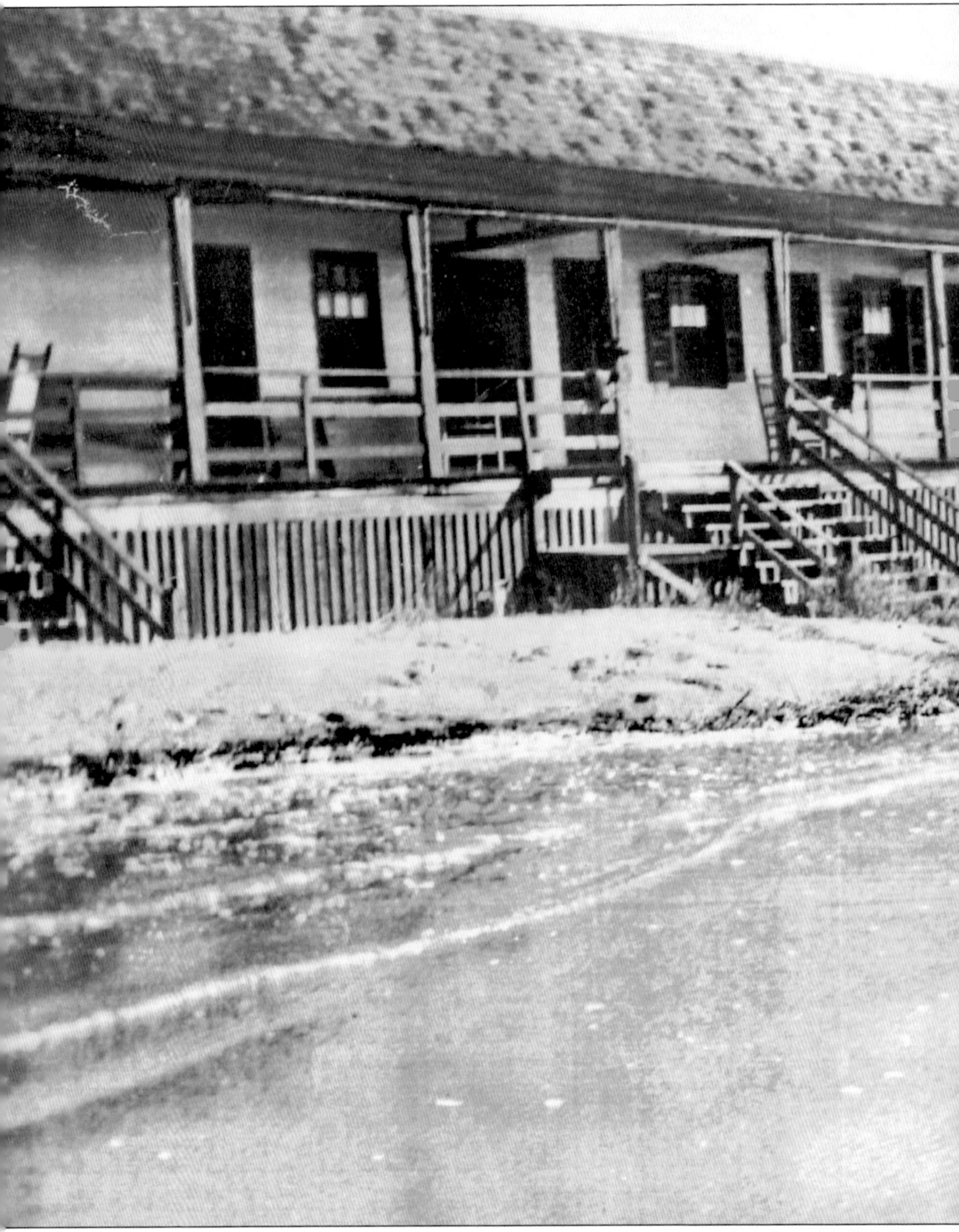

Boarding House Station 22 1/2. One of the numerous boarding houses that dotted Sullivan's Island in the early 1900s, this particular house was destroyed by a hurricane. To the immediate right in the photograph is the Johnson House at 2301 Atlantic. The area in front of these

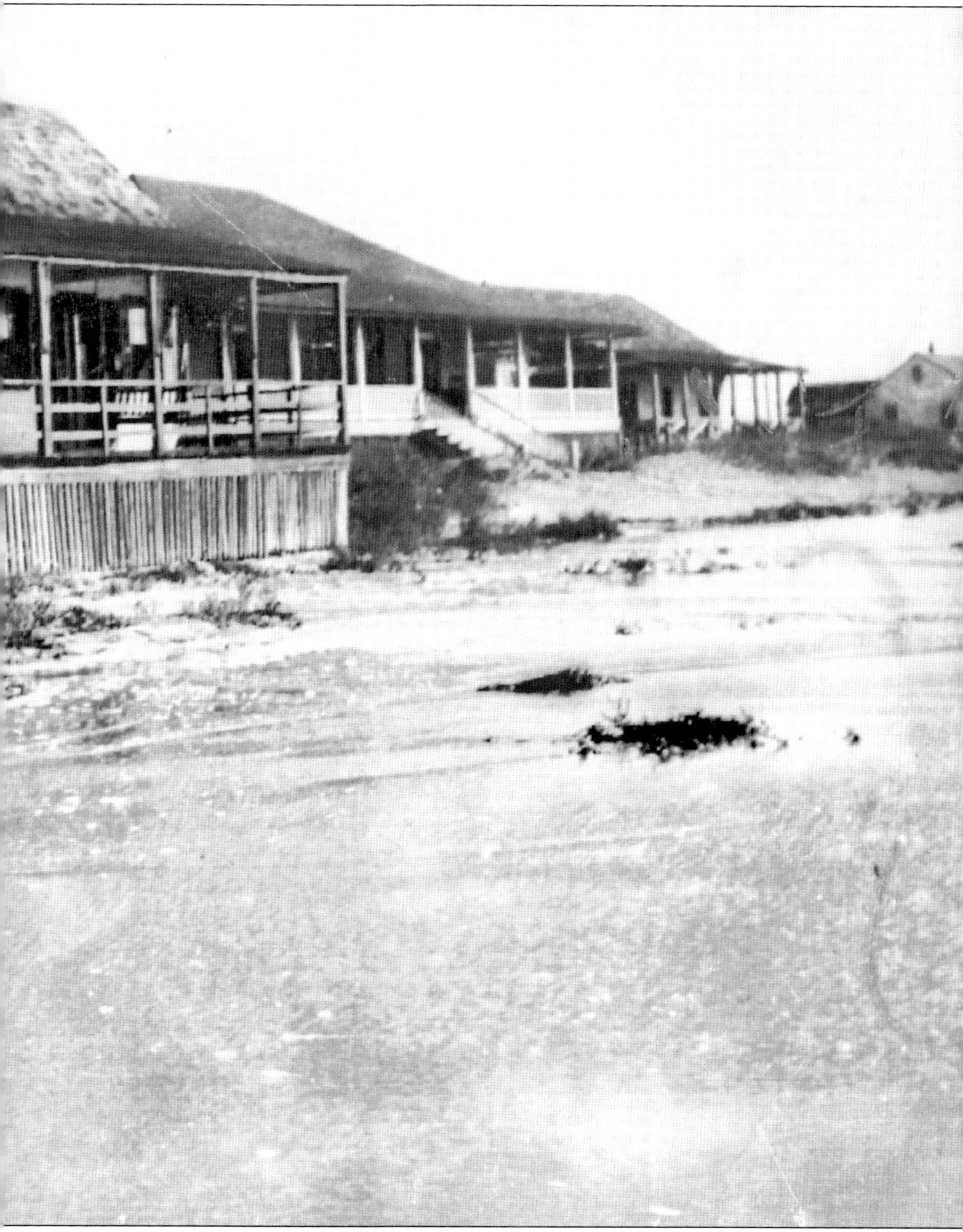

properties is now a greensward that stretches for some distance to a line of low-lying sand dunes that separate the lawn from the beach. (Courtesy of Marshall Stith.)

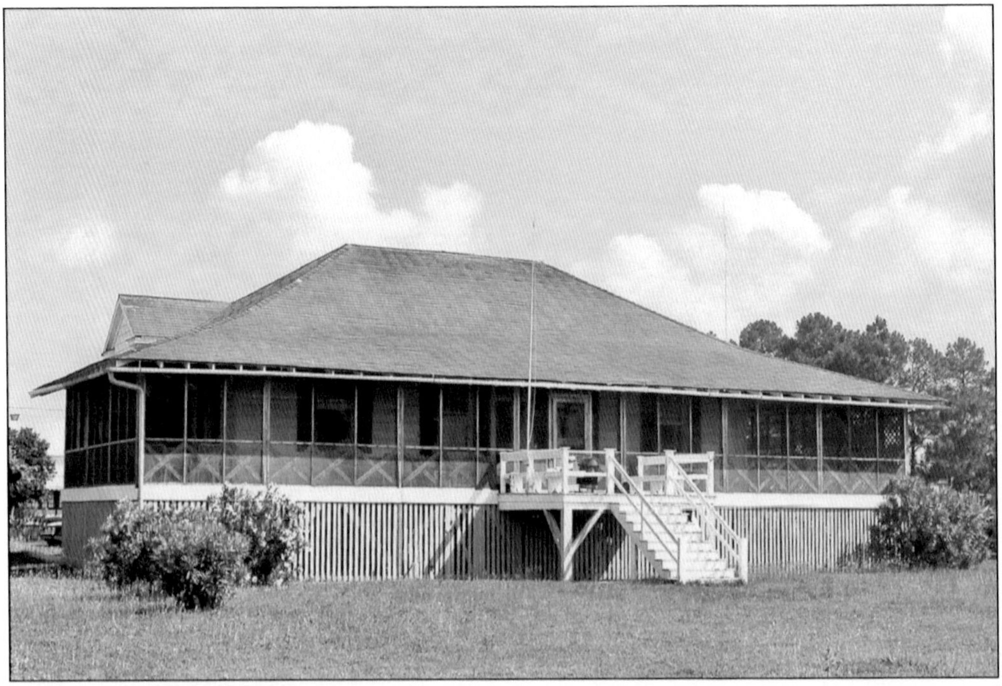

2301 Atlantic Avenue c. 1915. The Johnson House is similar to 2513 I'on Avenue and 2430 Jasper Boulevard. There is a hipped roof at the main block with intersecting gables and sheds at the rear additions. [Good early 20th-century example.] (Courtesy S.C. Department of Archives and History.)

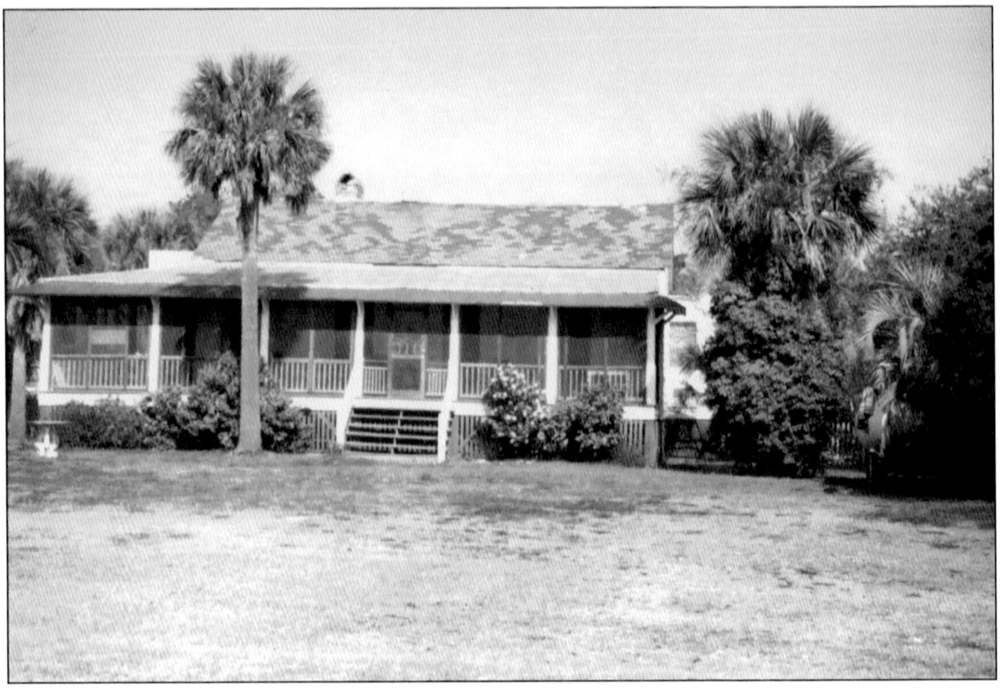

2414 Atlantic Avenue c. 1915. The house is shown on a 1917 plat and the 1924 Sanborn Map. [Typical early 20th century example; altered.] (Courtesy Marshall Stith.)

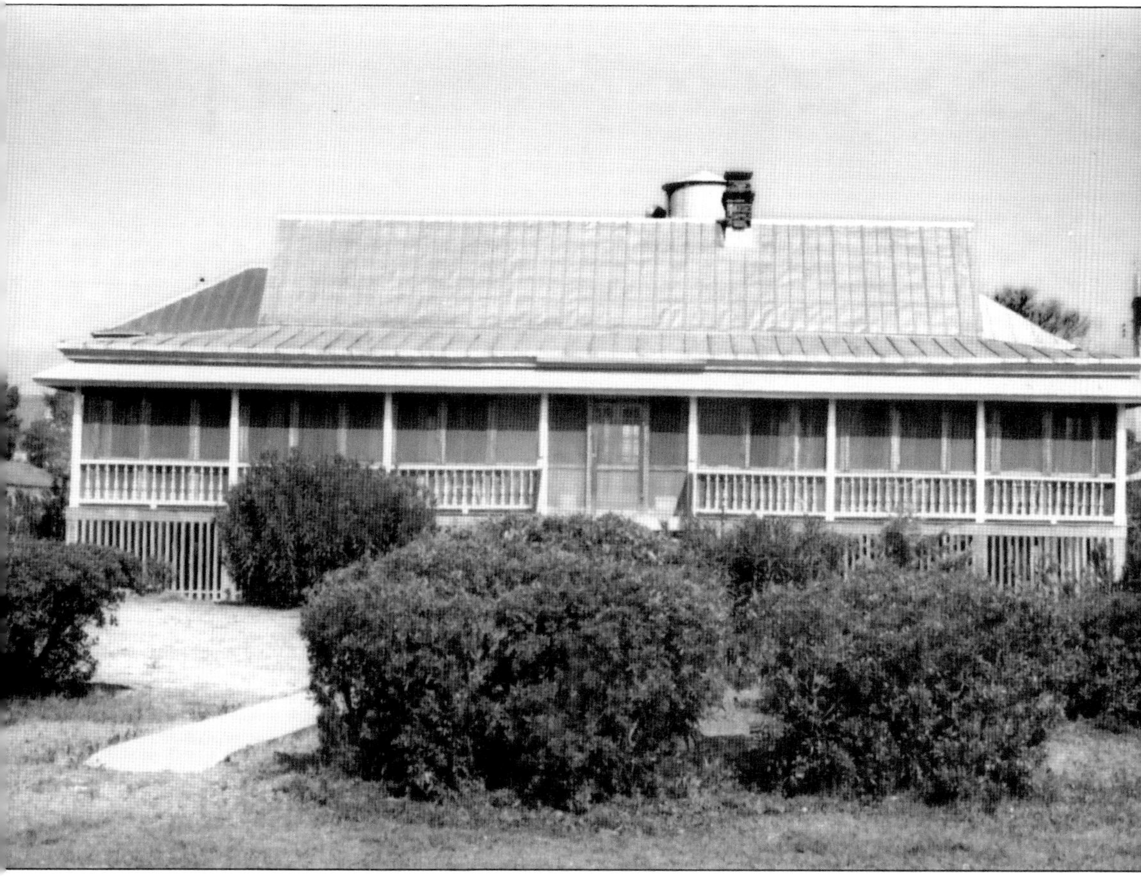

2424 Atlantic Avenue c. 1890. The house has a small rear section (a "keeping house" to fulfill leasing requirements) and was originally built for A. Olney Halsey (1872–1967), lumber dealer, civic and political leader, cartographer, and ferry boat commissioner. In the late 19th century at the University of Georgia, Halsey was captain of the school's first football team. He was president and treasurer of Halsey Lumber Company. Refuse from the mill was used to fill the pond that was between the old Charleston Museum and the old Municipal Yacht Basin. Nearby Halsey Boulevard was named for him. It was Halsey who obtained a copy of a map by John Culpeper from the British Museum that showed that Sullivan's Island was known by that name before Charleston occupied its present site. During his lifetime Halsey amassed an impressive collection of South Carolina maps. When the main house was built, doors and shutters used in the main were removed from a ferry. Mr. Halsey was a member of the Cooper River Realty Commission, who operated the ferry *Sappho* between Charleston and Mount Pleasant. The property later belonged to the Moore family and is now in the ownership of the Waring family. A second story has been added. [Good late 19th-century example; greatly altered.] (Courtesy Marshall Stith.)

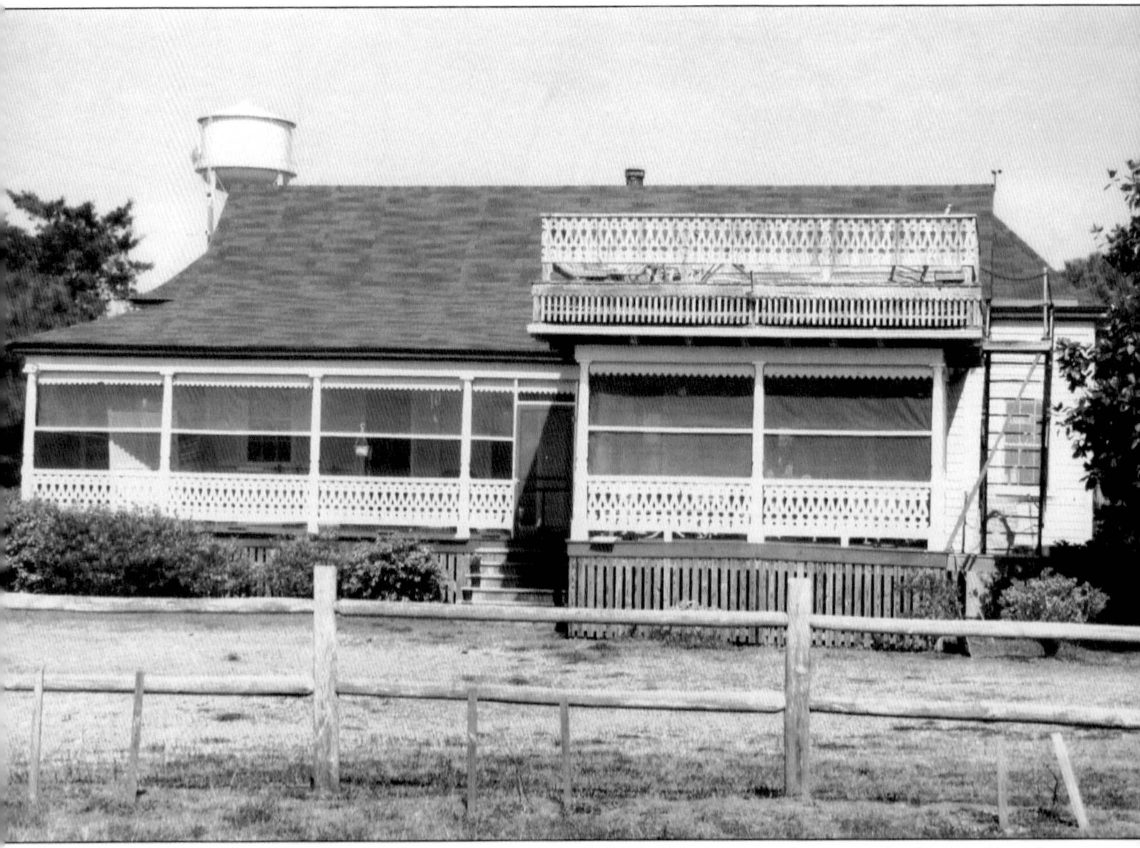

2501 Atlantic (2501 I'on) Avenue c. 1880. The Mauro House was built by the Hertz family, and the first plat was recorded by 1900. Previous owners include A.H. Bonnoit, Charles Mauro, Margaret Pringle Schachte, and Earl Jackson. The kitchen house was attached to the main house. The house was recently purchased by the Daniel Bruce family of Greenville and extensively remodeled. [Good example of late 19th-century island architecture; altered.] (Courtesy Marshall Stith.)

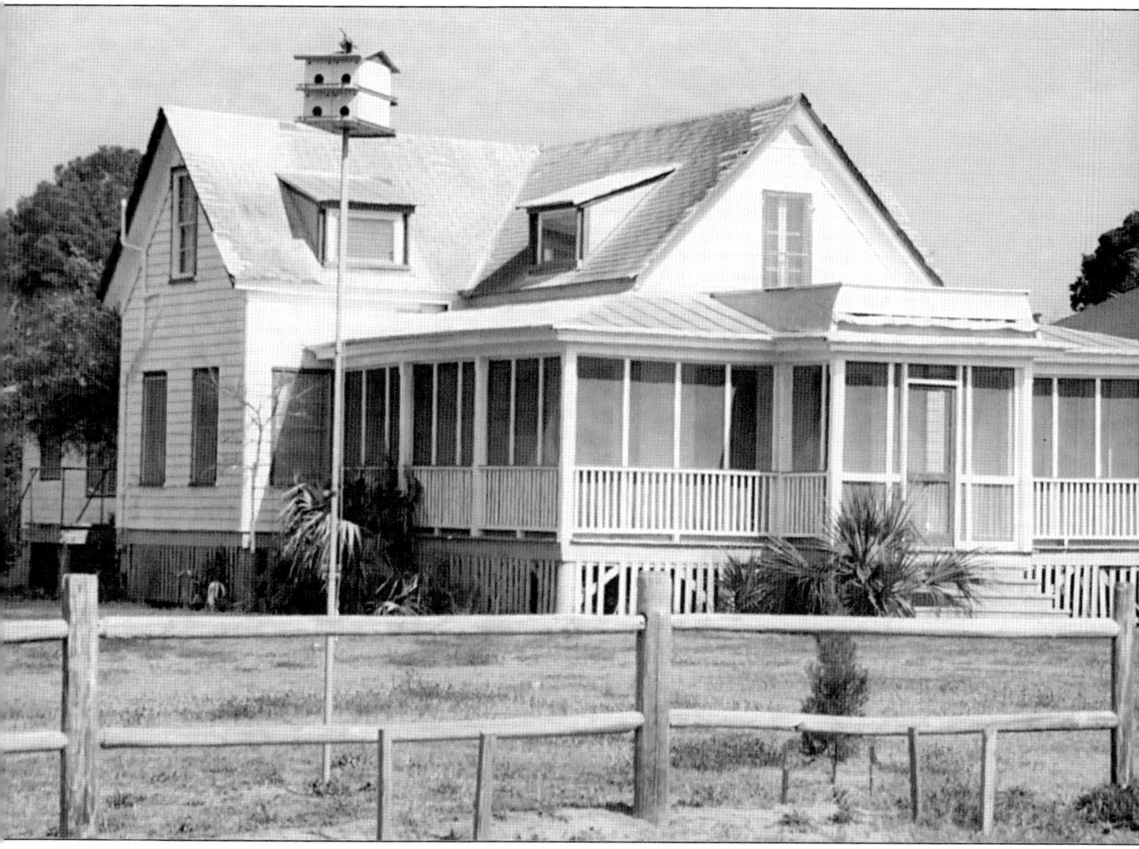

2508 Atlantic Avenue (or 2508 I'on Avenue). This house was built by a German family named Schwacke but later (*c.* 1927) became the summer home of the Stoney family. Thomas Porcher Stoney was mayor of Charleston from 1923 to 1931. During his administration, he was instrumental in establishing Charleston's first airport, a facility on James Island which was later transferred to the current location in North Charleston. While he was mayor a municipal golf course was laid out on James Island; Johnson Hagood Stadium and Thomas P. Stoney field were built; and the Gen. William Moultrie Memorial Playground opened. The house is built in the T-shaped historic plan with rear additions and enclosures. In 1927 the extreme rear of the house as a kitchen and servant's wing connected to the main house by a screened breezeway, which was later enclosed *c.* 1965. The rear of the house now has a modern wing after lightning was said to have caused a fire. [Good late 19th-century example; altered.] (Courtesy Marshall Stith.)

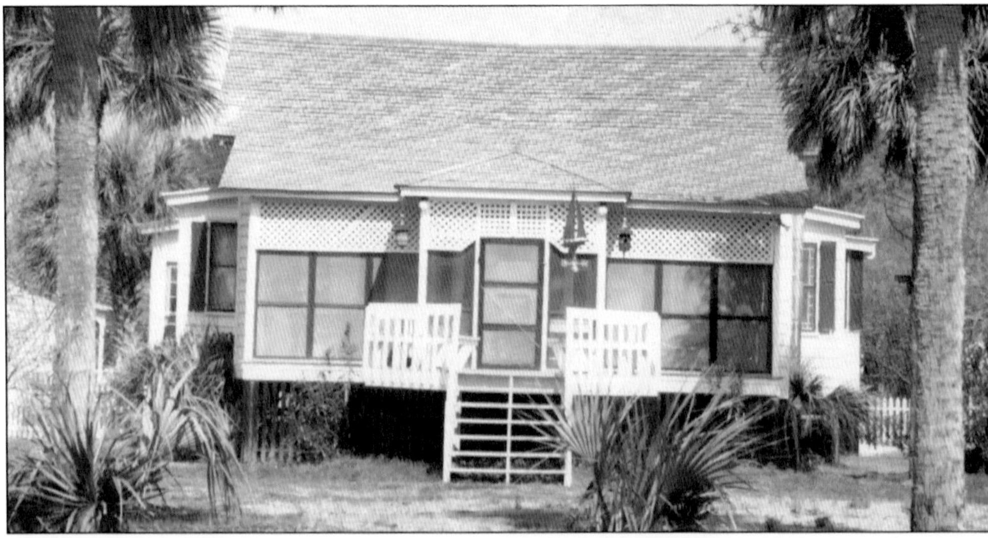

2520 Atlantic Avenue (Front) c. 1880. The house (Tranquility) was originally a four-room cottage divided by a central hallway. The back porch was later filled in to create additional rooms. The house has louvered attic vents at the gable ends. The windows have a single rectangular, clear glass light surrounded by small stained-glass lights. The entrance is in a projecting bay with side lights. The porch has lattice above the screening. Before Atlantic Avenue was extended in front of this property, the centerpiece of the front lawn was a pond stocked with brilliantly colored fish. Jack Krawcheck, owner of Krawcheck's Men's Wear, bought the house in 1928, and the Krawcheck family still summers here. [Good example of late 19th-century island architecture.] (Courtesy Marshall Stith.)

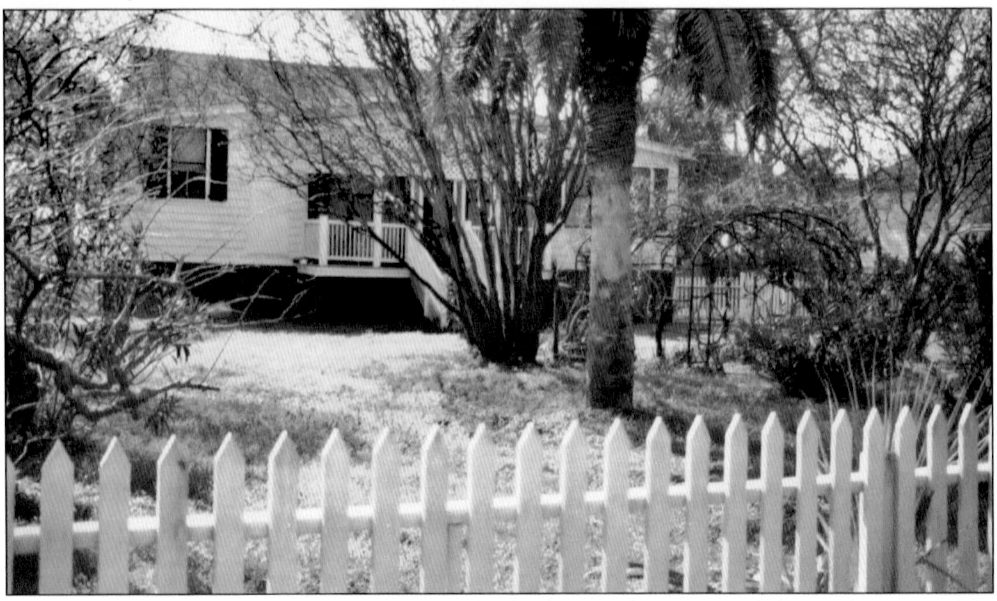

2520 Atlantic Avenue (Back) c. 1880. The back view shows part of the garden created by Jack Krawcheck when he summered on the island. During the winter he would come over every Thursday and Sunday to work in his island garden. Not visible in the picture is the building that housed servants' quarters and has now been made into a guest house. The bath house was destroyed in Hurricane Hugo. (Courtesy Marshall Stith.)

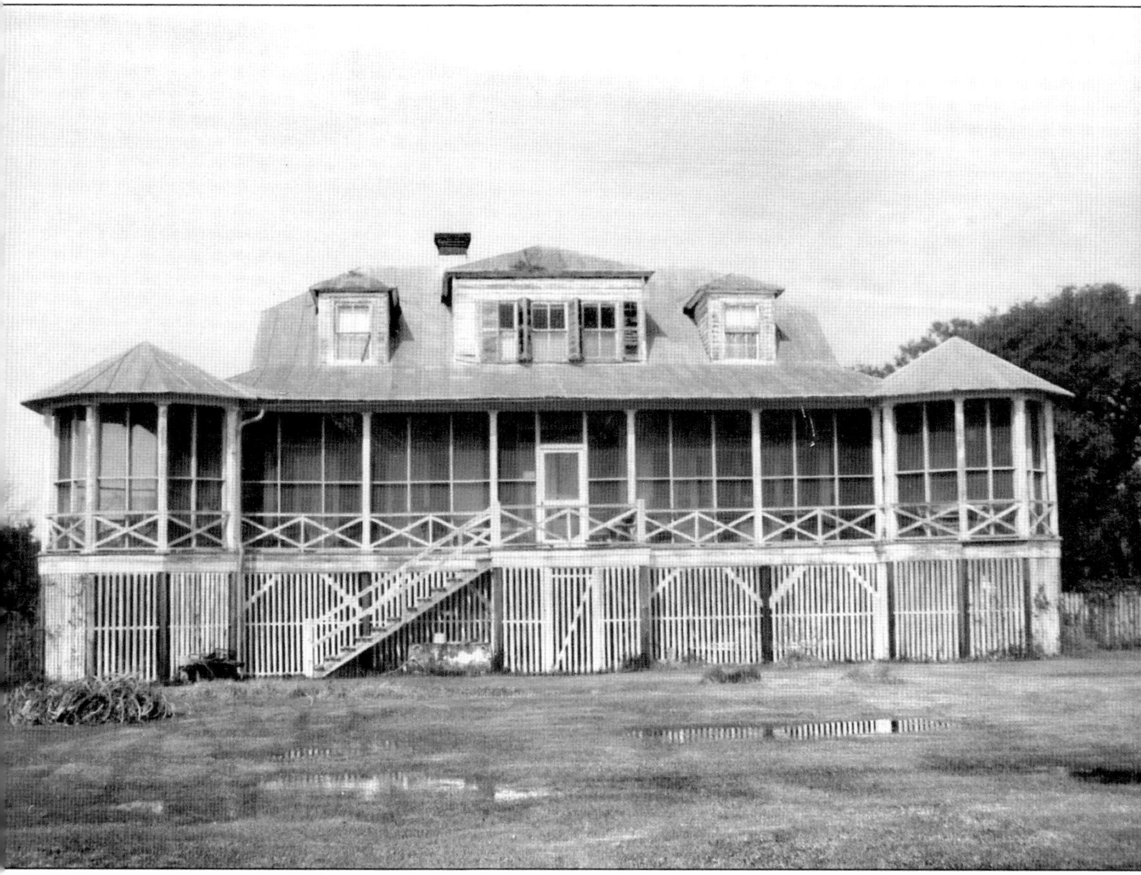

2673 Atlantic Avenue, 1889. The C. Bissell Jenkins/Simons House was a summer residence built for C. Bissell Jenkins on a lot he had purchased from Harriet Cross. The Trouche family acquired the property in the 1920s. It was purchased in the 1970s by Mr. and Mrs. Lewis Simons. The front porch extends with conical pavilions at either side of the façade. There is a porch at the rear elevation with paired rear entrance doors, transoms, and paneled shutters. There are three hipped dormers on the jerkin head roof and detached servants' quarters. [Excellent example of a late 19th-century beach house with minimal alterations.] (Courtesy Marshall Stith.)

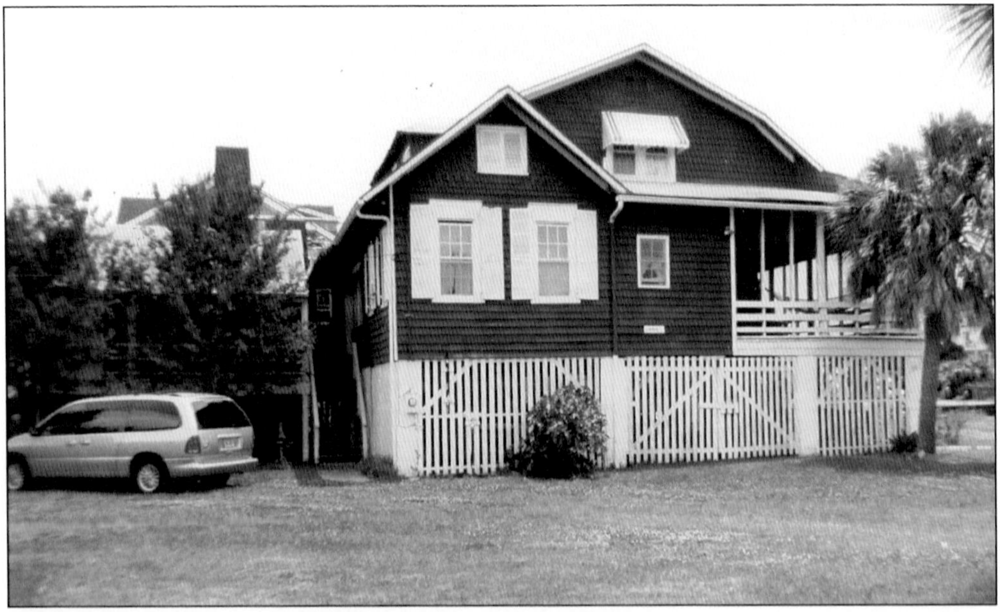

2702 Atlantic Avenue c. 1915. The house (The Island) was built for Titus Bissell Anderson and shows the craftsman influence. The house has a wrap-around porch at the façade and west elevation. The gambrel roof's gabled ends are shingled. (Excellent 20th-century example.] (Courtesy Ruth A. Hood.)

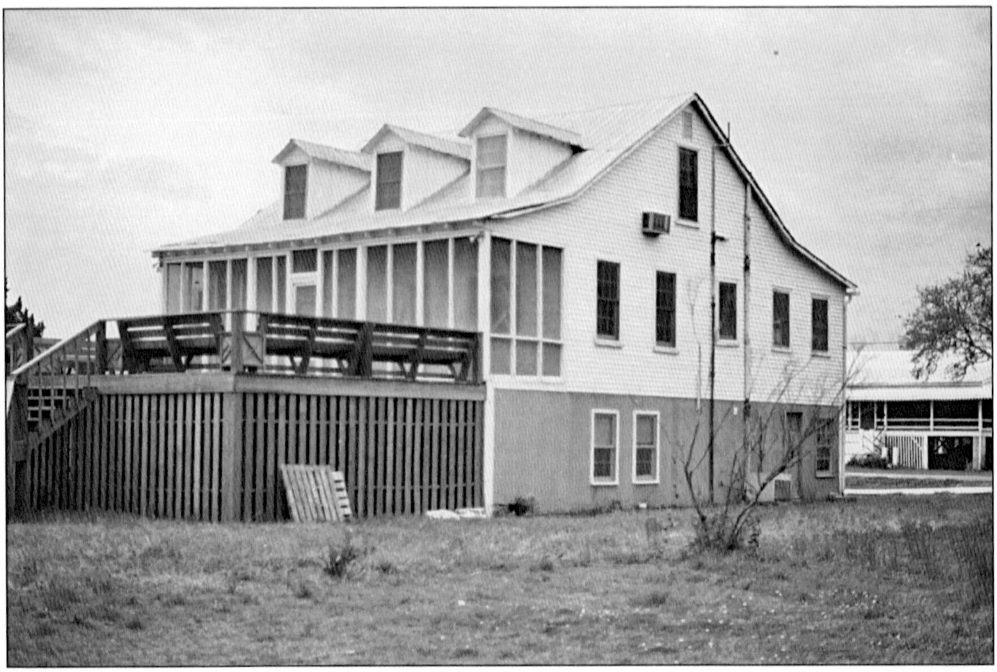

2720 Atlantic Avenue c. 1900. W.E. Whitelaw in 1906 received a title from the Township for this property, which he in turn conveyed to Lawrence Hamilton c. 1909. Hamilton left it in 1930 to his son Arthur, who the same year sold it to Leo and Gussie Livingstane. In 1960 Vernon Scott purchased the property and later sold it to W.E. Craver III. [Modest typical early 20th-century example; Moved.] (Courtesy Marshall Stith.)

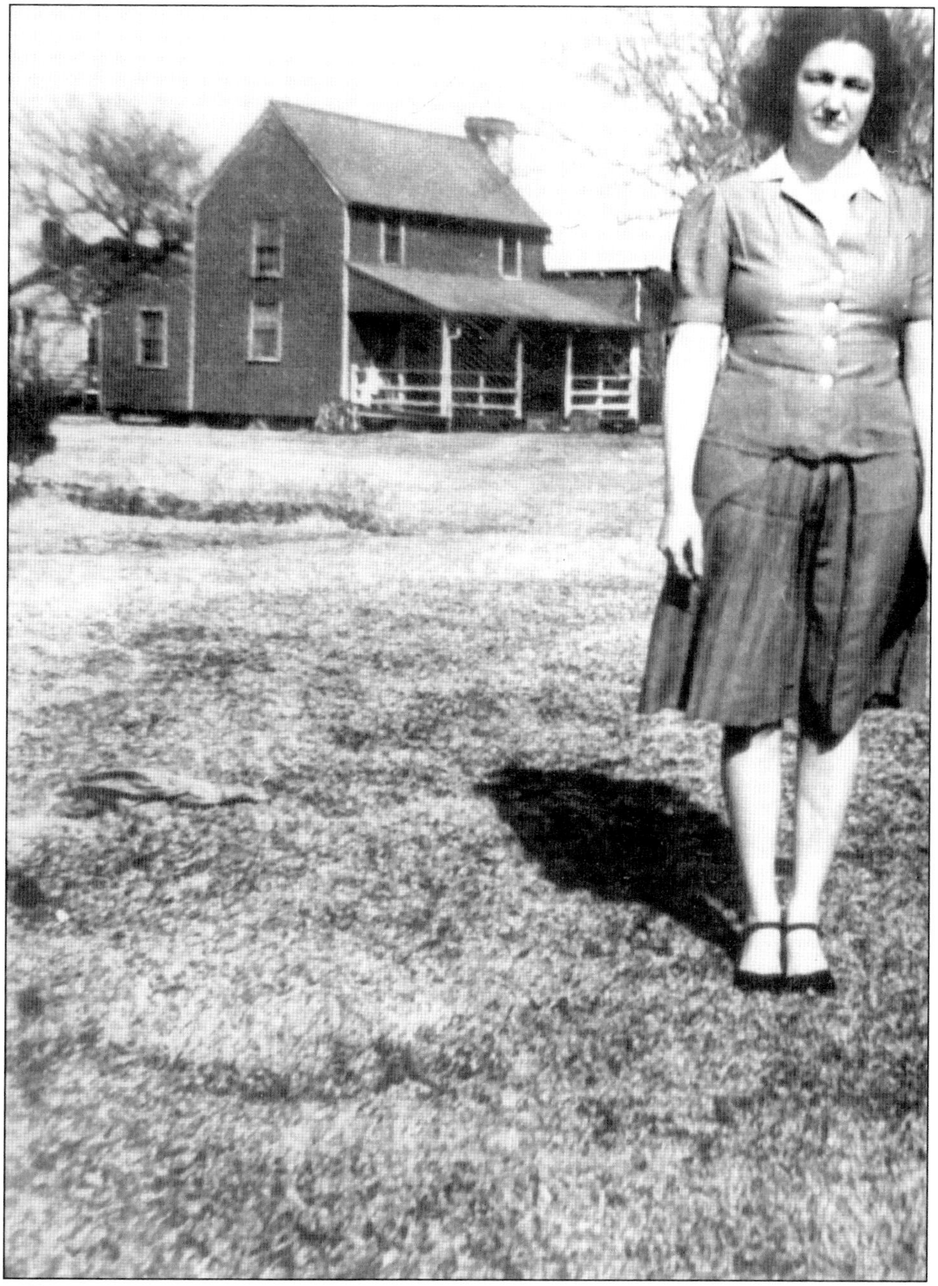

2520 Raven Drive c. 1907. Louis Napoleon Moore, operator of the last small farm on Sullivan's Island, bought the following parcels on July 12, 1900, from Elizabeth Portwig: one-and-a-half acres bounding northwest on the back beach; northeast and southeast on open land known as the "Myrtles;" southwest on lands of Joseph Whitesides's oyster beds near Sullivan's Island in a stream known as "the Narrows and Scott Creek;" and five acres (part of ten acres) of marsh land near Sullivan's Island that were confirmed to Elizabeth Portwig by Joseph Whitesides on August 11, 1893. This land above the highwater mark became lots 43, 44, 45, and 46 Raven Drive. Gertrude Moore Bloomingburg, one of Louis Moore's daughters, stands in front of the family homestead. [Gone.] (Courtesy Linda Dayhoff Smith.)

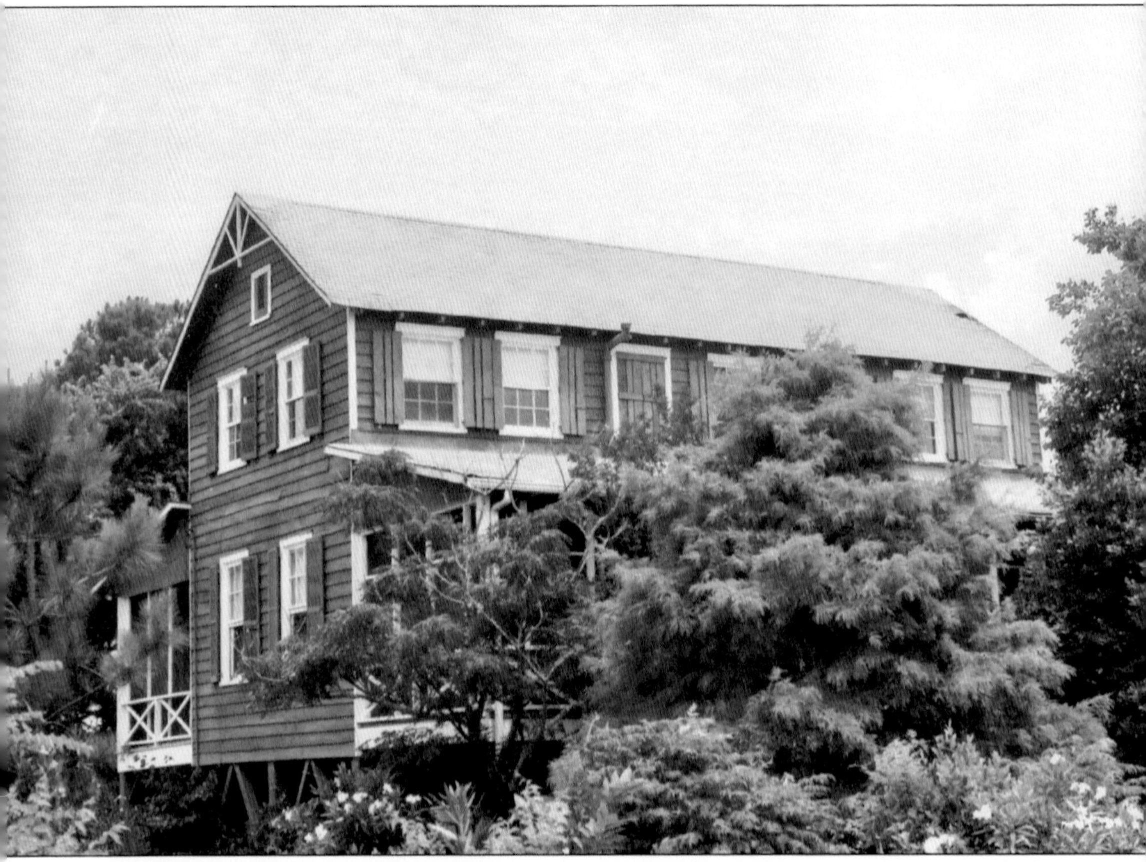

2708 Brooks Street c. 1904/1905. This house, known as the Jervey House, was built to face Railroad Avenue (now Jasper Boulevard), but the original rear has been used as the front since pre-1944 since it faces the ocean. The license to construct was given by the Town Hall to Benjamin McInnis on October 23, 1905. The license was transferred to Dr. Dougall Bissell. It is said that the dependency was the first structure, a "keeping house" built to retain the license to the lot. The license was transferred to Thomas Grange Simons Lucas. The Jervey family bought the property from the Lucas estate in 1944. [An elaborate example of an early 20th-century island residence.] (Courtesy S.C. Department of Archives and History.)

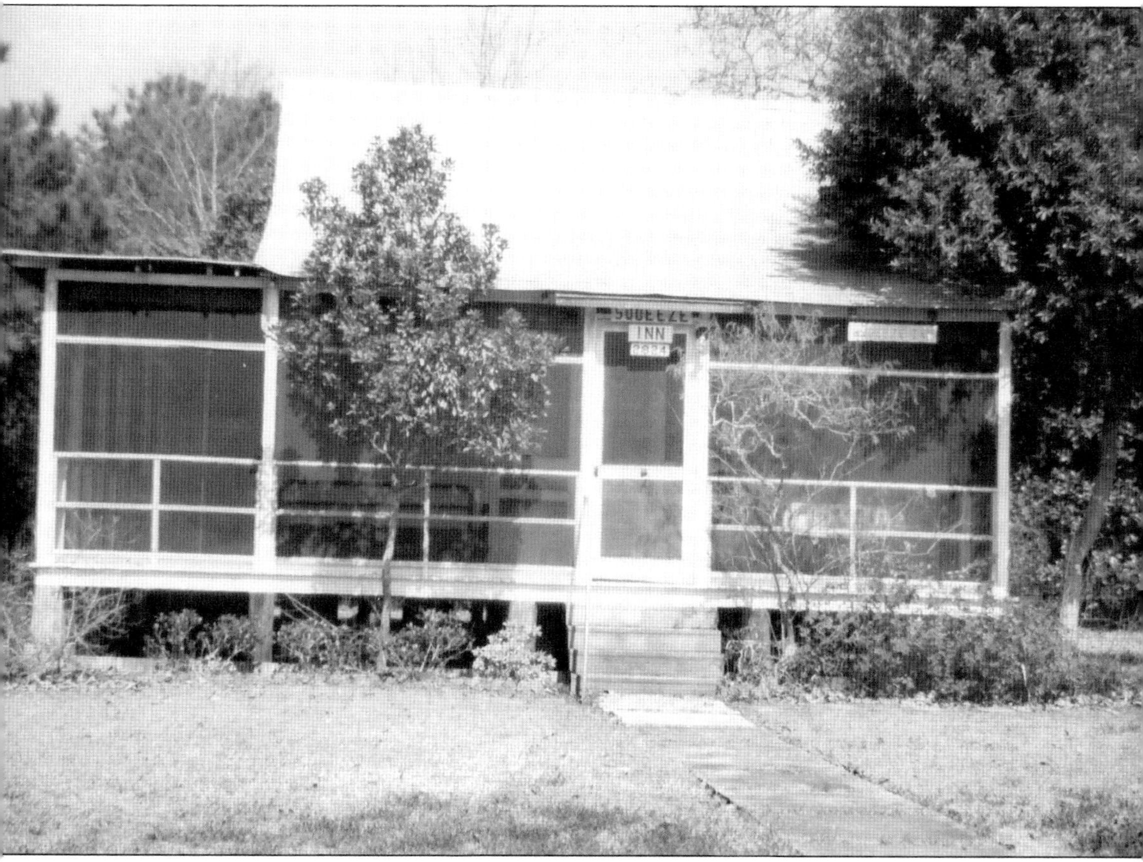

2920 Brooks Street c. 1910. This property (Squeeze Inn) was first mentioned August 15, 1906, as Lot 187 L, belonging to C.J. Cowperthwaite. The house is said to have weathered the 1911 hurricane and was sold in 1920 to Annie D. Tyler. It was sold two years later to Emily E. and C. Dunham Tyler. In 1944 W. Allison Siegling purchased the cottage. [Variation of "the island house" built prior to the Civil War through mid-20th century.] (Courtesy of Marshall Stith.)

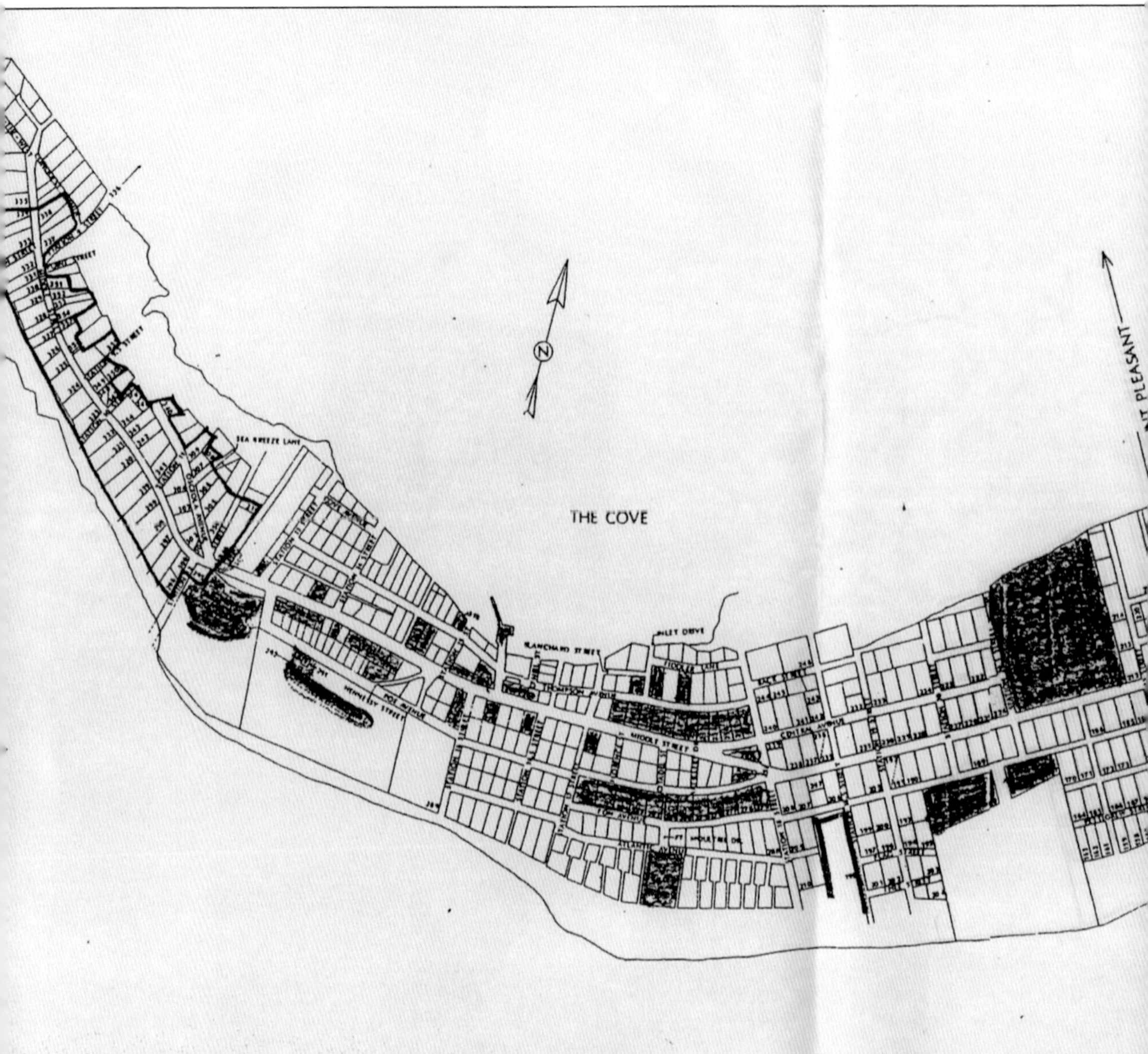

SULLIVAN'S ISLAND HISTORICAL AND ARCHITECTURAL INVENTORY MAP, 1987. The best available site number map is an enlarged-scale blueprint format. No reduction scale map is

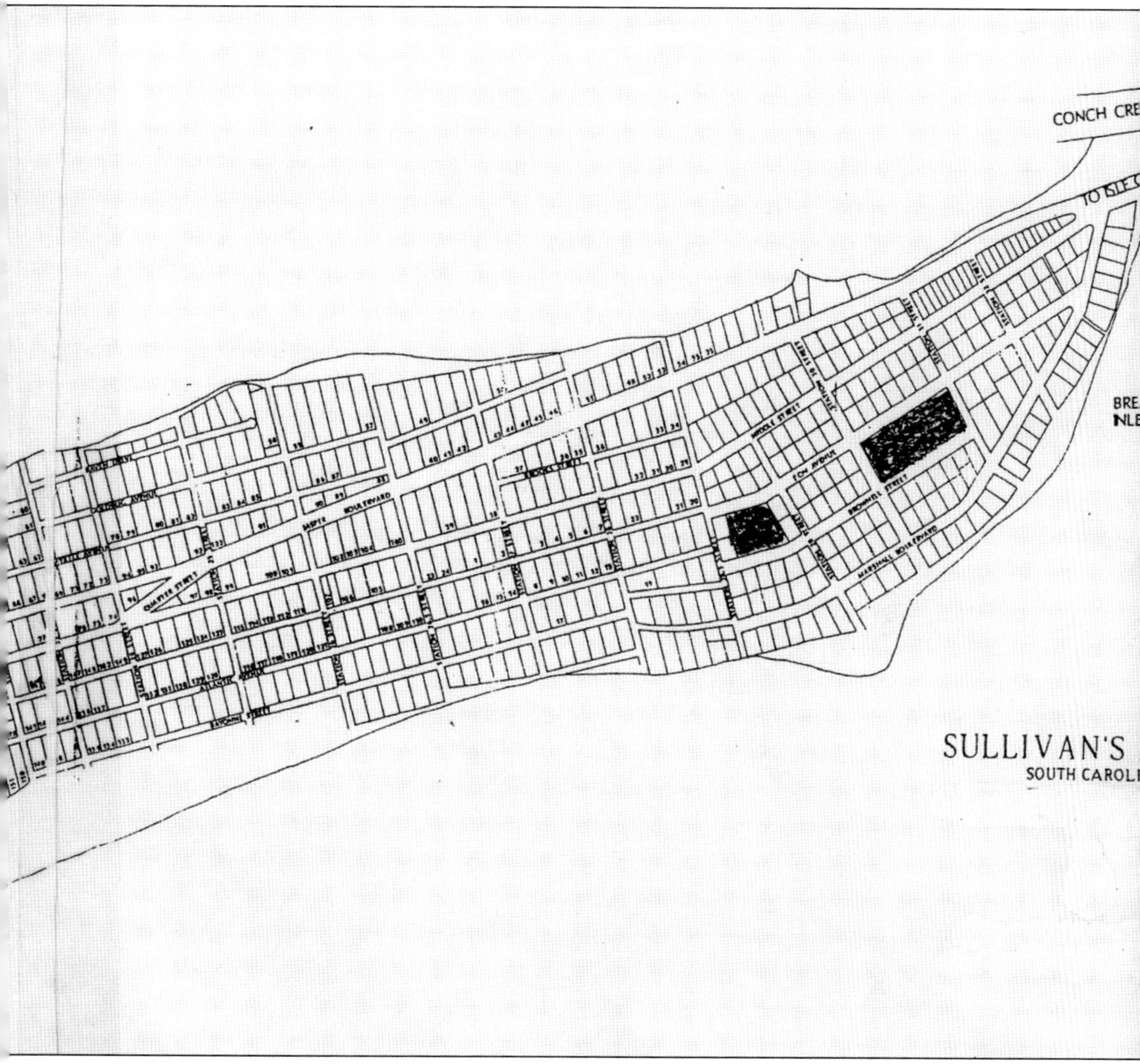

currently available. Site numbers used on this map are not used in the book but they show the extent of the survey. (Courtesy Preservation Consultants.)

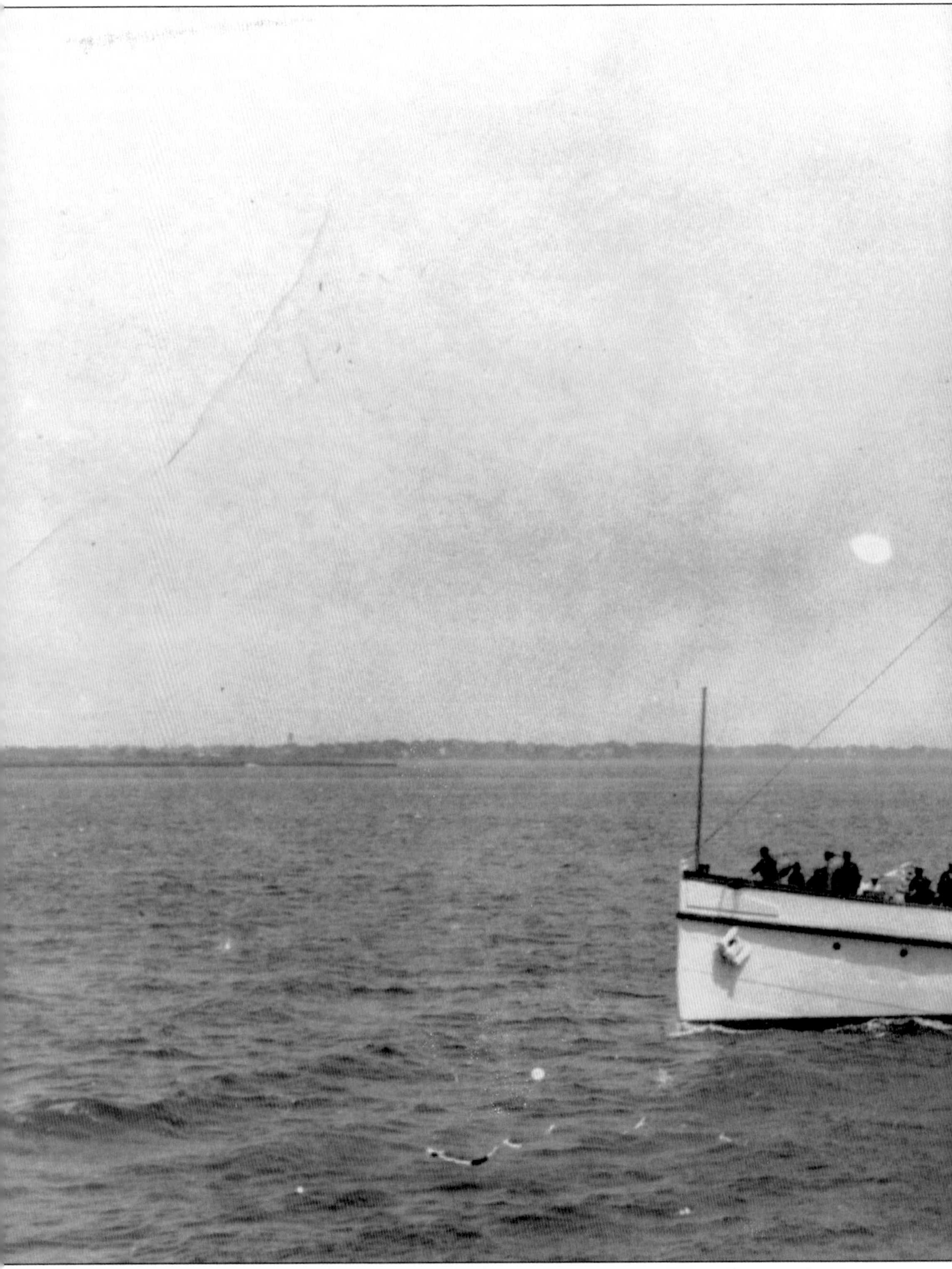

THE USS *SPRIG* CARROLL. This is one of the ferry boats used to carry residents and visitors to

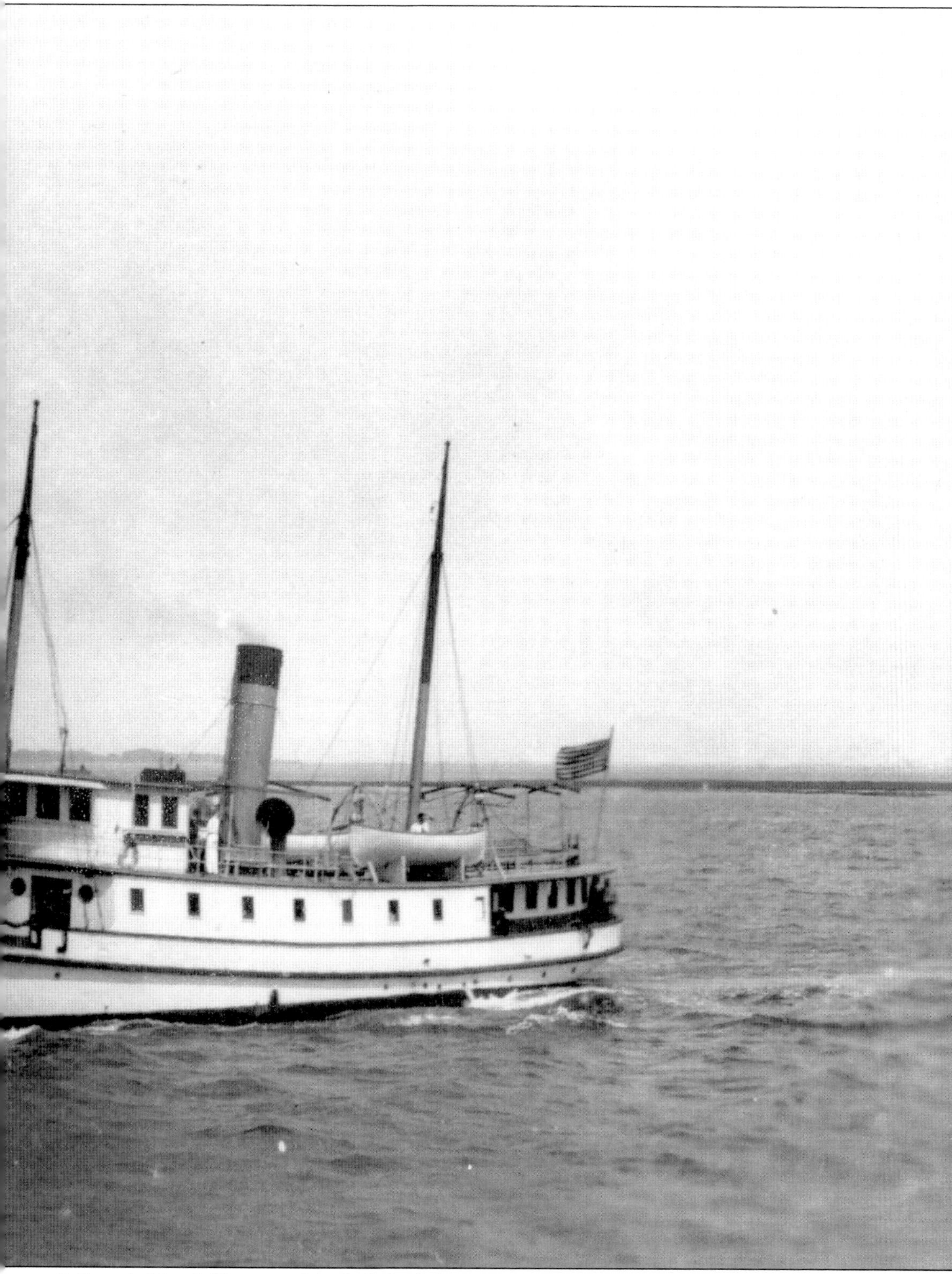
Sullivan's Island. (Courtesy Marshall Stith.)

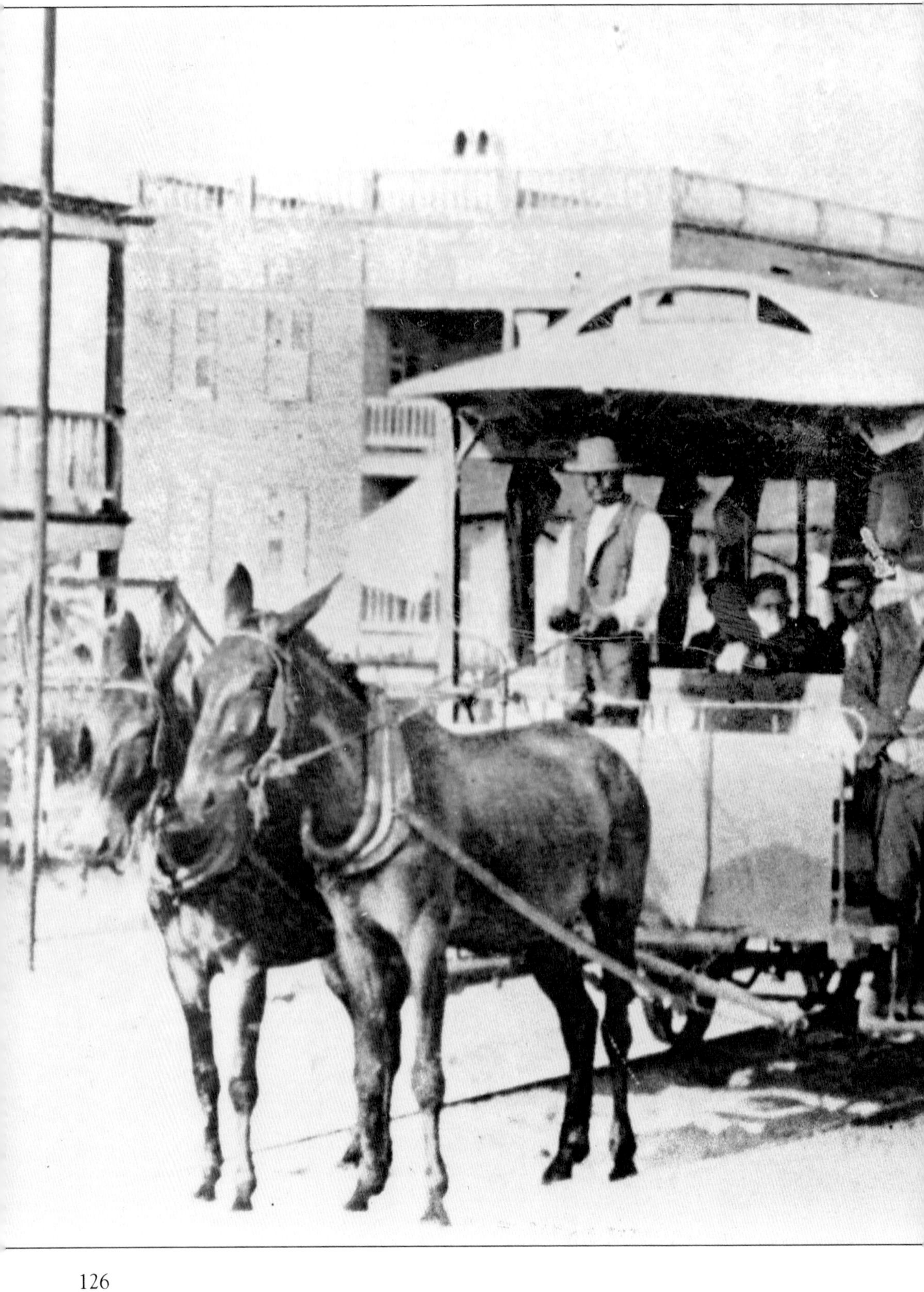

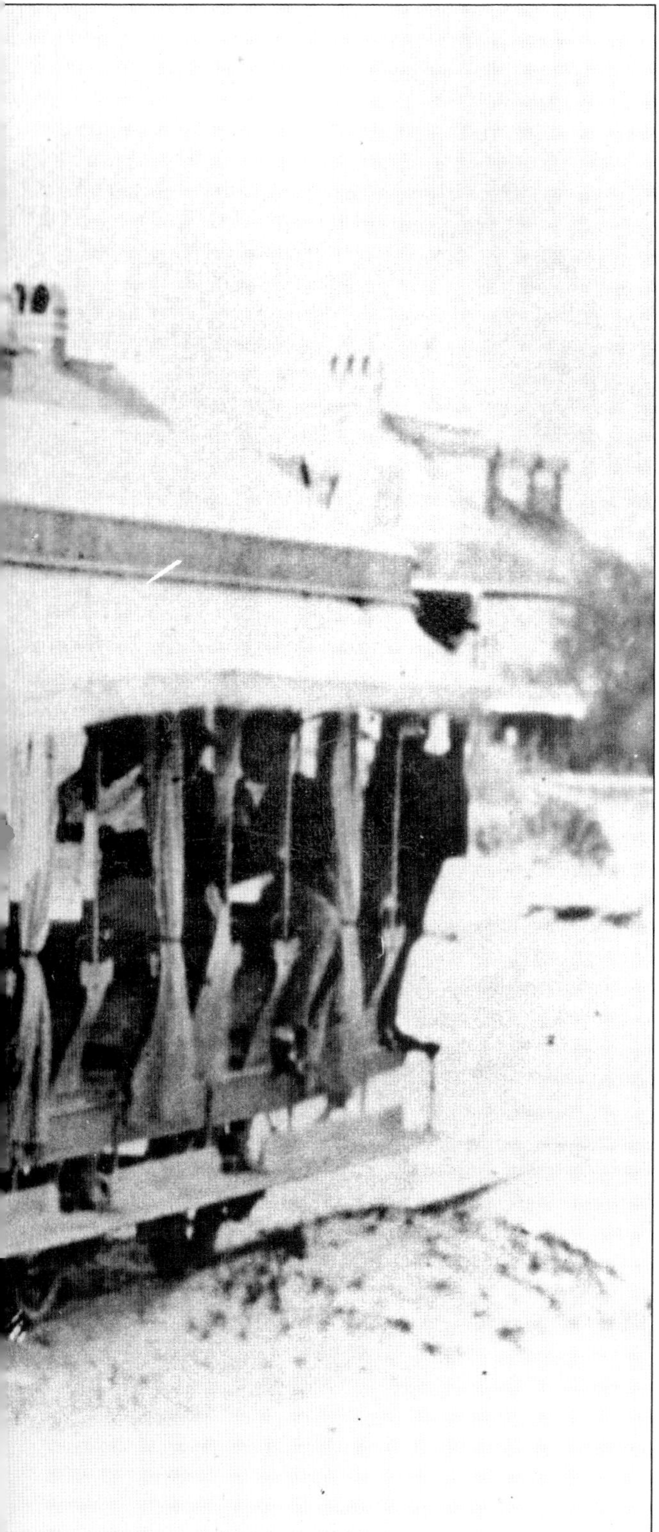

LAST TRIP OF A MULE TROLLEY IN JULY 1898. The 1890s brought major changes in transportation to the island. In 1898 Dr. Joseph Lawrence presided over the construction of a trolley line from Mount Pleasant to Sullivan's Island to Long Island (Isle of Palms) in order to promote the Isle of Palms as a resort. It was possible to bypass Mount Pleasant by taking a ferry directly from Charleston to Sullivan's Island where it was met by a horse or mule trolley. (Courtesy Marshall Stith.)

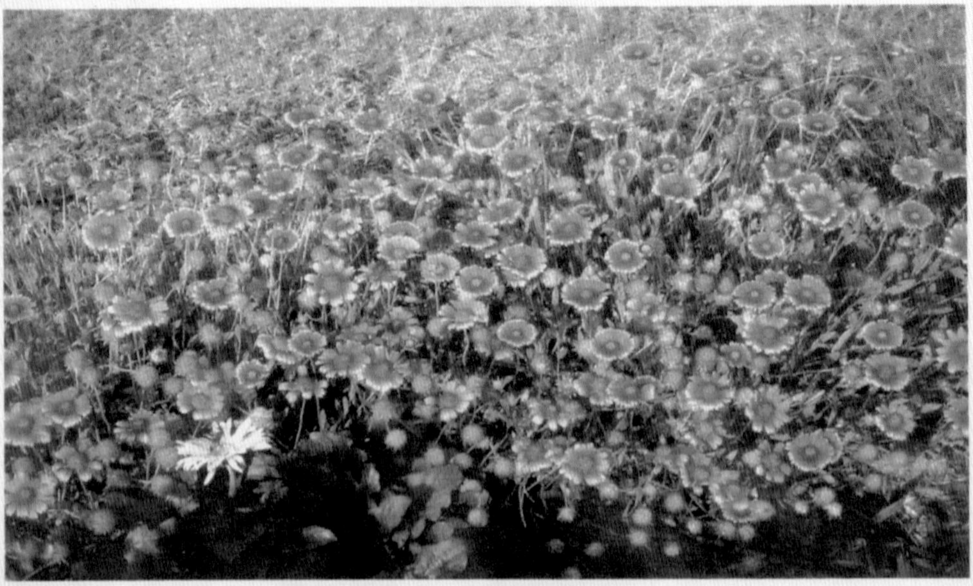

Island Flower

Friendliest of all Island flowers
On duene, in yard, and street,
Gailliardia brightens summer hours,
Where beach and gardens meet.

The sun tips every ruddy petal
Pale gold as harvest sheaves,
Its crownlets shine like burnished metal,
The moonlight frosts its leaves.

It glows in shades of reds and yellows
As bright as robin's breast
And smiles while bees, those trembling fellows
Plunder its treasure chest.

It fears no heat, no stormy weather,
No salt spray from the sea;
But spills its smiles and blooms together
With generosity.

So, like this plant, so gay, out-giving,
Our Garden Club salutes,
May our friendships prove as ever-living
And sturdy as its roots.

Helen von Kolnitz Hyer – Appointed South Carolina Poet Laureate – 1975

The Sullivan's Island Garden Club members treasure this written for the Club in 1960.

"ISLAND FLOWER." Helen von Kolnitz Hyer, South Carolina Poet Laureate 1975, praised island wild flowers in the following poem written for the Sullivan's Island Garden Club members in 1960. (Courtesy Make Macmurphy.)